## ABOUT THE AUTHOR

*Jon Hillson was in the heat of the battle as
a reporter for the Militant newspaper, a staff
member of the National Student Coalition
Against Racism, and an observer for the NAACP
in Charlestown and South Boston. A Boston-area
native, Hillson was active in the civil rights
cause and the antiwar movement; in the late
sixties he wrote for College Press Service and
Liberation News Service.*

# The BATTLE of BOSTON

## Jon Hillson
### Introduction by Robert Allen

PATHFINDER PRESS   NEW YORK

Printed in the United States of America
Library of Congress Catalog Card Number 77-72706
ISBN cloth 0-87348-470-3; paper 0-87348-471-1
Published by Pathfinder Press, Inc.
410 West Street, New York, N.Y. 10014

# Contents

Dates and Events  5

Preface  7

Introduction  9

Map of Boston  14

1. Boston Has a Near Lynching  15
2. The First Day of Desegregation  23
3. The Defeat of Jim Crow  37
4. The Machinery of Segregation  51
5. An Antiracist March and a Racist Challenge  63
6. The Siege of South Boston High  79
7. The Racists Don't Own the Streets of Boston  87
8. Labor Allies and Enemies  99
9. Cracks in the Racist Monolith  105
10. A Call to Action  117
11. Skirmishes on a Widening Front  129
12. The NAACP March for Desegregation  137
13. Racist Terror at Carson Beach  145
14. A Picnic Becomes a Battleground  155
15. The Beginning of Phase II  163
16. The Madhouse in the Schools  175
17. Black Students Tell Their Story  187
18. The Bigots Escalate the Violence  199
19. "People Have to Take Sides"  217
20. A Countermobilization Takes Shape  223
21. NSCAR Is Forced to Retreat  235
22. Mayor White's Peace Charade  245
23. The Racists Lose a Round in Court  257
24. Boston Today—the Struggle Continues  267
   Appendix: Judge Garrity's Busing Decision  275
   Index  281

# DATES AND EVENTS

1787  A petition to open Boston schools to Blacks is denied.

1849  Massachusetts Supreme Judicial Court declares school segregation legal.

1854  Blacks and Abolitionists win the outlawing of school segregation in Boston, but *de facto* segregation is reimposed.

1954  U.S. Supreme Court rules school segregation unconstitutional.

1965  Massachusetts passes first state law against *de facto* segregation: the Racial Imbalance Act. It is not enforced.

1972  Suit to desegregate Boston schools is filed in federal district court.

## 1974

June 21  Judge Garrity orders Boston schools desegregated.

September 9  ROAR antibusing rally draws 8,000.

September 12  First day of Phase I of busing; attacks on Black students and communities begin.

October 7  Mob of 500 attacks André Yvon Jean-Louis.

October 9  President Ford "respectfully disagrees" with Garrity decision.

October 15  A white student is stabbed at Hyde Park High School; the governor alerts the National Guard.

November 22  Racist school boycott drops attendance by 10,000.

November 23  Effigy of school bus is burned during halftime at South Boston-East Boston football game.

November 30  Coretta Scott King leads probusing march of 2,500.

December 11  Racists besiege South Boston High after a white student is stabbed.

December 13  Student teach-in against racism draws 1,200.

December 14  Antiracist demonstration draws 12,000.

December 15  Racist march draws 3,000.

## 1975

February 14  Founding conference of National Student Coalition Against Racism; Boston NAACP President Thomas Atkins calls for mass demonstration May 17.

February 15  Kenneth Edelin, a Black doctor, is convicted of manslaughter for performing a legal abortion at a Boston hospital.

March 19  ROAR rally of 1,300 in Washington, D.C.; Louise Day Hicks calls May 18 Boston rally to cap ROAR national convention.

April 10  ERA rally at Faneuil Hall broken up by ROAR.

May 10  Garrity orders expanded busing in fall—Phase II.

May 12   Supreme Court refuses to hear appeal of Phase I.

May 17   Probusing march draws 15,000.

May 18   ROAR rally draws 2,000.

July 27   Carson Beach mob attacks six Black bible salesmen.

August 2   Black community holds Commission of Inquiry into racist attacks.

August 10   Black community picnic at Carson Beach is attacked by racist mob and trapped by police.

September 4   Louisville explodes; 10,000 racists rally and rampage.

September 7   ROAR Boston rally draws 3,000.

September 10   Phase II begins; 1,900 police become target of racist attacks.

September 11   Racists hold first "Mothers' March."

September 22   Boston Teachers Union begins two-week strike.

October 8-20   White students walk out of South Boston and Charlestown high schools; Black students refuse to enter these schools because of daily attacks.

October 21   Black students testify before Judge Garrity about conditions in South Boston High School.

October 27   ROAR "National Boycott Day" demonstration draws 6,000; South Boston and Charlestown schools are empty.

December 9   Garrity puts South Boston High in receivership; NAACP office is firebombed.

December 12   ROAR holds "Day of Mourning."

## 1976

January 20-30   White student walkouts, sit-ins, and brawls at Hyde Park, Charlestown, and East Boston high schools.

February 15   Racist "Men's March" battles police.

February 19   City workers' demonstration is addressed by bigots.

February 21   NSCAR steering committee calls mass march in spring.

March 9   April 24 date is set for probusing march. Racists firebomb school buses.

April 5   Theodore Landsmark, a Black lawyer, is beaten on steps of City Hall.

April 18   Two Black bus drivers are severely beaten.

April 19   Coalition for April 24 holds meeting in city council chambers. White vigilantes attack a Black housing project; Black youths react by beating a white man into a coma.

April 20   Politicians raise hue and cry over violence; April 24 march is canceled; Mayor White calls "Prayer Procession for Peace" for April 23.

April 24   Fewer than 2,000 racists march in Washington.

April 29   Hyde Park High is evacuated after bomb threat; mob stones Black students.

June 14   Supreme Court refuses to hear appeal of Garrity decision but upholds Pasadena antibusing appeal.

June 22   End of second year of desegregation.

# Preface

This book concentrates on the experiences, personal insights, and big events that make up the battle of Boston. It also gives the historical background of the struggle.

I covered many of the events described—the demonstrations, news conferences, meetings, antibusing violence—as a reporter for the *Militant* newspaper from September 1974 to the fall of 1976. Because I was also a participant in the movement for desegregation, I was involved in discussions with many of the community leaders and came to know them in a way that reporters for the traditional media generally cannot. My activity included supporting projects of the National Student Coalition Against Racism, the Boston NAACP, the Coordinated Social Services Council, and the Boston Public School Crisis Intervention Teams. I was on the scene in Charlestown, South Boston, and East Boston from the start of the crisis.

Source material for the book, besides my own coverage and recollection, includes news copy from the *Boston Globe*, the *Boston Herald American*, the *Christian Science Monitor*, the *Boston Phoenix*, the *Real Paper*, the *New York Times*, and a number of Boston neighborhood weeklies. Especially useful were several important articles on the antibusing movement by *Real Paper* reporter Joe Conason. Where I rely on the coverage of the major dailies rather than my own material, the source is cited.

Two especially useful books were Jonathan Kozol's *Death at an Early Age* and Richard Kluger's *Simple Justice*. Kozol's prize-winning exposé of pre-1966 school segregation in Boston and Kluger's monumental study of the legal history of the 1954 Supreme Court decision are recommended to the interested reader.

Time and space limitations compelled me to select a small number of resource people for interviews. I wish to thank Black community leaders Thomas Atkins, Ruth Batson, Maceo Dixon, Ellen Jackson, Muriel Snowden, Mac Warren, and Percy Wilson for their cooperation. This group reflects the diversity of the broader leadership, and no slight of anyone else was intended.

*The Battle of Boston* concentrates on a crucial, untold side of the story—not the entirety of it. I have not explored here the important day-to-day work of probusing groups like the Citywide Education Coalition, the biracial councils, and neighborhood organizations. Such an undertaking would require many books.

In chapter 9, initials are used instead of last names; this was done for the protection of those interviewed, at their request. Fictitious names are used for the two Black Hyde Park High School students interviewed in chapter 18, for the same reason.

Finally, I wish to thank my editor, George L. Weissman, for his efforts in making the manuscript a finished product, and Susan LaMont, a Boston collaborator, whose criticism and encouragement were essential in preparing a worthwhile manuscript to which George could apply his craft.

Jon Hillson  
January 1977

# Introduction

This book tells the dramatic story of the struggle to desegregate the public schools in Boston. It is a story of courageous Black students who faced hysterical racist mobs to secure the right to an equal education. It is a story all too familiar to those of us who lived in the South in the 1950s and 60s and who witnessed the bitter struggle to implement the 1954 Supreme Court decision ordering an end to segregation in the public schools.

I was born and raised in the South. I was an elementary school student when the famous *Brown* desegregation ruling was issued. The Court ruled that segregation in the public schools was illegal, that the so-called separate but equal doctrine was unconstitutional because it created a racist inequality in the education of Black and white children. This decision was an important antiracist step by the highest court in the land; for the first time since Reconstruction the Court had ruled in favor of racial equality in education. But the ruling had not been an easy victory to obtain; rather, it represented the culmination of decades of court battles by NAACP lawyers and others to abolish Jim Crow laws. There can be no doubt that the Supreme Court decision was a great victory, and it signaled a turning point in U.S. history; but it also represented the start of a long period of struggle which has continued to this very day.

I remember that in 1954 many Black people were jubilant because we thought this court decision would bring instant desegregation of the schools and other public facilities. But this proved not to be the case. There is a vast difference between a court ruling on the one hand and *implementation* of that ruling on the other. By 1955 it was quite clear that southern politicians, businessmen, and other racist forces intended to defy the court ruling and maintain segregation. After all, racism was profitable to the white rulers of the South (and the North, too). Because of racial segregation and discrimination, Black workers could be exploited as a source of cheap labor, restricted to the worst jobs with the poorest pay; and the Black community as a whole was confined to impoverished districts with the worst health and educational facilities. At the same time racial hostilities between the white and Black communities were promoted for the purpose of preventing Black and white workers from uniting against their common enemy, the employers and politicians as a class. The history of these racial dynamics can be traced back to the origins of the plantation system and racial slavery.

So, of course, the white businessmen and politicians were going to oppose the desegregation decision because genuine desegregation would undermine their ability to manipulate and exploit both the Black *and* white communities: the breakdown of *racial* divisions between the Black and white communities would more clearly expose the *class* conflict between Black and white workers on the one hand and the capitalists on the other.

This the capitalists could not allow; so the rulers of the South trotted out the old racist tactics they had used so often in the past to prevent any progressive change. They launched a prosegregation propaganda campaign in the press, the churches, and the schools. They organized White Citizens Councils and other racist groups to mobilize ordinary white people to defend "white supremacy"—a myth that in reality meant supremacy for the white *rulers*.

The segregationists found ready support among racist politicians, including many in Congress. Senator James Eastland and other political figures aided and abetted the segregationist campaign. Some 101 members of Congress signed a "Southern Manifesto"—a document that refused to recognize the real issue of racism, instead blaming the court decision on the role of "outside agitators" and calling for organized resistance to "forced integration."

The segregationists came up with many schemes to obstruct implementation of the law. For example, they devised the doctrine of "interposition," under which they claimed that the states had the right to reject any federal law or ruling that the states thought was not in keeping with the Constitution. This was the old states' rights concept. Some seven southern states adopted interposition resolutions.

When this interposition doctrine proved ineffective in halting desegregation, the racists threatened to close down the schools altogether. This threat was actually carried out in four Virginia counties, but it was a futile effort.

Some of the more sophisticated racists soon realized that to get around the law they would have to confuse matters by pretending that racism and race were not really the issue, while finding alternate ways of keeping segregation. One device they came up with was the so-called pupil placement plans. Under these plans local school boards were empowered to designate which school each pupil would attend, according to certain sociological, psychological, educational, and aptitudinal criteria. Race as such was not mentioned, but the sophisticated racists realized that years of unequal education, combined with cultural diversity, created certain differences between Black and white students— differences that could be exploited to maintain racial segregation. These differences could be used as the basis for assigning Black and white students to different schools without using race as the overt criterion. Thus, segregation could be continued, but under a different name. This tactic was at least partially successful in slowing the process of desegregation. In fact, it required more than two hundred state and federal lawsuits to overturn the pupil placement plans; even after that, some survived in the form of "tracking" systems employed in certain school districts.

When the racists saw that their legal maneuvers were not going to be successful in stopping desegregation, they did not hesitate to use illegal means. They instigated violence against Black and white civil rights activists, and they incited cowardly mob attacks on Black school children. These Black youths were the real heroes and heroines of the struggle for desegregation in the South. These children had more courage and determination than all of the racist mobs put together.

It was the picture of these Black youths courageously walking to school through hysterical lynch mobs that provoked a massive outpouring of antiracist sentiment from the Black community and from progressive whites around the country. This massive antiracist protest finally compelled the federal government itself to step in to protect the Black children and implement the law of the land.

Black people were disturbed and angered by the widespread segregationist activity in the South after the Court decision, but no one was sure just what to do. It was in this context that Mrs. Rosa Parks, a Black woman weary from work, refused to give up her seat on a Montgomery city bus to a white man. She was immediately arrested, but this affront galvanized the Black community into action: people began organizing a massive boycott of that city's buses. The realization had come home that court decisions, while important, were not enough; progressive change could be achieved only by massive action involving thousands and thousands of people.

As fate would have it, a young Baptist minister, Martin Luther King, Jr., was named to head up the boycott. The choice of King was fortunate. Although he was inexperienced, King was open-minded; he quickly saw and articulated the importance of what the Black people of Montgomery were doing. Martin Luther King learned—and perhaps this was his major insight and message— that if the people themselves did not actively work for change, then no progressive change could be expected. He realized that masses of people in motion could change the course of history, and this insight revealed the way to break the deadlock that had developed since the 1954 Supreme Court decision.

It took more than a year for the bus boycott to succeed in desegregating public transportation facilities in Montgomery, but this struggle represented a clear victory for the tactics of massive, direct action.

Martin Luther King went on to lead other mass struggles in the South, and later in the North as well. In fact, in 1965 he led a march of some fifteen thousand people who were demonstrating against segregation in Boston.

I remember in the fifties that people used to say that racial segregation and discrimination were *southern* problems, as though these existed only in the South. But today it is clear that racism is not limited to the South; nor are the exploitation which racism rationalizes and the hatred which it breeds. Therefore, the struggle against racism has assumed national proportions, spreading to all parts of the country. Boston—the "cradle of liberty"—has become a symbol of the fact that the struggle for equality is far from finished.

Looking at the struggles in the South in the fifties and sixties, it is possible to see important parallels to what is taking place in Boston today.

First is the matter of what is really at stake in the struggle in Boston. What is the real issue? Put briefly, the real issue in Boston today, as it was the real issue in the South, is racism in the public schools; that is, the denial of the right of Black children to receive an equal education. In the past the segregationists tried to confuse matters by conjuring up the rhetoric of "forced integration" and "pupil placement plans." Today they try to confuse the issues by talking about "preserving neighborhood schools" and "opposing forced busing." But by their actions the racists have proved that what they really oppose is the right of Black children to have full access to an education equal to that of any white child. (Today's sophisticated racists are willing to accept token integration of a few Black *individuals* to forestall real desegregation, which means eradicating the discriminatory character of *institutions*.)

Second, in the South and in Boston the racists organized to oppose desegregation; the only effective way to counter this tactic is to build a broader and stronger antiracist movement. This means actively supporting the antiracist work of mass-based organizations such as the NAACP, the National Student Coalition Against Racism, and others.

Third is the necessity to avoid relying on the good intentions of politicians, including those in the federal government. Yesterday it was James Eastland who aided the racists and vowed to defend segregation to the end. Today it is Gerald Ford who encourages the racists when he talks about his opposition to "forced busing." Yesterday it was members of Congress signing the "Southern Manifesto"; today it is members of Congress signing antibusing riders and attaching them to legislation.

Nevertheless, it is still true that the local and federal governments have the responsibility and the power to implement the law of the land (and they never hesitated to implement the law when it favored segregation). But it is clear that the government will not move unless it feels sustained, organized pressure from the antiracist forces throughout the country. Only an independent, mass-based movement can assure implementation of progressive laws; reliance on the politicians only leads to disillusion and frustration. This was certainly the lesson of the civil rights movement, and Boston is no exception, as the compelling story in the following pages will show.

Robert L. Allen
September 1976

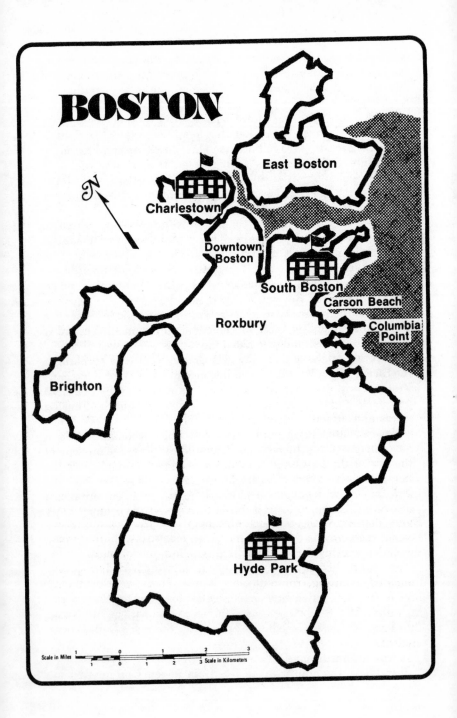

# 1

# Boston Has
# a Near Lynching

Monday, October 7, 1974, in Boston was a sparkling, unusually warm autumn day. As on the score of school days which had preceded it, the city was tense. Court-ordered desegregation of the school system had begun on September 12, with buses rolling from Roxbury to South Boston.

Since then, in South Boston, crowds of white students engaged in a boycott of the newly desegregated schools had, along with their parents, pelted outgoing busloads of Black students with rocks and bottles, sending them scrambling under the seats to protect eyes and faces from the showers of splintered glass.

André Yvon Jean-Louis was not a student, but he too had followed a route from the Black community of Roxbury into South Boston. He had done so daily for years now. He would drive his green Dodge into the neighborhood to pick up his wife after she completed her shift in the laundry where she worked. Jean-Louis had emigrated to Boston from Haiti in 1966.

It could have been any day that fall. Typical of South Boston now, there was a crowd on the streets. It was a big, surly, mobile band. There were schoolchildren as young as nine and ten, parents, and the ever-present knots of unemployed young men. Every day since the opening of school and the beginning of busing, such crowds would swarm on the sidewalks, spilling over the curbs, waiting for those rumbling yellow school buses.

The crowd this day numbered about five hundred. It was an animated, chatting, rambunctious crowd. Some were drinking beer in the sun, which was unusually hot for October. They were all waiting for the buses to come lumbering down the hill from the Patrick Gavin Middle School with their load of Black students—twelve-year-olds.

It was an antibusing demonstration waiting for a target.

Jean-Louis, the maintenance man from Roxbury on his way to

pick up his wife at the laundry, stopped for a red light at the intersection of Dorchester Street and Old Colony Avenue. That was where the crowd had gathered, several blocks from the school. It knew the bus route by now and was poised and waiting. Someone in the crowd spotted Jean-Louis. The instant the eyes of the whites met his, the Black man felt a sudden, terrifying awareness of who he was and who they were in the territory called Southie, the neighborhood where they stoned buses.

André Yvon Jean-Louis, Black and Haitian, minding his own business, had driven into a crowd of perspiring, angry whites on the prowl. They lacked but one ingredient to become a mob, and he had now supplied that. A shout crackled through the throng: "GET THE NIGGER!"

They rampaged towards the car. The Haitian frantically rolled up the windows and pushed down the door locks. The mob was on the Dodge in a second, rocking it like a toy, smashing the windows. The doors were torn off; Jean-Louis was dragged out screaming and beaten to the ground. Fists and feet banged into his face amid shrieks and cheers.

"OFFER HIM UP!" "LYNCH HIM!"

Two motorcycle police in the vicinity, on assignment to escort the buses on their way from Gavin school, drove slowly into the crowd. One officer tried to pull the assailants off Jean-Louis. Not a chance. The cop himself was jumped and thrown to the ground. His partner raced back to his motorcycle and radioed for help.

Now the mob was pressing in, each of the whites striving to get in a kick or some kind of blow on the body of the crumpled, groaning Black man. A white passerby moved into the crowd, pushing back the tormenters. Freed for a moment, Jean-Louis reeled away, attempting to run. He could only stagger.

The mob cornered him again, as pedestrians watched and drivers rolled up their windows. Hoots, whistles, shouting filled the air. Stunned and stumbling, Jean-Louis grabbed a stoop railing, trying to pull himself to a doorway. A young white opened the door, grimacing in disbelief as he looked into the Black man's face. *A haven.* But as Jean-Louis hung on, his jacket was grabbed from behind and someone slammed a sawed-off hockey stick down on his hands. He collapsed onto the pavement.

As he went down, he was given a fierce kick in the groin. The big white kid who delivered this kick turned to the mob, yelling, "I showed that nigger, didn't I?" He was answered with cheers of agreement. Jean-Louis could not move; he thought it was the end.

Mob attacks André Yvon Jean-Louis.

Suddenly the sound of a pistol shot froze the crowd. Patrolman Robert Cunningham had fired. Then he and another officer waded through the mob and lifted Jean-Louis to his feet. It was over. The bleeding victim hobbled between the uniformed escort to a police car, followed by jeers. Later, Cunningham would relate his motivation at that moment: "He is going to be dead if I don't fire."

The mob did not disperse. Its appetite had been whetted, not sated, by the near lynching. Just blocks away, Black elementary students in the John Boyle O'Reilly school were still waiting for buses—whose arrival the police had delayed because of the rampaging white mob. These were seven-year-olds, and they were trapped. The yellow buses would soon make vivid targets.

The only way out was to trick the mob. The police needed a decoy. For the past month, they had been using a big public transportation bus as a mobile rest unit. The local bigots—not yet hostile to the police as they would later become—might let it pass, thinking it was moving in for a pick-up of tired officers.

Two rows of police lined up outside the door of the building as a blue-uniformed sergeant entered the bus to drive it away. Then the Black children ran to the bus. Their departure was hastened by police who nervously hoisted them on board. Catching the startled mob off guard, the bus sped away. A rock banged off the rear of the vehicle as it drove off. The students, anticipating a fusilade of bricks, hit the deck. It was now a reflex. They were becoming veterans.

The spectacular assault on André Yvon Jean-Louis sent shock waves through Boston. Here was an incident which symbolized the brutality and bigotry inherent in the opposition to court-ordered desegregation. The photo of the Black man scrambling for the stoop, searching frantically for an escape, was a scene alien to Boston's image of itself.

Boston, the cradle of liberty and of the abolitionist movement, capital of Massachusetts—the state whose solitary majority for George McGovern in 1972 was still proudly proclaimed on bumper stickers reading, "Don't Blame Me, I'm From Massachusetts." This was Boston, the city of colleges and universities from which civil rights partisans had journeyed south to join in the "freedom rides" of the early 1960s. Boston, with its huge student and liberal population; where dissent against the Vietnam War had been early, loud, and large.

But now, in the fall of 1974, there was a new Boston emerging, or, more precisely, a side of Boston rarely shown, one ignored by the public image makers. This was the insular, ugly white underbelly, the "other" Boston whose violent actions over the course of the next two years would transform the identity of the city where the American revolution was born.

Boston is small for an American metropolis, its population hovering at slightly under seven hundred thousand over the past two decades. This inner city is ringed by a suburban belt of nearly two million. Boston is 17 percent Black, a comparatively small proportion for a major northern city; another 8 or 9 percent is Puerto Rican and Chinese. But the virulence of the opposition to court-ordered school desegregation was not due to the preponderance of the white population, but the way in which the social and political outlook of its key sectors had developed.

Irish Catholics constitute a majority in Boston. It was upon the massive Irish immigration in the second half of the nineteenth century and the early years of this century that the city's powerful Democratic Party machine was built.

The Democratic Party apparatus drew upon the pride and voting power of the downtrodden Irish, who suffered discrimination and exploitation by the Protestant founders and rulers of Boston, the Yankee patricians. These so-called Brahmins, whose archetypes lived on Beacon Hill and bore such names as Adams, Lowell, Saltonstall, and Cabot, sent their children to Boston Latin (if they attended public school) or to such famous private schools as Groton, Andover, or Exeter.

Boston proper is an old city. Its pinched, narrow streets wind and twist into dead ends and up and down hills and knolls—streets that are steep with the houses close together, streets that become playgrounds, streets that are like alleyways.

Boston's Irish immigrants just off the boats were crammed into tenements in South Boston, which soon came to be called "the Dublin of America." They would also move into Charlestown and, later, parts of Dorchester, then fan out into the more affluent neighborhoods of Hyde Park, West Roxbury, and Roslindale. The Italian immigrants settled in the city's North End (the site of the church from which Paul Revere received his signal) and across the harbor in East Boston.

Boston's Democratic Party machine—with its complicated network of patronage and cronyism, studded with party clubs and precinct and ward organizations—retains its decisive strength in the Irish ethnic voting bloc. This power base has delivered mayor after mayor. Its strength determines the composition of the city council and the school committee. The Italians, about 17 percent of the population, come in a distant second in ethnic voting clout.

It is the organization of these neighborhoods by the Democratic Party through its patronage power—its control of jobs in the civil service, the police and fire departments, and city construction projects, as well as party-based functionary positions—that the all-white political apparatus retains a vice-like grip on the city.

The ethnic neighborhoods are geographically separate: South Boston and Charlestown are peninsulas, ethnically rigid and ingrown. This special ethnicity has eroded a bit with the influx of other European nationalities, but not so much as to alter them fundamentally. "Southie pride" is a decades-old product of common national extraction, family ties, and the neighborhood identity of a self-contained community of forty thousand. For Charlestown, the analogous mood and sentiment is "Townie pride," and in East Boston there is a tough, more than skin-deep loyalty to Eastie.

Industrial development in Massachusetts in general, and in Boston in particular, had peaked long before the major Black migration to the North began with World War II. The postwar boom was modest in Boston. The growth of the Black communities in Detroit, New York, Chicago, and Newark was not matched in the state whose shoe and textile industries had gone south for the cheaper labor and the tax rebates offered there by local and state governments.

In Boston, jobs were on the decline along with the dwindling importance of the port as a center of trade and commerce. Jobs were scarce in South Boston and Charlestown, where shipping had once given employment. Coincident with the inauguration of busing, the Charlestown Navy Yard was closed. Teamster and longshore jobs were few and far between. In these neighborhoods of high unemployment, many would get lower-level city patronage and civil service jobs, or become police or firemen. As one traveled out of the inner city to Roslindale, Hyde Park, and affluent West Roxbury, the collars began to turn from blue to white, and the civil service workers—both city and state— occupied higher rungs on the employment ladder.

But if times were hard in such white neighborhoods as South Boston and Charlestown, they were tougher in Black Roxbury, predominantly Black North Dorchester, and the South End, where the majority was Black and Puerto Rican. State and municipal employment was practically shut off by discrimination and the virtual job-dispensing monopoly exercised by the Democratic Party machine. Hiring in the construction trades was dominated by an all-white building trades council. Most minority hiring was done by the universities, hospitals, and insurance companies. And here, wages were low and the workers for the most part without unions. Boston is a working-class city, but it is not a union town.

The year the buses began to roll, unemployment figures in South Boston and Charlestown were as high as 15 percent. The average annual income in depressed South Boston was barely over eight thousand dollars. In Charlestown it was slightly higher. But in the Black community, joblessness was over 20 percent, and the average annual income of the Black worker was two thousand dollars *less* than that of his or her counterpart in South Boston.

South Boston and Charlestown account for only 8 percent of the city's population. The unfavorable comparison between Black and white is even more striking when Roxbury is matched against the more affluent white neighborhoods.

Administering a system which featured widespread unemployment, deteriorating social services, and perhaps the poorest school system in the North, the Democratic Party needed something more than patronage, nepotism, and the dispensing of small favors to retain its base in the white neighborhoods. Therefore its message to its rank and file was: It is not only what you have, which may not be much, but what you might lose to them—to the Blacks. Fear of the Blacks became the machine's watchword as Boston's Afro-American population grew, as the civil rights movement campaigned in the South, as the struggle it inspired for school desegregation in Boston began in the 1950s.

The small-world insularity and intransigence of the white neighborhoods may on the surface seem quaint and appealing compared with the spread of suburban facelessness. But beneath that surface there was something sinister.

Whites had privileged access to jobs. White neighborhoods enjoyed greater city upkeep and services. There were housing projects in South Boston and Charlestown, but compared with the complexes of hovels in Roxbury, which had deteriorated under a policy of neglect and discrimination, they were relatively well maintained.

Black families virtually could not—and cannot—move into the white neighborhoods. From the North End to South Boston, from Hyde Park to East Boston, it was an uphill fight to find a color-blind landlord. And that was only the first hurdle. Ostracism and harassment were the normal greeting which Blacks faced.

The schools in the all-white neighborhoods glaringly reflected such discrimination. The physical plants were superior, the teachers more highly trained, the textbooks newer, the courses more advanced, and extracurricular activities more ample. Segregated education, which had been among the first targets of the early, southern-based civil rights movement, would also become a prime target of the movement for equality initiated by Boston's Black population.

Boston is called "the city of neighborhoods." Within the all-white enclaves, the anti-Black hatred and resentment nurtured by the political machine was easily mixed with neighborhood sentimentality based on ethnic myths and ingrown exclusivity. It was not the Yankees against the "micks" and the "wops" anymore; it had not been for half a century. Brahmin rule had long been broken. Directors of the city's banks and big businesses had Yankee *and* Irish and Italian names now, and only the timeworn tales of the old conflict existed. The Kennedys were multimillionaires now, not immigrants with calloused hands.

This was the background of a racially segregated city, a city whose better schools were off limits to a Black community ghettoized by job and housing discrimination. It was a city whose Democratic Party would rally and solidify its base over the years in opposition to the Black community's fight for social change. It fulminated about a "Black invasion" and a "Black power takeover." The banner of an attack on the last bastion of white ethnic strength, it warned, is "desegregation," and its weapon is the bus.

André Yvon Jean-Louis had not been aware of Boston's history or the combination of explosive elements that created, the time bomb ticking away. An immigrant from an impoverished island, he was just minding his own business and was almost beaten to death. He was Black, a "bonehead" in Southie parlance, a flesh-and-blood manifestation of what opposition to "forced busing" was all about.

# 2

## The First Day
## of Desegregation

In South Boston they had begun to cluster early that September morning on G Street, angry, nervous, and bitter. Among the five hundred or more were students boycotting classes, mothers pushing baby strollers, fathers going to work an hour or two late.

Waiting for the yellow buses, they massed on Day Boulevard, stood in groups at street corners, not quite sure where the buses would turn as they wound their way to the old yellow brick building at the top of the hill—South Boston High School.

These were the locals, the Southies, who had been promised the buses would never come. They had been told as much by the Boston School Committee since 1965, when the state legislature passed the Racial Imbalance Law, a modest desegregation order aimed at the Boston school system. It would never be implemented, the school committee had pledged.

They had been counseled to disregard the law, to resist it, in meetings of the Home and School Association throughout the city. (This predominantly white organization, Boston's version of the Parent Teacher Association, is prohibited by its statutes from criticizing the school committee, a provision binding it to segregation.) They had heard defiance from the city council and had been reassured that no action was to be feared from the mayor's office.

And most of all, they had been heartened and spurred on by their favorite, their very own Louise Day Hicks. She had gone to bat for them—as a power in the Home and School Association, on the school committee, in Congress, and now on city council.

Louise Day Hicks knew the Democratic Party inside and out. Her father had been an important, respected judge in South Boston, and she had been raised in the rough-and-tumble politics of the neighborhood. The wheeling and dealing, the petty favors, the backroom arm-twisting sessions—Hicks was privy to them all. She had twice been an unsuccessful candidate for mayor. Her usefulness to the rulers of Boston was defined by her stewardship of the antibusing movement, which she had helped build with parental dedication.

Hicks is a big woman, six feet tall and husky, middle-aged, with a pleasant, round face which gives a deceptive impression of softness. Her voice is unique: high-pitched, it always seems on the verge of trembling, and it skillfully modulates statements which uniformly mention "*all* the people of Boston, Black and white." Grandmotherly innocence and seeming sweetness ooze from her. But beneath the public image is a tough, astute politician. Her years of experience and single-minded opposition to desegregation have built a network of contacts and supporters. Her personal apparatus and influence extend deep into the Home and School Association, the school department bureaucracy, and the patronage-ridden city government.

That morning, Louise Day Hicks was up early, mobile in her golden Cadillac. For all the worry she professed in behalf of "*all* the people of Boston," for all her decorous dread in anticipation of desegregation, she, perhaps more than anybody else, knew exactly what was going to happen.

South Boston had been paired with Roxbury for the first stage of school desegregation ordered by Federal District Judge Wendell Arthur Garrity less than three months before. The busing plan, known as Phase I, based on an outline submitted by the state board of education, was a fleshed-out version of the state's old Racial Imbalance Law.

Of all the areas included in the busing plan, the South Boston–Roxbury district was expected to be the principal trouble spot. In anticipation of Judge Garrity's decision, the antibusing leaders had organized a mobilization of some twenty thousand on April 3, 1974, to call for repeal of the Racial Imbalance Law. But with Judge Garrity's ruling of June 21, the state statute became unimportant; federal antisegregation law now took precedence.

On September 9, after a summer of furious antibusing organizing, a throng of eight thousand had gathered in City Hall Plaza to protest Phase I and boost the projected boycott by white students. Senator Edward Kennedy arrived at the rally and attempted to reason with the demonstrators. The Kennedy mystique—the Irish family that had made good—was fast evaporating with the senator's refusal to oppose the Garrity order. Kennedy emphasized his understanding of antibusing feeling, but repeated his support for busing, unpleasant though it might be, to achieve desegregation. That was by no means enough for the foes of desegregation at the City Hall demonstration. He was jeered; as he left the podium, unable to break through the din of the heckling, he was jostled and shoved. The angry crowd pressed in on him. He was their own, they thought, one of us. He *owes* us. Now, betrayal! The shout was audible through the tumult. "Why don't you put your one-legged son on a bus for Roxbury," yelled an enraged bigot, referring to the Kennedy child whose leg had been recently amputated. It was getting ugly. "Let your daughter get bused there so she can get raped," someone screamed.

*Raped in Roxbury.* That was one of the fear-mongering threats spreading through antibusing neighborhoods.

A shower of tomatoes splattered on bystanders, spraying Kennedy as escorts pushed the crowd back. The glass doors of the John F. Kennedy Federal Building shut fast as the senator was hustled inside. Outside, white fists pounded on the panes, shattering them.

It was a taste of things to come.

The attitude of the police was anything but discouraging to the antibusing resistance. Despite the assault on Kennedy, the *Boston Globe* noted that "low visibility of the police remained policy" for the opening of school.

Boston Mayor Kevin White, the city's chief elected official since 1967, had always been uncomfortable with the Racial Imbalance Law. He had never shown himself a firm supporter of desegregation during the nine years of the city's obstruction of that state law. Now he faced the reality of Judge Garrity's order. As resistance to it sharpened amidst pledges of defiance from the all-white, all-Democratic city council and school committee, he waffled further. The mayor's contribution to a harmonious opening day of school was a media campaign urging "calm."

The crowd bunched up at the gates of South Boston High School was anxious and ready for action. In its hands were the implements of opposition to "forced busing"—beer cans, rocks, bottles, watermelons, bananas. The fruits would be tossed, bursting on the buses, after being used as props for imitating the antics of monkeys and apes, as the Black youngsters got off the vehicles.

Graffiti were everywhere, brightly splashed on the walls, streets, and boarded-up windows of South Boston: *Niggers suck; No niggers in South Boston; Niggers eat shit; Bus 'em back to Africa; Boneheads beware; French-fried niggers for sale.* As publicity came to South Boston, with television shots of the racist obscenities, there were half-hearted attempts to wash the epithets off the walls or to paint over them. But for every such effort, a dozen more slogans appeared.

They were disciplined, the fifty-six Black students who entered the buses at Bayside Mall, the site of an abandoned, boarded-up shopping center little more than a mile from the high school. Some had some from Roxbury, but most had walked from nearby Columbia Point, a stark complex of high-rise public housing on a small peninsula across the inlet from South Boston's Carson Beach. More than that half mile of water, however, separated the whites of Southie from the Blacks of "the Point."

As the crowd milled around the high school gates, workmen scrubbed the building door clean of a freshly painted "Niggers go home." It was getting warm early. It was going to be a hot day, and already it was uncomfortable waiting for the buses.

The sound of bus motors was not strange to South Boston. There were the city buses, the buses for parochial school students, the school buses for field trips, and the school buses which had transported thirty thousand students, among them South Boston youth, before desegregation began. But today every ear was listening for the sound of approaching buses.

Today, they sounded louder than ever.

The air was shattered by hoots and catcalls as the buses rolled up onto G Street. The mob surged towards them, pounding on their sides with fists and clubs. A rock slammed off the front of the lead bus. The police cordoned off the sidewalk approach to the building. The Black students, fearful and hesitant, waited for the order, then moved out of the vehicles rapidly, entering the school as the chorus of boos and chants—"Go back to Roxbury," "Niggers suck"—became deafening. The bigots did monkey dances, imitated apes scratching their armpits, and dangled bananas from their hands.

Then the Black students were inside.

The morning would be occupied by a drama of small forays and pushing matches between the police and groups of whites, and bottles being smashed on the pavements. In Roslindale and

Hyde Park, groups of racists stoned buses transporting Black students.

That afternoon the buses departed from South Boston High without incident. Much of the crowd had moved down to Day Boulevard, where the buses leaving the Gavin school and the L Street Annex made easy, slow-moving targets.

Screaming, taunting phalanxes of racists lined the road for several hundred yards, heaving what they had picked up on the beach, on the streets, in backyards. The screams of Black students, some of whom were as young as eleven, filled the inside of the buses as window after window was shattered. The toll: eighteen buses damaged, nine Black students injured by flying glass. Three buses suffered a double dose of the terror. Confused by the frantic scene, one driver had made a wrong turn, and was forced to lead his small caravan through the rock-throwing gauntlet a second time. There were no arrests.

The scene would be repeated regularly for weeks.

Thomas Atkins, the president of the Boston branch of the National Association for the Advancement of Colored People (NAACP), had sensed what was coming. He had warned the mayor, the FBI, the Justice Department, and the Boston police where the trouble would be. While a student at Harvard in the early 1960s, he had participated in the struggles against school segregation in Boston. Twice elected to the Boston City Council, he was aware of the racism in that body; he also had a firsthand knowledge of Louise Day Hicks.

Atkins and other Black leaders had pressed for maximum law enforcement and security for the Black students. The mayor, however, would not directly confront the bigots. Strict enforcement of the busing order was anathema to him. It would mean a showdown with Hicks and other powers in the Democratic machine. He would attempt to ride out the storm with appeals to "rationality."

Atkins's view is that the violence was predictable—and most of it avoidable. "Political decisions were made not to clear the crowds away from around South Boston High School," Atkins recalls. "Political decisions were made not to arrest people seen throwing rocks and bottles at the children on the buses. Political decisions were made to take a go-slow, take-it-easy approach—at all costs." Such political decisions were made by Mayor Kevin White.

That first day of school—as Black children picked glass from their hair and told stunned parents how they had ridden home beneath the bus seats to the sound of rocks hitting the vehicles—Mayor White was preparing to go to Freedom House in Roxbury. The auditorium of this community center, which the *Boston Globe* nicknamed "the Pentagon of the Black community," was packed with bitter, angry parents. They cheered calls for a National Guard mobilization in South Boston. They applauded and whistled as Patricia Bonner-Lyons, a two-time candidate for the school committee, demanded that Louise Day Hicks be arrested for incitement to riot.

Tough, shrewd, and ambitious, from an old political family, White had been mayor for seven years. He had built an impressive personal machine that combined the traditional apparatus with his own innovations. Normally he exuded confidence; now as he began to speak he was nervous. In one day his low-key public relations campaign for compliance with the law "for all the children's sake," a continuation of a ten-year attempt to straddle the issue, was in ruins.

"It's not the Lord's guarantee," he told the parents, "but I'm asking for a second chance. And if I can't produce, I'll fight alongside you." The next day, more buses were stoned, and White had flunked his second chance. He would never "fight alongside" the Black community.

NAACP President Atkins called for a Black boycott of South Boston schools for September 13, a Friday. That weekend there began to be attacks on Blacks at subway stations in or bordering South Boston. Blacks were beaten up on streetcars. One Black man, pushed in front of an onrushing subway train, narrowly escaped death. A hangman's noose was strung up at the Andrew Station stop with a grim warning smeared on a wall: "Niggers stay out." Racists in South Boston made a target of nearby Columbia Point. Sniper fire shattered windows and tore out chunks of brickwork in the housing projects there. White-hooded nightriders fired wildly at the buildings from speeding cars.

On Sunday, September 15, Atkins withdrew his call for a boycott, stating his assurance that revised law-enforcement plans were "adequate to the task" of carrying out the court order. South Boston was not the only trouble area, however. On September 13, stoning of buses had also been reported in Forest Hills, Jamaica Plain, and Roslindale.

As Atkins urged increased Black attendance and strict self-discipline by the students, the antibusing leadership was preparing a provocative blast at the Black community itself. A joint statement entitled "A Declaration of Clarification" was issued by Louise Day Hicks, South Boston State Senator "Billy" Bulger, and South Boston State Representative Michael Flaherty. It poured oil on the fire with such statements as these:

> It is against our children's best interest to send them to school in crime-infested Roxbury. That is the issue. All of the rest is only a distraction. . . . There are at least one hundred Black people walking around in the Black community who have killed white people during the past two years. . . . Any well informed white suburban woman does not pass through that community alone, not even by automobile.

The racists were now headed by a new organization, Restore Our Alienated Rights, whose acronym ROAR was devised to show fierce opposition to desegregation. The nucleus of ROAR had been pulled together by Hicks in February of 1974 under the temporary name of the Save Boston Committee. Its by-invitation-only meetings in a City Hall hearing room had regularly drawn upwards of two hundred people. They anticipated that Judge Garrity's decision in the school case, which was expected at any moment, would be unfavorable. They came from all of Boston's white neighborhoods, from the grassroots of the Democratic Party machine, from the Home and School Association chapters; some of them were members of Massachusetts Citizens Against Forced Busing, the organization responsibile for much of the lobbying against the Racial Imbalance Law.

The nominal head of the Save Boston Committee was John Kerrigan, a Dorchester lawyer who had been the chairman of the Boston School Committee since 1967. Kerrigan was a foe of busing to the marrow of his bones and vocal in his hostility towards Blacks. Angered, for example, by the coverage of Phase I by ABC's Black newsman Lem Tucker, Kerrigan would blast the reporter as "one generation out of the trees—I bet he loves bananas."

Kerrigan was also a bitter foe of the mildly liberal *Boston Globe,* and over the years seemed to have developed a visceral hatred for reporters—"media maggots"—in general. Nonetheless he sought them out in order to tout himself as a champion and inspirer of white resistance. He wore a windbreaker with "Boston School Committee" on the back and the nickname "Bigga" on the sleeve. What did it mean? he was once asked. Smiling, he replied that he had acquired it in the army because of "the prodigious size of my genitals. . . ." He, indeed, was the one to "save Boston."

Hicks had coined the name ROAR in late May, inspired by a toy lion in the back seat of a friend's car. "I said," Hicks would recall, " 'maybe we could ROAR!' " The Save Boston Committee had organized the massive demonstration in City Hall Plaza on April 3. The September 9 rally was called by ROAR, which by then was headed by Hicks.

Besides utilizing and consolidating all the preexisting organizations, ROAR introduced a new form. These were "information centers," storefront operations not formally tied to ROAR but staffed by trusted cadres of the organization. The South Boston Information Center, its facade draped in red, white, and blue bunting, was the first to appear. Others would rapidly follow in Hyde Park, West Roxbury, the North End, East Boston, and later Charlestown. They were the mainsprings of the rising ROAR machine, capable of mobilizing hundreds in picket lines or demonstrations on short notice through their "telephone tree" network. Focal points of organization and solidarity for the activist white high school students against busing, they were also community centers for the racists' propaganda and agitation.

On all levels, ROAR was secretive, and would become more so as the struggle deepened. In the course of the spring, its weekly citywide meetings moved into city council chambers under Hicks's sponsorship. Wary guards would keep watch for "infiltrators."

Chief among the ROAR bouncers was city council member Albert "Dapper" O'Neill. Boisterous and flamboyant, white-haired and on the heavy side, O'Neill was an old Boston pol, legendary for rambling speeches and boastful of his constant companion—a .38 caliber revolver. A buffoon and an embarrassment to proper Bostonians, O'Neill postured as a "friend of the little man." Highly popular as an antibusing champion, he had been made an honorary lieutenant colonel in the Alabama State Militia by Governor George Wallace.

O'Neill had fulminated against antiwar "rowdies" during the days of demonstrations against the Indochina War. If he had seemed an anachronism when that movement commanded Boston's streets, he was now riding high with the bigoted crowds who took to the same streets to oppose desegregation. O'Neill had a particular base of support among the "beat cops," the rank-and-file Irish and Italian police whose opposition to busing he cultivated and voiced. This fact was not reassuring to Black parents whose children rode the buses into hostile neighborhoods where those men were the first and last line of defense against white mobs.

The antibusing movement, ranging from elected officials to their foot soldiers on the phone lists of the information centers, had brought powerful pressure to bear on Mayor White's administration to abdicate its law enforcement responsibilities. The lack of response to their challenges emboldened the bigots in the all-important first days.

In the wake of the Hicks-Bulger-Flaherty "Declaration of Clarification," the stoning of school buses spread throughout the city, with South Boston's new Black students bearing the brunt of the terror. On September 18, a rifle bullet shattered the front door of Jamaica Plain High School. The next day in Hyde Park High School, fighting erupted in the corridors as outnumbered Black students were jumped and beaten by gangs of whites.

That week, the Ku Klux Klan came to Boston. A quietly organized rally of five hundred in an all-white section of Dorchester took place without the presence of the major news media. But one reporter, Joe Klein of the Cambridge-based *Real Paper*, found out about the meeting and attended it. The main speaker was David Duke, Grand Dragon of the Knights of the Ku Klux Klan. He was greeted by the football cheer—"Here we go, Southie, here we go!"—that had become a rallying cry of the bigots.

"The tide is beginning to turn against forced race-mixing," the Grand Dragon declared. "It is our duty as white people, proud of our heritage, to help return civilization to this continent. . . . The federal government is taking little white children out of their homes and sending them into Black *jungles*."

To Duke's statement, "We don't believe Negroes fit into modern society," the crowd shouted back, "They're not Negroes; in Southie, we call them *niggers!*" Here the pretenses were down. Race hate was not disguised by the code words of the politicians.

"The real issue isn't education," Duke responded. "The real issue isn't a school here or a school there . . . the real issue is *niggers!*" The crowd went wild.

The Nazis also arrived, setting up shop on West Broadway in South Boston, and swastikas appeared on walls alongside the

Graffiti in South Boston, 1974.

Police guard entrance to South Boston High.

three *K*'s that had gone up the day after Duke's speech. The Nazis were the fringe, to be sure, exercising little influence. But their presence was symbolic.

On September 23, after suffering nearly two weeks of sniper fire and nightriding terror, Black residents at the Columbia Point housing project announced the formation of "community observation patrols." Blasting police failure to furnish protection, they demanded federal marshals. NAACP President Thomas Atkins backed the demand as "totally justifiable." Days later the Boston police would move into "the Point" like an occupying army, patrolling the roofs with M-16 rifles and breaking up community demonstrations, while across the inlet their colleagues stood by as white hooligans pelted the school buses with rocks.

The spectacle stunned Roy Wilkins, national executive director of the NAACP. On a fact-finding trip to Boston, he appeared with Black parents from the projects at a news conference, supporting their attempts to secure the area against terrorist attacks.

Despite the mobs, the violence, the street and subway assaults on Blacks, Boston's news media did not give a picture of what was going on. In a September 19 *Boston Globe* roundup of the day's events, for example, one could read, "Other students were injured and buses stoned in Roxbury, Dorchester and South Boston." For weeks into the fall, such curiously laconic statements, coupled with generally glowing reports from City Hall and the school department about the relatively smooth implementation of desegregation, were standard journalistic procedure.

Was there an effort to manage the news? For weeks, suspicions and rumors were rife among the leaders of the Black community about a "media pact," a virtual agreement by key decision-makers in the communications industry to gloss over the turmoil. Otherwise, why had the *Boston Herald American*'s headline announced on September 13, "Calm Prevails As School Opens" and the *Globe*'s proclaimed, "Boston Schools Desegregated As Opening Day Generally Peaceful"? How else explain that when a three-hundred-car motorcade organized by ROAR had blocked the *Globe*'s delivery trucks at its plant on September 21, and when shortly afterwards shots shattered windows in the *Globe* building, there had been no editorial response?

High-level meetings between Mayor White and major figures in the media were known to have taken place, but they took great pains to dismiss the idea of a pact. Rumors, nonetheless, persisted.

The *New York Times,* not given to sensationalism, had reported a different Boston scene than that described in the local media. Its banner headline read: "Violence Mars Busing in Boston; Mayor Bans Street Gatherings in South Area."

The contrast between local and national coverage was explained by Mayor White's efforts to muffle the media impact of the white resistance. His or his staff members' meetings with television and radio station managers, editors, and publishers had been generally successful. "Sensational" events—mob violence, bus stonings, Klan rallies—were to be downplayed; simultaneously the mayor supplied laundered news of the success of the busing plan through daily briefings that gave the appearance of "control" of the situation.

The national media simply rejected the "pact," earning the animosity of White, the antibusing leaders, and other civic figures for "distorting" Boston's image. As a large national and international news corps assembled in Boston for the opening of school in the fall of 1975, the *Herald* would print an unprecedented front-page editorial rebuking the out-of-towners for sensationalism, telling them there was no story in Boston and rather undiplomatically inviting them to go home.

Thomas Atkins knew of the behind-the-scenes meetings which resulted in the pact. "Political decisions," he recounted, "were made to seduce the media into a 'we will report only positive news' kind of euphoria." Mayor White, according to Atkins, had persuaded the media to make "a complete, 180-degree reversal on the way they report news." Bad news was no news. Only radio stations WEEI, the city's CBS all-news outlet; WILD, a station geared to the Black community; and Cambridge's progessive, low-budget WCAS refused to buckle to the pressure. The NAACP leader thought the media pact was entered into "in good faith" by the communications outlets. It revealed, he concluded, their "willingness to get raped."

For every occurrence that was modified or managed into insignificance, there were scores of unreported incidents that demonstrated the depth of anti-Black hatred behind the antibusing movement. For example, there was the occasion when a child dressed in a sheet and hood was sent running by his mother through the hall of the L Street Annex School, shouting, "The Klan is coming, the Klan is coming."

Another incident: a pickup truck dragged a Black effigy by the neck through South Boston's streets with a sign reading, "This is what's coming to you, niggers." On another occasion teachers had to close the windows of the Dean school to stop white students from throwing eggs through them at the Black students. And in Hyde Park High School the bathrooms had become combat zones, where Black women students dared go only in groups.

With the daily stoning of buses and the myriad threats and acts of harassment, a tapestry of racist violence was being woven. A psychology of resistance was being set which drew strength from the oratory of the antibusing lawmakers and encouragement from the silence and default of the officials charged with enforcing the law.

Both the "low visibility" of the police and the media pact were purportedly features of Kevin White's plan to help implement Judge Garrity's order. In actuality they reflected the mayor's accommodation to the promised resistance of the racists.

On the state level, two liberals were running for governor: incumbent Republican Francis Sargent was being challenged by Democratic State Representative Michael Dukakis. They too had a pact—one that was quite public. They would refrain from discussing "the busing issue" in the fall campaign. That was Boston's problem.

On the national level, President Ford entered the battle less than forty-eight hours after André Yvon Jean-Louis's narrow escape from the South Boston mob. Ford had been carefully briefed on events in Boston since the schools had opened, and he certainly knew of the Jean-Louis beating, which had burst into the national media.

He may not have known of the less spectacular events of that awful day: A mob of two hundred had smashed bus windows in Roslindale after chasing a group of ten Blacks—who had attempted to eat in a local snack bar—back into the high school. Police had decided not to send buses to South Boston High School for the second school day in a row because of the huge rock-throwing crowds on Day Boulevard. Ford *had* been told, however, that the Boston NAACP had demanded that federal troops be sent to the exploding city.

At his press conference on October 9 Ford was asked about the Boston crisis. After the ritual of deploring the violence there, he declared, "The court decision in that case, in my judgment, was not the best solution to quality education. I have consistently opposed forced busing to achieve racial balance as a solution to quality education, and, therefore, I respectfully disagree with the judge's order."

Ford's statement was embraced by Boston's antibusing leaders, who could deplore violence with equal facility. Now the president of the United States had with a few words undercut the authority of Judge Garrity's order in the middle of the crisis.

The stakes were big in Boston. A Black fourteen-year-old, Kenneth Farmer, bused to the L Street Annex, had a gut inkling of what was going on when he told his friends, "They say no niggers are coming to Southie. I say if they run us out of here, they'll run us out of Roxbury. We got a right to go to any school in Boston."

It seemed a simple enough proposition. That right had roots in a history of struggle which had a profound influence in Boston. It would be tested in blood and fire before Christmas. But the very scope of that test and the forces it marshalled in battle evidenced that the issue was not just one for Boston. American society was entering a new period of crisis, and the birthplace of the American revolution was suddenly at its storm center.

# 3

# The Defeat
# of Jim Crow

The National Association for the Advancement of Colored People had traveled a long and painful road to bring the challenge of school segregation to the U.S. Supreme Court in 1952. Founded in 1909 as a multiracial organization committed to securing Black equality in all spheres of life, the NAACP was up against huge odds. In 1896, the Supreme Court had affirmed as the "law of the land" principles of racial segregation based on white supremacy.

Ruthlessly enforced, the policy popularly known as Jim Crow had made Blacks in southern and border states a pariah people, forbidden by law and custom the political rights of American citizenship. Black students trudged miles to ramshackle Black schools, often walking past newer, all-white facilities. Sometimes they were bused past white schools, or watched white students ramble past them in the yellow vehicles to superior facilities.

Movie theaters didn't admit Blacks, or required them to sit in the balcony. There were "colored" Coke machines, drinking fountains, toilets. Restaurants barred Blacks. They were denied the right to attend regular state colleges and universities. They were kept in economic bondage in menial jobs. Blacks fought America's wars in Jim Crow units and were killed and brought home to be buried in "colored" cemeteries. Jim Crow was the *law*. The sign "white only" haunted Blacks from childhood to death.

There had been no NAACP in 1896 when the Supreme Court, by an eight-to-one decision, approved the right of states to legislate segregation. A Black man named Homer Adolph Plessy had been arrested for refusing to leave the "white only" car on a Louisiana railroad train, thus breaking a law passed in 1888. He and the group of Blacks with whom he organized the challenge to the statute believed that his Fourteenth Amendment rights to equal protection under the law had been violated. New Orleans Municipal Court Judge John Ferguson did not. The appeal, *Plessy* v. *Ferguson*, wound its way to the U.S. Supreme Court. The decision would not be difficult for the high court to make.

Racism, North and South, was on the rise. Below the Mason-

Dixon line and in the border states, the emancipating principles of the Civil War and Radical Reconstruction had been over-thrown. The Ku Klux Klan, the Knights of the White Camelia, and other white racist organizations had triumphed through a campaign of naked terror. Lynching and other extralegal acts were abetted by the police and state militia. State and city statutes had imposed Jim Crow segregation in the southern and border states. The White House had nodded its approval.

This had been the growing reality and national mood in the two decades of expanding aggression against Blacks since the fall of Reconstruction. Now the Supreme Court was about to bestow upon the drive a constitutional blessing.

The Fourteenth Amendment enforced "the absolute equality of the two races before the law, but in the nature of things it could not have been intended to abolish distinctions based upon color, or to enforce social, as distinguished from political equality," the high court stated. "Laws permitting or even requiring [racial] separation where [the races] are liable to be brought into contact do not necessarily imply the inferiority of either race to the other. . . .

"We consider the underlying fallacy of the plaintiff's [Plessy's] argument to consist in the assumption that the enforced separation of the two races stamps the colored race with a badge of inferiority. If this be so, it is not by reason of anything found in the act, but solely because the colored race chooses to put that construction on it."

Jim Crow, with its fiction of "separate but equal," was as American as apple pie. For the next two decades, the whole of American culture was permeated with white supremacy. Popular songs bore such titles as "All Coons Look Alike to Me" and "If the Man in the Moon Were a Coon." National magazines published "fact" and fiction depicting Blacks as inferior beings. Columbia and Yale spawned professors in the social sciences whose common view was the genetic inferiority of Blacks. Harvard adopted white-only policies in its dormitories. The country itself was on the verge of the Spanish-American War, in the early, colonialist phase of imperialism.

The *Plessy* v. *Ferguson* decision, the legal buttress of the Jim Crow system, was the ultimate target of the NAACP from its birth. The NAACP based itself on a strategy of fighting for Black rights in the courts. However saturated with racism the judiciary was, suits could still be filed and appeals could be carried up the legal ladder. The Democratic and Republican parties were bastions of white supremacy; the American Federation of Labor, based on all-white crafts, itself practiced Jim Crow.

The NAACP's victories came slowly. In 1915 the Supreme Court ruled against the "grandfather clause," a subterfuge for keeping Blacks from voting in several states. In 1917 city ordinances requiring Blacks to live in certain sections of a town were struck down. In 1923 the conviction of a Black was overturned because Blacks had been excluded from lists of prospective jurors.

The NAACP, in defending isolated victims of Jim Crow, in bringing suits which challenged whole sections of discriminatory law, found openings because of the contradictions between Jim Crow law and the U.S. Constitution. But it was unable to contest the essence of *Plessy* v. *Ferguson*.

Not when the president of the United States, who was also a former president of Princeton University, regarded Jim Crow as "not humiliating, but a benefit" for Blacks. Liberal Democrat Woodrow Wilson stoked the fires of racism. And as America moved into the 1920s, Washington, D.C., was a citadel of segregation: Jim Crow in housing, public accommodation, employment, education, and public facilities. The cue had come from Wilson, the nation's chief law enforcement official, who refused to speak to Black audiences and never opposed the epidemic of lynchings that enforced Jim Crow.

Wilson *introduced* segregation into America's center of political power. Shortly after his inauguration in 1912, Jim Crow became the official hiring and promotion standard in the postal service. Soon to follow were the Bureau of the Census, the Bureau of Engraving and Printing, and the Treasury Department. Cafeteria seating and toilets were marked off "for white only," and the Senate gallery was segregated. Purges of Blacks in a number of governmental departments came later.

The NAACP was not deterred. There were setbacks, to be sure, but it stood firm as the voice for Black rights, growing in size and influence through the years.

In 1941, with preparation for World War II well under way, A. Philip Randolph, leader of a Black union, the Brotherhood of Sleeping Car Porters, called for a mass march on Washington to demand that America's booming war industries end racial discrimination in hiring. The march never took place; President Franklin D. Roosevelt headed it off with the reluctant appointment of the Fair Employment Practices Commission. Roosevelt, who never supported the campaigns for an antilynch law or other civil rights legislation, paid only lip service to Black rights, and the FEPC was mostly a paper organization. But the call for the march had generated a momentum that was not without effect, and was a harbinger of things to come.

Under pressure to live up to its wartime rhetoric against Hitler's racism, the Roosevelt administration joined an NAACP-backed suit against the "white primary" system of the Democratic Party in Texas. This Jim Crow practice, which in effect barred Blacks from voting, was thrown out by the Supreme Court in 1944.

By now the core of the NAACP legal team included Charles Huston, who would become the dean of Howard University Law School, and a young attorney named Thurgood Marshall, later to be appointed U.S. solicitor general and finally elevated to the Supreme Court. Marshall, an architect of NAACP court strategy, had his sights on *Plessy* v. *Ferguson.*

The year 1944 marked the appearance of *An American Dilemma* by Gunnar Myrdal, a Swedish sociologist. This two-volume work was a painstaking documentation of the brutality of the Jim Crow system. It had an especially disturbing effect upon public opinion at this time because the portrait of white supremacy under law punctured the propaganda ideal of a color-blind democracy waging war against the Nazis' racist barbarism.

Dramatic economic and social changes growing out of World War II would set the stage for the defeat of Jim Crow. The Black population had begun to shift. Sharecropping, long the basis of southern agriculture, was giving way to mechanization. Blacks were being forced off the land and into southern cities; the massive trek to the industrial North continued. Moreover, Blacks were demanding payment on the wartime boasts about democracy. Now the fight was at home. Blacks had not bled overseas to return to miserable bondage. New moods were generated, new aspirations. For Blacks, the "V for Victory" salute had a second meaning: victory at home, as well as abroad. It was the "Double V" in the Black community.

The postwar revolutions by nonwhite peoples in Asia and Africa against colonialism had an inspiring effect upon Black Americans. In addition, the U.S. government needed to improve its image with these newly independent states. This was hardly served by the overt racism of Jim Crow.

Such bigotry was most glaring in the armed forces. In 1948 the government decided to desegregate the army, an act whose implications reverberated deeply through the Black population, North and South. This was a signal to the NAACP to press ahead.

The U.S. was under greater international scrutiny than ever before; its racial policies were steadily under fire from abroad. As a concession to internal and foreign pressure, the Democratic Party put a modest civil rights plank in its 1948 platform. Black community after Black community was challenging segregated education. Parents filed suits in Delaware, South Carolina, Virginia, and Kansas. All of these cases were lost in the lower courts and they all went to the Supreme Court. Each of them contained the basis of a confrontation with *Plessy* v. *Ferguson.* In the past, the NAACP, defeated on appeals challenging any aspect of the "separate but equal" doctrine, had given up doing so as impractical. Now times were beginning to change.

The road the NAACP had traveled was forty-three years long when, in 1952, the Supreme Court combined the five separate appeals, placing the case of a young Black student, the first alphabetically of a number of Black plaintiffs, at the top of its list. Her name was Linda Brown. She had walked miles to a run-down all-Black school when an all-white school—better kept, better staffed, just plain *better*—was a few blocks away. The Black plaintiffs had been fighting the Topeka school board and its Jim Crow system for five years, and *Brown* v. *Topeka Board of Education* was now before the court of last resort.

Of all the cases before the court, none had come out of such a heated battle as that of *Briggs* v. *Elliot,* in Clarendon County, South Carolina, the heart of Jim Crow country. The NAACP had considered this the pilot suit. But the Supreme Court chose not to place the South Carolina case at the top of the list. To do so would have made action upholding the appeals seem like a head-on assault on the South. Topeka, in the border state of Kansas, would serve better, taking off some of the heat.

Events were creating a climate which could produce the decision; from the sweeping changes in the Black population to the desegregation of the army and the stunning impact of the colonial revolution on the American government. As Martin Luther King, Jr., would remark in an early speech, "Whether we want to be or not, we are caught up in a great moment of history. . . . The vast majority of people of the world are colored. . . . Up until four or five years ago most of the one and one-quarter billion colored peoples were exploited by empires of the West. . . . Today many are free. . . . And the rest are on the road. . . . We are part of that great movement."

The Truman administration, too, was conscious of the phenomenon King described. As it prepared to turn the reins of government over to the Eisenhower regime, it would file a friend-of-the-court brief in support of the NAACP appeals. Segregation, the brief contended, was indeed unconstitutional, a thorny problem for Washington—"the window through which the world looks at our house." Later, Secretary of State Dean Acheson would make similar remarks. Propelled by world historic events, the rulers of America were making a conscious shift in policy.

On May 17, 1954, the Supreme Court announced its decision. "Does segregation of children in public schools solely on the basis of race, even though the physical facilities and other 'tangible' factors may be equal, deprive the children of the minority group of equal educational opportunities? We believe that it does. . . .

"To separate them from others of similar age and qualifications solely because of their race generates a feeling of inferiority as to their status in the community that may affect their hearts and minds in a way unlikely to be undone. . . .

"Whatever may have been the extent of psychological knowledge at the time of *Plessy* v. *Ferguson,* this finding is amply supported by modern authority. Any language in *Plessy* v. *Ferguson* contrary to this finding is rejected.

"We conclude that in the field of public education the doctrine of 'separate but equal' has no place. Separate educational facilities are inherently unequal. Therefore we hold that the plaintiffs and others similarly situated for whom the actions have been brought are, by reason of the segregation complained of, deprived of the equal protection of the laws guaranteed by the Fourteenth Amendment."

The decision itself took pains not to assault Jim Crow verbally, nor to excoriate the grotesque legal argumentation that had bolstered *Plessy* v. *Ferguson*'s authorization of white supremacy. Once consensus had been reached that "separate but equal" was a violation of the Fourteenth Amendment, the justices had debated for months how to avoid tackling the "southern system" head on. The wording should be stern but cautious enough not to ruffle the sensibilities of the Jim Crow states. The meaning of such formulations was clear to Black leaders who, while hailing the decision, would note that it had not called for dismantling of racist school systems.

In fact it would be more than another year before an implementation decision would come from the high court. In the *Brown* decision of May 17, 1954, the justices held that racial discrimination in public education is unconstitutional. The implementation ruling of May 31, 1955, added that "all provisions of Federal, State or local law requiring or permitting such discrimination must yield to this principle." Thurgood Marshall had sought a fixed date for the dismantling of segregation, but the court merely called for a "prompt and reasonable start toward full compliance."

From the very beginning of the historic hearing, there was an atmosphere of apprehension, as if a high explosive was being handled in the courtroom. The judges, compelled by powerful international, domestic, and governmental pressures to make the decision, had then seemed to take fright. Choosing Kansas instead of South Carolina was an act of deference to Jim Crow. Then they had delayed their consensus order, seeking language to soften the blow. They had waited more than a year to outline implementation; and that edict was ambiguous enough to *not* be taken as an order mandating immediate dismantling of the system it had declared onerous, evil, and unconstitutional. The time elapsed had allowed the Jim Crow forces to recover and rally. Declarations by racist governors, senators, legislators, and mayors, repeated month after month, would soon begin to dissipate the mood which had followed the decision—in both the North and the South—that the Supreme Court had *outlawed* school segregation at long last and that there was no alternative but to accept the "law of the land."

Experience would dampen Black America's initial state of euphoria. Now, for the first time since Reconstruction, the law was on its side; but it was going to take a fight bigger than anyone could have imagined back on May 17, 1954.

"Legislation and court orders tend only to declare rights," Martin Luther King, Jr., once noted. "They can never thoroughly deliver them. Only when people themselves begin to act are rights on paper given life blood." The *Brown* decision was an impetus to act, and the initiatives it inspired came first from individuals.

Emmett Till, a fourteen-year-old Black from Chicago, was

visiting relatives in Mississippi in 1955. The whites who lynched him claimed he had whistled at a white woman. They seized him, demanding he tell them that whites were superior to Blacks. Emmett Till refused, and they killed him. That "crazy nigger" just couldn't be dealt with, his murderers told *Life* magazine.

Perhaps it was the rising mood generated by the *Brown* decision that influenced Emmett Till's mother to ship his body back to Chicago as an anguished protest. That seemingly minor, private act became the spark for social action by masses of people. A quarter of a million turned out to view the victim's body. Protest meetings rapidly spread throughout the country—twenty thousand in New York City; six thousand in Detroit; three thousand in Cleveland and in San Francisco; eight thousand in Los Angeles; nine thousand in Washington, D.C. In Chicago five thousand people demanded that federal troops be sent to Mississippi to protect Blacks.

An all-white jury freed Till's murderers. Blacks who testified against the terrorists were threatened, one of them "disappearing" after a mysterious arrest. Till's uncle was forced to flee the state. The FBI investigated and harassed organizers of protests against the lynching.

But the eruption of protest on an unprecedented scale around the lynching of Till was a symptom of the rebellion gestating within the Black community. In December 1955 a Black woman named Rosa Parks—a longtime NAACP member—refused to give up her seat on a city bus to a white man—the proper, legal thing to do in Montgomery, Alabama. She was arrested. Months earlier, perhaps nothing would have happened. But now there was the *Brown* decision. E.D. Nixon—the local NAACP leader and a trade union organizer—sought out Martin Luther King, Jr., to head a bus boycott. It mobilized the city's Black community in a solid front and aroused national attention and support. After a long struggle the buses were desegregated. And the news coming from the deep South was of a movement being born: the civil rights movement.

It faced perilous obstacles. The white supremacist "Dixiecrats," who had bolted the Democratic Party in 1948, were back in the fold. The Supreme Court had remanded implementation of the *Brown* decision to the lower courts, a time-consuming process quite in accordance with the "go-slow" sentiment of Congress and the White House. It would take the *action* of Blacks and their supporters to *compel* the break-up of the Jim Crow system.

In 1957, Little Rock, Arkansas, became the center of the fight to desegregate the schools. Governor Orval Faubus, elected as a liberal and a racial moderate with the support of the state AFL-CIO and NAACP, became the hero of the Ku Klux Klan and the White Citizens Council by defying the desegregation order and fomenting mob action against entry of Black students into the lily-white schools. President Eisenhower at first made excuses for the racists. At a news conference in early September, he asked for understanding of the emotions of southern whites who feared "mongrelization of the races." But the events in Little Rock excited national and worldwide indignation and finally forced a distinctly reluctant Eisenhower to send in federal troops. Bayonets held off white mobs; the schools were desegregated. The racists had suffered a stunning blow, and supporters of civil rights were inspired by the victory.

Still, the real surge was yet to come. It broke on February 1, 1960, in Greensboro, North Carolina, as Black students engaged in a sit-in. They marched into the F.W. Woolworth department store and sat at the "white only" lunch counter. Ordered to leave, they refused. They were arrested for disobeying the hated Jim Crow laws, which were unconstitutional under the *Brown* decision. But the Black students would return, often with white supporters, time and time again, throughout the South. The target of such actions was the entire range of public facilities segregated by Jim Crow: beaches, trains, restaurants, movie theaters, parks, bus terminals.

The struggle would spread to the North, awakening support on the campuses—which were then still passive as the result of McCarthyism. Woolworth stores in Boston, New York, and Chicago were picketed by protesters demanding the end of the company's southern policy. The development of support in the North was both useful and necessary for the victory in the South, and decisive for the new student movement that was beginning to evolve.

The Freedom Rides were organized, and thousands of white and Black students and northern supporters of civil rights journeyed south to take up the struggle against Jim Crow in massive protests, marches, pickets, sit-ins, and demonstrations. Nonviolent, the troops of the civil rights struggle faced police clubs, blackjacks, and electric cattle prods. Attack dogs were unleashed on them. They were soaked and driven to the ground by high-pressure streams from fire hoses.

They did not buckle to the legalized mayhem of the police or to the extralegal violence of Klan nightriders or White Citizens Council vigilantes. Their fortitude won the admiration and sympathy of millions of Americans who watched the battles that raged throughout the South.

Moreover, white racist resistance to Black rights was now visible to the whole world. America's vicious "racial policy" was exposed, and the movement to overcome it was gaining international support.

The scenes of major confrontation shifted rapidly. Birmingham, Alabama, became the center of the struggle in 1963, as boycotts, marches, demonstrations, and pitched battles with the police shook the city to its Jim Crow roots. Here in an urban setting, brutal police commanded by the notorious "Bull" Connor were met with a hail of bricks, bottles, rocks—sometimes rifle fire—as they drove demonstrators back into the Black community. The pleas of Martin Luther King, Jr., for passive resistance became unavailing with the mass of urban Blacks once police violence passed a certain level.

Black pleas for federal troops had steadily been dismissed by President John F. Kennedy. His emissaries' advice was to "cool things down." The fruit of such a policy was bitter. Racist terrorists, emboldened by Kennedy's refusal to act and smugly confident of support from city officials and Governor Wallace, assaulted the Black community regularly.

On September 15, 1963, the Sixteenth Street Baptist Church in Birmingham was rocked by a bomb. Four young Black girls attending Sunday school there were killed. Finally, Kennedy sent in federal troops. In Detroit, a quarter-million people, virtually the entire Black community, took to the streets in a historic show of power and determination. In Chicago, fifty thousand marched. The country had been staggered by the Birmingham bombing; the Jim Crow bigots faced growing isolation.

The names and places of conflict would span the South: Selma, Alabama; Oxford, Mississippi; St. Augustine, Florida; Memphis, Tennessee. Soon afterwards, the gigantic march on Washington would take place. The movement expanded northward not only through actions of sympathy and solidarity but in the beginnings of protest against local discrimination in housing and education—in Chicago, New York, and Boston.

There would be more killings of civil rights leaders and

activists, both Black and white. Federal troops were sent to Mississippi to protect James Meredith, a young Black man, as he entered the University of Mississippi. That first night at "Old Miss," racist mobs raged against the troops. Hundreds were injured and arrested, and two died in the fighting.

The civil rights battle was electrifying the country. New organizations rose up to lead the struggle. The Student Nonviolent Coordinating Committee—called "Snick" after its initials—animated and organized tens of thousands of Black and white students to join the crusade.

"All deliberate speed," the tempo prescribed by the high court's implementation decision of *Brown*, was proving to be a snail's pace of enforcement. Only action and protest had brought actual gains. The scope of struggle, moreover, was opening new fronts against Jim Crow every day. And with every day of delay and evasion by the government, new thousands of Blacks began to question the role of their "friends" in Washington and the nature of the two parties which ruled the country.

Shortly after the massive civil rights march on Washington, where Martin Luther King, Jr., delivered his "I have a dream" speech, President Kennedy called a high-level meeting of a hundred industrial and corporate leaders. His message was simple and clear: the civil rights struggle had to be taken out of the streets. To accomplish this, Jim Crow had to go. The federal government would begin to move on enforcement. Out of this emerged the 1964 Civil Rights Act and the 1965 Voting Rights Act.

In 1964, however, a new element was introduced in the struggle. The mass movement in the South against Jim Crow had exercised profound influence on northern Blacks, most of them confined to the misery of the ghettos. Racism was not "the law" here, but racial oppression was the fact. In 1964 Harlem exploded in a rebellion touched off by the police killing of a Black youth. In 1965 Watts, the Black community in Los Angeles, erupted as if in visceral response to the spectacle televised live from Selma, Alabama, where Blacks were facing intense violence from police and white vigilantes. In 1967 Newark's impoverished Black community rose up. Hundreds of cities would experience similar blowouts, culminating in the national outburst caused by the assassination of Martin Luther King, Jr., in 1968.

The mood of challenge to the government was spreading, heated by the growth of opposition to the war in Vietnam. The civil rights movement and the new wave of protest against the war overlapped in leaders, activists, ideas, and anger.

Tactical differences had existed for some time in the civil rights movement between the older, established NAACP and the newer organizations involved in direct protest actions—King's Southern Christian Leadership Conference and the Congress of Racial Equality. Throughout the period of turbulence, the NAACP had maintained steadfast confidence in and concentration on the courts. While local units of the NAACP participated in demonstrations, more often than not it was the newer organizations that initiated them. The NAACP, after two generations of legal battles and lobbying, believed that relief could be won through pressuring the Democratic Party. This position was also held by SCLC and CORE, but these two organizations engaged in direct protests, street actions, and civil disobedience as the most effective means of pressure.

SNCC, the radical wing of the movement, was opposed to reliance on Democratic politicians. Much of their distrust came from bitter experience in civil rights battles. Also, many SNCC activists were influenced by the intransigent Black nationalist leader Malcolm X, who declared that the "Democratic Party is responsible for the racism in this country, along with the Republicans." SNCC evolved into an all-Black organization, nationalist in consciousness and revolutionary in direction, but it was unable to develop a strategy of involving the masses of Blacks in struggle for social change. Its radical perspectives dissipated into small-group confrontations and adventurist concepts as the organization met systematic harassment and repression from the government.

While the politically isolated militants encountered the iron fist of victimization, the government offered the moderate, pro-Democratic Party wing of the movement the velvet glove of concessions. Poverty programs and community service projects from President Lyndon B. Johnson's "Great Society" patronage bag may have been meager compared with the largesse enjoyed by other segments of society, but the jobs and funds were the glue that held former activists to the Democratic Party. And, in fact, the Democratic Party *did* open up, drawing Blacks into administrative and elective posts as part of the national, state, and city governmental apparatus.

This co-opting of the Black leadership was reflected in the decline of mass protest and action—which had wrung the social and political concessions from the government in the first place. Jim Crow had not been killed by government edict, but by a decade of sustained and militant protests. Now the leaders of such protests, and a key layer of activists, were either dead or demoralized, frustrated, and isolated—or else snugly ensconced in the party which had originated, administered, and defended Jim Crow for almost a century. That party could make cosmetic changes, to be sure. Racism now existed without the legal facade of Jim Crow, but it remained a living reality of social, economic, and political oppression.

Blacks—as a people, a nationality forged during slavery and subsequent forms of oppression—remained second-class citizens. Their exploitation provided American business and industry with a cheap source of labor; job discrimination meant billions of dollars in profits. Racism was not simply irrational ideas or the legal trappings of Jim Crow, but the bedrock of a system. It was used to justify America's foreign wars against "lesser races." It was the source of ghettoization of the inner cities, the Black communities confined to deteriorating slums.

Now, at the end of the 1960s, *de jure* racism, the "lawful" segregation of Jim Crow authorized by *Plessy* v. *Ferguson,* was dead. But the racism institutionalized *de facto,* through centuries of oppression, still presented an enormous hurdle to full social equality.

By the 1970s the civil rights movement was dormant. The Black power wing, first in SNCC and later in the Black Panther Party, had been politically isolated and then physically crushed. CORE had become the merest shell of its previous self. With the death of Martin Luther King, Jr., the decline in direct action, and the increasing grip of the Democratic Party, SCLC dwindled in size and influence. Although estrangement from the goverment was greater than ever before in the Black community, there were no action-minded leaders capable of turning the frustration into protest for change. By the early 1970s the Democratic Party, through thousands of Black officials—mayors, congresspeople, state legislators, executives in community agencies and projects—constituted an influential force in the Black community. Its political perspective manacled the Blacks who looked to it as the vehicle through which change would be brought about.

With the decline of the newer, more militant organizations of the 1960s, the NAACP was soon to be the only strong national organization of Black Americans. It would continue pressing in the courts for Black rights, expanding its scope to include suits for affirmative action and against the death penalty and housing discrimination. But it would not cease its campaign for complete school desegregation. Now, with Jim Crow buried in the South, that would include targets in the North.

The 1960s had seen a forest fire of social protest sparked by the *Brown* decision. It had taken virtually a war to implement the order—more than a decade of pitched battles that tapped the militancy of Black America. The energy and strength of that movement had done much to shake America out of the fear of the McCarthy era, setting the stage for a new challenge to the government: opposition to the war in Southeast Asia. A radicalization had been born, manifesting itself in rebellious attitudes against governmental authority and traditional morality. It permeated the youth—on the college and high school campuses, in the armed forces, the church, the prisons.

The *Brown* decision, as a legal pronouncement, was not so resounding, not at all a clarion call. But what it inspired was another matter. As the basis of all future legal and legislative decisions affecting Black rights, *Brown*'s strength came from the struggle required to give it "life blood," to turn legal edict into reality. Furthermore, the spectacle of a confident, fighting movement gave the lie to the stereotypes and myths about Black inferiority and stimulated a new generation of Black writers, artists, educators, and agitators to cultural and intellectual expressions of race pride. Through the struggle, Blacks had hammered out a new identity, while educating millions of whites, winning many of them as supporters in action, isolating the retrograde elements and Jim Crow partisans.

As the 1960s came to a close, it was apparent that America's thinking on the "race problem" had undergone a drastic change in the course of the struggle inspired by *Brown*. That new consciousness is a material force in America. It is a roadblock to retreat. Though quiescent through the early 1970s, the Black community still would register gains in the fight for democratic rights; the legacy of the 1960s remained strong as a moral and psychological reserve that could still be drawn on.

In no city would *Brown* come alive—and come under challenge—as in Boston. And that challenge would make *Brown* itself appear somewhat less invulnerable than before. Its standing would become inextricably intertwined with the campaign for school desegregation in Boston.

# 4

# The Machinery
# of Segregation

Slavery had been abolished in Massachusetts during the American Revolution. Many of Boston's Blacks were former slaves; others had come as free people from the West Indies. Yet their children were denied access to the public school system of the city and barred from private schools.

In 1787, a West Indian Black named Prince Hall, who had fought in the Battle of Bunker Hill, led a delegation to the state legislature with a petition. "We are of the humble opinion that we have the right to enjoy the privileges of free men," it stated. "But that we do not will appear in many instances. . . . One is the education of our children which now receive no benefit from the free schools in the town of Boston. . . . [This is] a great grievance. . . . We now feel the want of a common education [denied our children] for [no] other reason [than that] they are black. . . ."

The petition was denied.

In 1798 Prince Hall set up his home as an all-Black school. In 1800 the city of Boston refused to support it. In 1820 the city fathers opened a handful of segregated schools for Blacks. Boston had a Jim Crow system—if not by name, then by deed. The crumbling, rundown Black schools were inferior in every respect.

One Black five-year-old, Sarah Roberts, would walk past five all-white schools to the hovel reserved to "the colored." Her father filed suit in his daughter's name against the city of Boston, after being rebuked by officials for trying to enroll her in the better, white institutions. In 1849, in a historic decision, the Massachusetts Supreme Judicial Court ruled against Sarah Roberts. The decision implied that a variety of social "relations" and "conditions"—prejudices—could be the basis of laws and statutes that were constitutionally valid. Black rights thus had no fundamental legal guarantee.

The *Roberts* v. *City of Boston* decision, which in effect

authorized two school systems, one for white and one for Black, became the precedent a generation later for federal court rulings giving approval to Jim Crow. Though it did not utilize any "separate but equal" formula, it became the chief legal reference point for the noxious *Plessy* v. *Ferguson* decision in 1896.

School segregation in Boston was legally ended in 1854, in response to agitation by Blacks and abolitionists. But discrimination in employment and housing left the Black community vulnerable to the loss of previous gains, and in the period of racial reaction following the betrayal of Radical Reconstruction, Boston's once strong abolitionist fervor became weaker and weaker. There was still struggle and protest, much of it articulated by the militant Black editor William Monroe Trotter in his paper, the *Guardian*; but through the machinations of the Democratic Party officials who ruled the city, a system of *de facto* school segregation was steadily imposed. No battle would be opened on this front until after World War II.

In 1950 Ruth Batson was a young mother with children in the Boston schools. She had grown up in a political household; both of her West Indian parents had been followers of Marcus Garvey, the Black nationalist leader. She visited the school buildings her children attended and was shocked by their condition. She went to the Boston School Department to protest, but to no avail.

Ten years later, she sought out the Boston NAACP, again complaining about the schools, and was put in charge of the group's newly formed education committee. Now the wheels began to turn. The rising protests in the South, the *Brown* decision, and the new mood in the country were setting the stage. Batson's committee compiled a staggering proof of the woeful educational system imposed on Black children. From per-pupil expenditures to teacher assignment, from educational resources to physical plant, the Black students received the least. It came under the heading of *de facto* segregation, discrimination that was part of the social fabric of the city. The NAACP's education committee wrangled over the term for some time. It seemed a bit radical. The idea that the Boston School Committee was *organizing* segregation never, Batson would recall, crossed their minds.

In January 1963, a group of Black mothers gathered to protest the miserable conditions in the school their children attended. They had been buoyed by the struggle down South. Now they were prepared to take on the Boston School Committee, if necessary. Backed by the NAACP, they demanded a public hearing. It was refused.

In March, as the state legislature began hearings on housing discrimination, the NAACP brought forward its findings, focusing the light of publicity on a situation the school committee had previously kept hidden.

In May, more than ten thousand marchers converged on the State House in the first of the city's big solidarity demonstrations with the southern civil rights struggle. The theme of the march was support to the Blacks in Birmingham battling for equality, but several of the speakers drew a straight line connecting that battle to the unfolding campaign against discrimination in Boston. One of them, James Reeb, a white Unitarian minister and militant civil rights partisan, urged a Black boycott of the schools to dramatize the issue of *de facto* segregation—a suggestion that sent a chill up the spine of the school committee.

That body finally agreed to hold a hearing, but only on the condition that *de facto* segregation could not be discussed. The NAACP attended the hearing, which began on June 11. "The room was jammed," Batson recalled. The NAACP presented fourteen demands to remedy discrimination. It was a heated, bitter confrontation. "They rejected everything we said," Batson noted, adding, "That meeting was when the war began."

The fervor of the fight swept through the Black community and inspired white support. An unprecedented school boycott took place; eight thousand Black students stayed home. "There was ferment everywhere," Batson recalled. "Everyone was a volunteer. There was a lot of sacrifice."

More militant Blacks led by Rev. James Breeden came forward in the boycott, strengthening the movement started by the NAACP. "I was elated," Batson recalled. "We had a coalition." CORE, SCLC, the churches, community activists, and white supporters joined in the united effort. Throughout the summer mass picket lines and rallies were held in front of the school committee offices. Thomas Atkins, then a student at Harvard Law School, joined in the fray, taking on a "temporary" job as acting executive secretary of the Boston NAACP. It lasted two years.

In the fall, Melvin King, a young Black activist from the NAACP education committee, another of the new militants of the rising struggle, ran for the Boston School Committee. There was something special about this campaign. The candidate was a fighter, backed by all of the civil rights forces. He ran independently from the Democratic Party in the election, utilizing his campaign to mobilize support for the desegregation struggle.

He did not win, but the campaign accomplished a lot. More Black voters turned out than ever before; in some Black districts King's candidacy drew as much as 90 percent of the vote. At this time Louise Day Hicks was gaining the spotlight among the racists; she ran as an opponent of desegregation, saying: "There is no segregation in Boston. I deny its existence." King would outpoll Hicks by as much as fifty to one in some areas of the Black community.

In 1964 a united Black community drive was the basis of "Freedom Stay Out Day" in Boston. The one-day boycott on February 26 was part of a national show of support for the civil rights movement as well as part of the campaign to fight discrimination locally. In New York City 360,000 students had stayed home on February 4, three weeks before the date of the Boston mobilization.

Massachusetts Attorney General Edward Brooke, a liberal Republican who would later become the nation's first Black senator since Reconstruction, ruled the Boston stay-out illegal. His decision reflected mounting pressure by the city's bigots to stem the new movement. It had little effect.

For weeks parents, community organizations, and white activists had carefully mapped plans for "Freedom Schools"—one-day institutions developed as part of the boycott. It was a huge undertaking: a faculty of two thousand was organized; churches, agencies, and homes became classrooms; massive publicity was organized. On February 25, a rally of three thousand in Roxbury kicked off the boycott. The next day, more than eight thousand Black and one thousand white students attended the Freedom Schools. Later in the day, eighteen hundred Blacks and whites marched in a blizzard to City Hall to protest segregation.

The growing struggle not only voiced the demands for equality in education; it revealed that the opponents were hell-bent on preserving segregation. This much was admitted by school committee member William O'Connell, who declared: "We have no inferior education in our schools. What we have been getting is an inferior type of student."

The continuing fight against the school committee was sometimes spurred in tragic ways by the battles in the South. In

March 1965 James Reeb, the white minister who had been a key figure in the Boston drive, was killed along with James Lee Jackson, a Black man. Their murderers were vigilantes stalking civil rights activists in Selma, Alabama, then the latest center of confrontation between Black equality and Jim Crow. In Boston thirty thousand people turned out for a massive memorial for Reeb. The struggle he had died in was on both sides of the Mason-Dixon line.

A month later, Martin Luther King, Jr., returned to Boston, where he had been a student at Boston University. He was aware of the struggle in the city and had backed the Black student boycott. He tried to visit the W.L.P. Boardman school, a prime exhibit of segregation that was a target of Black parents' protest, but was refused admittance. The next day he led fifteen thousand Bostonians to the State House to demand an end to *de facto* segregation.

King also had a meeting with Hicks, who, Ruth Batson says, "treated him like dirt." Hicks and the bigots she represented were, however, in a distinct minority, isolated and demoralized by the tumult raging about them. The pressure for Black rights had made an impact. With the mass action led by King, it had reached a turning point.

Rev. Vernon Carter, the fiery civil rights activist from the All Saints Lutheran Church, conducted a 114-day, round-the-clock picket and vigil at the school committee offices, which was joined by thousands as the weeks stretched out. The aim of the vigil, like other protests of the time, was to demand passage of the proposed Racial Imbalance Act in the state legislature. Carter's individual action reflected the Black community's sentiment for the law. He stood before the school committee offices as a daily reminder of the months and years of parents' meetings, pickets, demonstrations, and marches that had gone on before.

On August 18, 1965, the act was signed into law. Massachusetts became the first state to outlaw *de facto* segregation in education. At the time, Black youth were being educated in a clearly inferior system of schools. Nine out of ten predominantly Black schools had been built before World War I. Their staffs had the highest percentage of provisional and substitute teachers—those without tenure or experience. Per-pupil expenditures were one-third less than in the mainly white schools. Ten percent less was spent on textbooks; 19 percent less on library and reference materials; 27 percent less on health care.

Moreover, the attitude of the predominantly white teaching and administrative staff was anti-Black. This would be brought to the attention of the nation in *Death at an Early Age,* a best-selling book by Boston schoolteacher Jonathan Kozol. Kozol, fired in a highly publicized controversy in 1965 for his unauthorized use in a Roxbury school of a poem by Black author Langston Hughes, stripped the veneer of lies from Boston's school system. The book's publication in 1967 alerted America to the simmering crisis. Locally its devastating exposé of the Boston School Committee was a powerful blow to the bigots' defense of their system.

The Racial Imbalance Act defined segregation in only one of its facets. "Imbalanced" (or segregated) schools were those that were majority Black. All-white schools did not fall within the scope of the new law. Busing to achieve "racial balance" was thus a requirement and remedy which fell on Blacks only. They would be transported to all-white schools. At least that was what the law said. It was never implemented.

With its passage, the mass struggle against *de facto* segregation subsided. Within the Black community, a period of waiting for implementation began, although dissatisfaction with the law itself was evident: Why not the white schools? Why should we alone bear the burden of busing?

Amidst the frustration growing out of the initial victory, the principal leaders of that struggle went off, in Thomas Atkins's words, "in a lot of different directions." Ruth Batson became involved in the newly founded METCO (Metropolitan Council for Educational Opportunities), which organized Black students to be bused into white suburban schools. Melvin King became a Democratic state representative from Roxbury. Paul Parks, another key member of the NAACP education committee, was appointed head of the Model Cities program in Boston. Atkins himself left the NAACP to work on urban renewal problems, and later was elected to the Boston City Council.

The struggle on the school issue continued in the annual efforts of antibusing state legislators to repeal the Racial Imbalance Law. The Boston School Committee embarked on a relentless drive to sabotage the law, appealing it in the courts, obstructing it in practice, and all the while organizing segregation in a cold, methodical fashion. A new movement was arising: the antibusing movement.

As the 1960s wore on, as the national civil rights movement was divided and its leadership was being drawn out of the streets and into the Democratic Party, the bigots buttressed the dual school system in Boston. To those who pointed to existing *de facto* segregation and the busing requirements for racial balance, the school committee had a stock answer: Boston's was a "freedom of choice" school system. Black and white parents alike could avail themselves of the "open enrollment" program allowing free transfers to any school in the city. On paper, this program meant busing was unnecessary.

Ellen Jackson, a young Roxbury mother, took up the school committee's offer in 1965 by founding Operation Exodus, a program which attempted to utilize "open enrollment" for Black students. Unable to get city support, she scratched for private funding, running up huge debts over the years.

The experience of Operation Exodus confirmed the pattern of organized segregation. Information was withheld from Black parents regarding available places in all-white schools. Interviews with parents were required; this was a device, supplementing the noting of telltale Roxbury addresses on written requests, to facilitate refusal of transfers to Black pupils. If and when Black students made it into the all-white schools—mostly in Hyde Park and Dorchester—they were segregated in seating arrangements (even placed in hallways and corridors) and urged by guidance counselors to leave the school. At some schools, doors were chained shut by administrators. At one, desks bolted to the floor were removed, to make seats "unavailable."

At its peak, Operation Exodus involved eleven hundred students. As it ended in 1970, Ellen Jackson went to work for the state board of education, an agency which officially supported desegregation but was unable to dent the resistance of the Boston School Committee.

In 1971 and 1972 a group of Black parents again went through the process that Ruth Batson had begun in 1950 and that in effect had dissolved with the incorporation of Operation Exodus into the school structure in 1970. But this time it took only a few months to find that all avenues for redress of their grievances—the city government, state officials, voluntary programs—had been exhausted. After several meetings, they sought the advice of lawyers they knew would be sympathetic. They learned there was only one resort left: the federal courts. From the start, the Black parents' appeal was "as grass roots as any you could find," according to Atkins. Community organizations and agencies were rapidly involved, providing more plaintiffs. A battery of lawyers was assembled. The suit, contending deliberate segregation of the Boston schools, was prepared. The national NAACP agreed to provide expenses for the painstaking legal work through its independently chartered "special contributions fund." The lead lawyer was Harold J. Flannery, a veteran of the civil rights division of the Justice Department, head of the Harvard Center for Law and Education. The team was rounded out with other lawyers from the Harvard center and from the Boston firm of Foley, Hoag, and Eliot.

In March of 1972 Federal District Judge W. Arthur Garrity, Jr., had been chosen by lot from a panel of judges to receive the envelope marked *Tallulah Morgan et al., Plaintiffs* v. *James Hennigan et al., Defendants.* The envelope contained the summary of what would prove to be legal dynamite, blowing apart the carefully constructed dual school system.

Arthur Garrity, tall, bald, and bespectacled, was not known for making waves. It was said that in private conversation he was not enthusiastic about busing. But as the facts of the Boston situation unfolded in his court, there could be no alternative. In 1971, the year before the appeal was filed, and in 1973, the year Garrity spent in considering his decision, the Supreme Court issued two rulings which were, in addition to *Brown*, his legal reference points.

In 1971, by a unanimous decision, the high court upheld mandatory busing in *Swann* v. *Charlotte-Mecklenburg Board of Education*, affirming a lower court order desegregating schools in the North Carolina district. In 1973, with one dissent, a sweeping court-ordered busing plan was upheld in the Colorado case of *Keyes* v. *Denver School District No. 1. Swann* and *Keyes* were the application of the line of *Brown* to situations in which there was segregation not mandated by law. *Brown's* blow against legislated Jim Crow was now directed against *de facto* segregation. Racial discrimination was racial discrimination regardless of form.

Three months after the appeal was filed in federal district court, the Department of Health, Education and Welfare began hearings on the withholding of $10 million in federal funds from the Boston school system. Previously, upwards of $50 million in state aid had been withheld from the city, in an attempt to compel the school committee to comply with the Racial Imbalance Law. But the school committee, firmly in the hands of bigoted foes of "racial balance," was adamant about keeping the schools segregated at any cost.

In early 1973 Federal Administrative Judge Lawrence Ring found against the school committee. Boston, his decision proclaimed, was operating a dual school system, separate and unequal. This was added to the mountain of testimony before Judge Garrity.

The school committee's lawyer, James St. Clair—later to become Richard Nixon's attorney in the last months of his crumbling presidency and to achieve notoriety for his racial slur against a senator from Hawaii during the Watergate hearings—was unable to find an out for his clients. His main defense was that neighborhood segregation was solely responsible for the racial composition of the schools and that this disproved the malice attributed to the school committee by the Black plaintiffs.

The evidence showed otherwise. Segregation began at the elementary school level, with pupil assignment supervised by invariably white superintendents. In a given district, two of five schools might be entirely or majority Black, the remainder all-white. Students normally went from these elementary schools to junior high or middle schools and then to high school according to geographical "feeder patterns" which maintained segregation. Blacks who tried to transfer into the white schools were usually frustrated by the administrators of the "open enrollment" plan, while thousands of whites transferred every year.

Another factor discouraging Black transfers was the dual grade structure. Black students went to 5-year elementary, 3-year middle, and 4-year high schools; the whites had a 6-3-3 setup. This arithmetic penalized Blacks who transferred to white schools by forcing them to go through an extra change of schools. For example, Black students finishing elementary school could try to transfer into white elementary schools for sixth grade; but that would mean changing schools again the next year to attend junior high. Their education would be less disrupted if they simply went on to sixth grade at middle schools in the Black system.

Within the structure itself were special "advanced" classes at the elementary level. These courses were taught only in all-white schools. They prepared the students for the city's predominantly white accelerated "examination schools"—Boston Latin, Girls' Latin, and Boston Technical High School. The entry tests for these schools were found by the Massachusetts Commission Against Discrimination to be culturally biased and discriminatory, a finding not contested by the school committee, which voluntarily abandoned them. Subsequently, new tests devised by the school committee would be junked by Garrity, who found them also to be discriminatory.

Boston Technical High School, overwhelmingly white in teacher staff, administration, and student body, stood as a telling refutation of the claims of the segregationists who protested the busing of white students into the "high crime area" of Black Roxbury. The Hicks-Bulger-Flaherty "Declaration of Clarification" of 1974, which hysterically promoted that view, overlooked the example of Boston Technical High School. It was in the center of Roxbury, and had been for years. White students were bused across the city to it, and had been for years.

Indeed, busing had been used to *maintain* an entire system of segregation, as thousands of white students, through initial elementary school assignments and "open enrollment," were bused into all-white schools. In some cases—where Black and white neighborhoods bordered one another or where neighborhoods were racially mixed—what would have been naturally integrated schools became, as the court put it, "racially identifiable"; that is, they were segregated through busing.

"Neighborhood schools" meant white schools, better schools. White students were bused out of their neighborhoods to such schools on the basis of easily obtained transfers. White students from West Roxbury traveled miles to the Charlestown High School Technical Annex for vocational programs that did not exist for Blacks. And from all across the city white students were bused to "Tech High" in Roxbury. Racist feeder patterns were set up to bus Black students away from nearby white schools—arbitrarily prohibited to them despite the promised "freedom of choice."

"Forced busing" was hated only conditionally by the racists. They themselves used it as part of the system of white privilege. But when the law used it to give equal education to Blacks, that was another story.

Racist hiring of teachers and administrators was rampant. In

1971, 35 percent of the students were Black, while 94 percent of the teachers were white. There had never been a Black principal in any of the city's predominantly white schools. Many of Boston's newest teachers—the least trained and qualified, many of them products of predominantly white Boston State College—were initially assigned to the Black schools. These functioned as a revolving door for them. After serving the two years necessary for seniority and the option to transfer, they were on their way out. These were the "provisional teachers." Their back-ups were the less qualified substitute teachers. On any given day, all-Black schools were staffed 20 to 30 percent by substitute teachers.

In vocational education, the white high schools had on-the-job training programs tied in with businesses and the all-white building trades. Of the white students in vocational education, 70 percent were involved in such training projects, earning two thousand dollars a year in the process. There was simply no parallel in the all-Black schools.

"Open enrollment" for white students meant transferring out of neighborhoods like Dorchester—where the closest high school was fed by Black middle schools—and this meant increasing segregation. What would have been a mixed, neighborhood high school became majority Black—and thus neglected by school officials.

Also, it became underutilized. On the other hand, all-white schools to which white students transferred became overcrowded. When the state board of education, before the development of this process, had suggested "mobile classrooms" as additions to alleviate crowding in the Black schools, Hicks and the school committee had vehemently rejected such proposals as educationally deleterious and physically unsafe. But when white transfers, intensifying segregation, bulged the overcrowded schools beyond capacity, the use of "mobile classrooms" became standard operating procedure. They were simply given a new name: Hicks called them "demountables."

The Black plaintiffs' facts, figures, and charts, demonstrating nearly a decade of resistance by the school committee to the state law, constituted a devastating documentation of the segregated system. As if in anticipation of Watergate, Garrity listened to tapes of school committee deliberations, recordings kept by the committee itself. The bigots' own words confirmed the obvious.

Segregation meant that Black students had been consigned to the worst of everything. It was a system rooted in the segregated neighborhoods, to be sure, but cultivated and nurtured by the school committee. Above all, it was a system of *force*.

On June 21, 1974, nearly two and a half years after the filing of the Black parents' suit, Judge Garrity released his decision. Sharp, unusually free of legalese, it aimed a dagger at the heart of the pernicious system: "The defendants have knowingly carried out a systematic program of segregation affecting all of the city's students, teachers and school facilities and have intentionally maintained a dual school system. Therefore the entire school system is unconstitutionally segregated." The judge's order required the dismantling of the entire structure.

# 5

# An Antiracist March
# and a Racist Challenge

After the effort culminating in the Racial Imbalance Law and
the ensuing frustration with its ineffectiveness, the leadership of
Boston's Black community had disintegrated, with individual
leaders "going their separate ways." But as the long waiting
period for Judge Garrity's decision began to draw to a close,
many community leaders anticipated a favorable decision which
would inevitably include busing. Among these were Otto and
Muriel Snowden, and they took steps to meet the situation. They
were social workers, who had founded Freedom House in Roxbury
in 1949. The Roxbury center had achieved a well-deserved
prestige for its representation of the Black community's interests
in the fields of housing, urban renewal, and social projects. In
late 1973 the Freedom House Institute on Schools and Education
was formed to work with parents and students and to monitor the
desegregation process. Ellen Jackson became director of the new
project.

Boston's NAACP branch had suffered a period of decline. In
1973 Thomas Atkins, then serving in Governor Francis Sargent's
cabinet as Secretary for Communities and Development, began to
work with the branch, but his official duties kept him from more
than marginal participation. By 1974 the branch's problems had
intensified, and, when the new president became ill, Atkins
assumed leadership of the organization. Judge Garrity's order
had by now been released, and it was vital to rebuild the NAACP
branch to take the heat from the infuriated antibusing forces.

Concern for the safety of students who would be bused brought
together two young Black leaders, Pat Jones and Percy Wilson.
Jones was the director of the Lena Park Development Center, a
large community agency, and Wilson was director of the Roxbury
Multi-Services Center. They went to see Ellen Jackson to tell her
that the Freedom House Institute's approach to the opening of
school lacked an essential item: protection of Black students
being bused, and organization to inhibit any retaliation against

violence they might encounter. Concern about security had brought them to Freedom House initially; later both would become immersed in the desegregation issue itself.

Both their agencies joined with Freedom House to form the Freedom House Coalition; the coalition drew in Ruth Batson, now an associate professor of psychology at Boston University specializing in community mental health, and other individuals— professors, community workers, and participants in the struggle for desegregation. The coalition and the NAACP would be the principal support mechanisms for the Black community as desegregation began.

Less public in its posture, but carrying on the vitally needed parent counseling in the neighborhoods—including South Boston—was the Citywide Education Coalition, which supported desegregation within the context of its general educational activity.

Over the summer, the Freedom House became the locus of practical preparation for the beginning of busing. On the first day of school, more than eleven hundred phone calls deluged the agency with questions from alarmed Black parents. Volunteers from scores of community organizations and churches tried to answer them; scores more were in the streets and at bus departure points to aid the Black students. But for all the meetings, question-and-answer sessions, conferences, and discussions that had taken place over the all-too-fleeting months of July and August, for all the discipline of the Black students and the relative restraint of the Black community in the wake of the early violence, cooperation from the city government was dramatically lacking.

Percy Wilson drily called Mayor White's "Peace with Progress" slogan a strategy for evading any confrontation with the racists. At a meeting with White early on in the crisis-ridden situation, Wilson broke with the mayor. In private, White had told Black leaders of a "contingency plan" reaching all the way to the White House for the mobilization of federal troops. As the violence mounted, the call for troops came in unison from the Black community: clergymen, politicians, the NAACP, and members of the Freedom House Coalition. Push was coming to shove, and *Mayor White had no plan.* Worse, his policy of "low visibility" for the police assigned to the buses only encouraged the racists. "He lied to us," Wilson said.

"I knew South Boston," Ruth Batson recalled. "I knew what

was going to happen. But we had no input in the decisions. What shocked me was, the mayor did nothing. We were like poor souls going to his office. The decisions were already made."

Batson is something of a maverick. As a young woman, she was the first Black to run for school committee in five decades. As the central public figure in the early days of the desegregation fight, she earned the hatred of the racists' rising star, Louise Day Hicks. Short, plump, animated, she often speaks out without concern for convention or diplomacy. It is a style that has earned her respect. In 1974, at the age of fifty, she plunged back into the middle of things. In a recent conversation, Batson looked back over the two years since busing began and expressed dissatisfaction with the confidence the Black leaders had had in the officials. "Everybody seemed to be looking to be on the mayor's good side. There was always this jockeying: Will the mayor invite me? Will I go to this?—that kind of thing," she recalled.

White had built up a base of support in the Black leadership in the course of two campaigns for mayor that had pitted him against fellow Democrat Louise Day Hicks. "He has always been perceived as less bad than something else," Atkins explained. His support in Roxbury, "has always been based on 'lesser evilism.' He was 'less bad' than Louise Day Hicks and electable." A political foe of White since his days on the city council, Atkins "had no confidence" in the mayor.

The government was looked to for law enforcement, but it was not neutral. It sided—nationally and locally—with the resistance. Compelling it to move against racist violence required an independent show of strength by the Black community. That was the lesson of the early civil rights movement. That was the reality in Boston. The absorption of the Black leadership into and around the Democratic Party and its politics in the decade after the 1963-65 upsurge paralleled the national pattern of the evolution of the civil rights movement: *Out of the streets.* The irony in Boston was that a wing of the Democratic Party was organizing a direct action movement *in the streets*—against desegregation. It was a campaign marked by violence, accommodated to by politicians, like White, who publicly took their distance from the bald racism of the antibusing footsoldiers. His balancing act was to promise, cajole, and pressure the Black leadership not to act independently, while he gave backhanded support to the bigots.

Batson, since the early sixties a public figure in the Democratic

Party in Massachusetts, did not trust the setup being revealed during that first autumn of desegregation. The lack of political independence had created a "tremendous vacuum" over the years, she said. "Everybody was looking to be in, for the position. You couldn't trust them [the Democratic Party establishment]. This always seemed to happen to Black folks. You have to stick up for your integrity." This vacuum was why "we were like poor souls" going into Kevin White's office. Over the years, the leadership had been "split up, jockeying for positions, for invitations. People were played off against each other."

The big mobilizations of the Black community which had won concessions were far in the past. The city's Black Democrats had a six-member caucus in the state legislature, and poverty programs and community agencies dotted Roxbury. The ending of mass actions and the subordination of the struggle to the maintenance of the status quo demanded by the Boston, the statewide, and the national Democratic Party now meant that a big price would have to be paid. "We had," Ruth Batson said, "no clout."

Prior to the opening of school, according to Atkins, a group of Black leaders who "believed Kevin White at his word" sought to reach an accord with him. "The promise went this way," Atkins recalled. "If you will provide police protection [they told White] we will speak highly of you and your role." White agreed. But when the moment of truth came, the deal was off. White's betrayal—not only of private promises but of his legal responsibilities as mayor—"put our children on the chopping block."

In the fall of 1974, ROAR took to the streets in car caravans for twelve consecutive Sundays, mobilizing an average of three thousand at the rallies which concluded the horn-honking motorcades. City Hall was theirs; ROAR planning sessions took place there secretly every Wednesday night. White made no effort to stop such gatherings, which were mapping sabotage of the desegregation order.

In the streets, the buses were vulnerable, slow-moving targets. In the schools where white resistance was highest, Black students were outnumbered and faced hostile teachers and administrators. Their lot was a steady barrage of abuse.

Vigorous protest against such a many-sided racist campaign was needed to compel enforcement of the law. That, however, required a break in the city administration's hold on the Black leadership. The Black leadership was by no means happy with the relationship. It had implied "inclusion" in the government, in the Democratic Party, in the system; but it was, in fact, a noose. Some thought that if there was no rocking of the boat the crisis might pass over and government would assume its responsibilities. Black protest could, some leaders thought, only serve to sharpen antibusing resistance.

In those all-important early days when the city administration's policy and tone were being set, Ruth Batson recalls that she "wondered why no one called a march." From the first day of school, such Black leaders as Atkins, Ellen Jackson, Percy Wilson, Pat Jones, and the members of the state legislature's Black caucus were vocal—demanding troops, indicting the bigots, refusing any halt in the desegregation process.

There were few voices raised in their support, however. In the gubernatorial campaign, for example, Democratic contender Michael Dukakis and incumbent Republican Francis Sargent subtly competed for the antibusing vote by avoiding the issue of desegregation. Only the Socialist Workers Party candidate for governor, Donald Gurewitz, brought it up, making it the central issue for him and his running mate for lieutenant governor, Ollie Bivins, a Black student from Boston University. They received substantial media coverage, for candidates of a small party. Their message on the crisis in Boston reached tens of thousands through the airwaves, meetings, and campaign literature.

The first significant public protest in this period in Boston came on September 26 in the form of a meeting called on short notice by the Young Socialist Alliance and the Ujima Society, a Black organization at the University of Massachusetts in Boston. Five hundred people, many of them Black South Boston High School students, filled the auditorium of the National Center for Afro-American Artists in Roxbury. The director of the center is Elma Lewis, an older Black leader, who had played a key role in preparing for the school opening. Her center is a much-used community resource.

The meeting was a speak-out to report the truth about South Boston and the police occupation of nearby Columbia Point. It crackled with intensity as parents, students, and Columbia Point representatives told of victimization. The hall resounded with applause, cheers, and chanting. Before the meeting could chart future action, however, a shout that "the Point's in trouble" caused hundreds to run out to the rescue. It proved to be a false alarm. The meeting was an indicator of the anger building up in

Roxbury. It had been supported by a wide array of community leaders, including William Owens—soon to be the first Black elected to the Massachusetts senate—who addressed it. Though they had been notified about the rally, the first of its kind, the Boston media did not report it. But word filtered out into the community.

On October 6, the day before the mob attack on André Yvon Jean-Louis, upwards of seven hundred people, most of them white, many of them radicals, marched to the State House in support of Black rights. Initiated by Youth Against War and Fascism, the action reflected the hesitations of the organization's leadership and many of the participants about the validity of busing, but it vocally opposed the racist resistance to it.

On October 8, the state legislature's Black caucus called an emergency march in the wake of the mob beating of André Yvon Jean-Louis. Three hours later, Kevin White issued a ban on all parades and marches. The Black caucus rescinded the call for the march, only to reissue it on October 11, after the ban was lifted. On forty-eight hours' notice, with virtually no apparatus to build the action, more than seven hundred and fifty marchers turned out, stepping forward from Carter playground, in Roxbury. Virtually all Black, they were joined at the Boston Common by hundreds of white supporters, who swelled the crowd to fifteen hundred.

The biggest cheer went up for Tanya Poe, thirteen, a Black South Boston student. "My cousins came home the first and second days all bloody," she related. "People don't want us to stay, but we're not going to run. The cops don't do nothing, the teachers don't do nothing. . . . I am not going to run." She received an ovation with fists in the air. Speakers backing her up were Tom Atkins, State Representative Royal Bolling, and Melnea Cass, the eighty-year-old, near legendary Black community leader known as the "Mother of Roxbury." They urged that the buses be packed with Black students. The next day more than four hundred Black students filed into buses to South Boston, the biggest turnout since school had begun.

In the days leading up to the march, Black legislator William Owens had gone to South Boston alone, transacting business at a local bank. He aimed to prove, he had said, that Blacks had a right to go anywhere in Boston. He had added that he would be willing to lead a march to prove it. Soon his words would take on flesh and blood. The Jean-Louis beating combined with Gerald

Ford's blast at Judge Garrity had created strong sentiment for further protest. This was made clear at the October 13 march and rally on the Common.

In this period campus teach-ins, organized by coalitions of student groups launched by the Young Socialist Alliance, drew audiences of more than five hundred at area colleges. In Roxbury, especially, Socialist Workers Party gubernatorial candidate Donald Gurewitz's supporters sold thousands of copies of their newspaper, the *Militant*, which featured the Boston crisis. Its insistent theme was that a marching, protesting movement of Blacks and whites was necessary to enforce the law in Boston, because the Democratic Party could not be relied on. It argued that the power of the Black community and its white allies lay in making their numbers visible in the streets, demanding that the government do its job.

On October 15, a white student inadvertently walked into a big brawl in the corridors of troubled Hyde Park High School. He was stabbed. The school was closed as a new deluge of antibusing propaganda flooded the media. Governor Francis Sargent alerted the National Guard.

The city was boiling. Every day was marked by fights, walkouts, the gathering of bitter, combat-ready white crowds near the schools. It had taken the stabbing of a white student, nearly a month and a half after the beginning of the desegregation plan, to compel mobilization of the guard—which, as it turned out, would not be deployed. Hyde Park High School was second only to South Boston in turmoil. Bus stonings had been common. The Blacks there were outnumbered. Children of ROAR members in the school carried the message of resistance. The scope of harassment and police abuse of Black students had driven the bused students to desperate lengths, a handful of them coming to school with weapons to defend themselves.

Mayor White's "law enforcement" policy had produced numerous Black victims and now a white.

The National Guard mobilization, however, brought a short period of uneasy calm in the schools and on the streets. It was the first of the many "lulls" in the battle, a break in the action. In the Black community, these moments would give rise to hopes that the worst was over. For the racists, they were a time to regroup, to prepare new challenges to the desegregation order.

During this hiatus, however, there was no real abatement of tension. ROAR's Sunday rallies continued. Not a school day would pass without a bus stoning, a corridor fight, an attack on a Black in the subway or on a street corner. Relative peace was not the absence of war: it was a brief period of small explosions that were the harbinger of larger eruptions bound to occur.

The members of Youth Against War and Fascism who had initiated the antiracist march of October 6 did not remain idle in the month of foreboding. With little publicity, they formed an Emergency Committee for a National Mobilization Against Racism. The organization worked quietly, circulating a letter to hundreds of prominent Black and trade union leaders, civil libertarians, and individuals prominent in the movement against the war in Vietnam.

The letter accurately spelled out the situation: "The forces of racism and reaction in this country are mobilizing and gathering strength in every corner of the United States, using the recent events in Boston as their rallying cry. Their code word is 'antibusing.' But their real symbol is racist mob violence against Black school children. They have gained strength and confidence from the fact that there has been no sufficiently massive outcry against these attacks."

The letter urged a countermobilization, a "demonstration that would bring together the largest possible number of people who are against racism, who are against the racist attacks on Black school children, and who are for the elementary democratic right of these children to go to any school in safety." Supporters of the idea could send their names to the group if they were "in agreement with such a nationally called peaceful mass action." No date was projected.

In late October the Emergency Committee set up headquarters in an office in Cambridge's Central Square shopping area. The work of the Emergency Committee began to take on an increasingly public face moving into November, although no action had, as yet, been announced.

On November 14, State Senator William Owens, flanked by members of the staff of the Emergency Committee, told the Boston media, who packed the State House news conference room, that on December 14, thousands of people would come to Boston to protest the racist violence.

"We're here today in recognition of the fact that racism continues to exist in education in the city of Boston and in other major cities across the country. We have watched a bigoted and racist School Committee disobey the law for nearly ten years. We have watched antibusing forces demonstrate on a weekly basis," Owens said.

"Our voices must be heard and we appeal, therefore, to every individual, every organization, every city and every state to join with us in a demonstration to let the School Committee and others similarly situated know that we will no longer tolerate the injustices that are being perpetrated on our children.

"We must link our arms, Black and white and march together for the right of all children to go to any school in safety. Let our voices and our presence say: 'NO to institutionalized racism, NO to racist mob violence, NO to racism in education, NO to the Boston School Committee.' Our message must and will be heard around the world."

With hundreds of endorsers and the authority of a rising, young Black politician, December 14 was now out in the open and on the map.

Five days later, on November 19, a second demonstration was announced, less ambitious but of special importance in the germinating response to the racists. A dozen ministers, rabbis, and priests gathered in historic Old South Church to call a demonstration for November 30 to support busing. The joint statement of the clergymen was simple:

"The tension and violence of the past several weeks have created a division which we, the residents of Massachusetts, cannot condone. We feel what is needed is a strong, unified voice in Greater Boston for the peaceful implementation of desegregation. We cannot afford to let violence drive us apart. Let us get together with and for our children so that they can get together. Let us try to end injustice and guarantee quality, integrated education for all children."

The proposal had been discussed informally for weeks. The call was issued by the Committee for Quality, Integrated Education. This ad hoc grouping had been initiated by the Citizens for Participation in Political Action, a statewide lobbying organization based in Boston, which functioned as a liberal wing of the Massachusetts Democratic Party. The group's racial justice committee, a longtime supporter of desegregation, was at the time heavily involved in backing passage of a school reform referendum in the fall elections. If passed, it would abolish the school committee and place the educational system under the control of the mayor.

The aim of the November 30 march was to mobilize white

support, particularly in the suburbs. The involvement of the clergy was central to the achievement of this end. With only eleven days before the action, the committee had its work cut out. Despite the scant time, however, there was widespread public concern the group could draw on, a desire to march against ROAR and for desegregation.

An apparently ideal situation existed now: a local demonstration on November 30 to be followed by a national action on December 14. This was a one-two punch aimed at the racists, which could force an end to government inaction and heal the wounds of a desegregation process that had been battered by unanswered defiance.

The November 30 action began to gain support in Boston immediately. Thomas Atkins became involved in the planning. Ellen Jackson, Otto and Muriel Snowden, Black legislator Melvin King, and scores of other Black and white Bostonians joined in backing the effort.

Something, however, was not going right with the plans for the December 14 march called by Senator Owens. When supporters went to the Emergency Committee's office to sign up as volunteers or inquire about citywide and campus meetings to publicize the demonstration, they got vague answers at best. The logistical and political preparation required for an ambitious undertaking such as a national demonstration was great. The November 30 march, with its local aims, had more modest requirements, and those were under control. Regular meetings discussed what had to be done in the short period remaining. But the situation in the Emergency Committee was different.

A small staff occupying a tiny office had been set up, hardly sufficient to meet the needs of a large action. No meetings to discuss plans were set. Further, the staff members appeared to have an ambivalent attitude toward the November 30 march, as if it were a threat to December 14. They were not sure whether they supported it. December 14 appeared stalled.

Traditionally, the office for a mass protest action has served as a political and organizational center for assembling and coordinating the activists—members of community organizations, unions, support groups, campus committees—to build the action through leafletting, bill posting, fundraising, publicity, and speaking tours. This requires scores and scores of volunteers. Fundamentally, it necessitates a perspective to find, inspire, and organize them. A coalition of forces is necessary.

The Emergency Committee, with a staff of seven, waited for the activists to come. It was unable to reach out and attract support. Such a weakness meant fundraising would be doubly hard. The Emergency Committee made up for this lack by making those who did wander in pay for leaflets and posters, a manner of raising money which was inefficient and counterproductive. It implied organizational incompetence and hardly encouraged volunteers to return. Information about the action, discussion, the means for participation—all were lacking. There was no coalition.

This situation, which daily eroded the potential size of December 14, conflicted with the enthusiasm that had been generated by the initial call for the demonstration. Owens, occupied with assuming his senate seat, was hard to get hold of. His seemingly solitary political command over the action served further to inhibit the expansion and growth of a team of supporters. Moreover, the staff was entirely new to Boston. Because they all shared the political perspective of Youth Against War and Fascism, they viewed the Emergency Committee as their private preserve.

These radical activists were known in the left for an approach to politics marked by confrontation. In the antiwar movement they had not built the mass demonstrations of the 1960s and 1970s, but had engaged in small physical confrontations and split-offs at the fringe. Ultraleft rhetoric combined with confrontation defined YAWF's view of "militant action." Buoyed by the success of the October 6 demonstration it had initiated, the group had gone on to envisage something much bigger for December 14. The idea had achieved material existence with Owens's assumption of responsibility for it.

But the practical inexperience and political sectarianism of the Emergency Committee could not be overcome merely by the group's initial good intentions. The building of the action had been stopped. The December 14 march could be either a historic mobilization of support for desegregation, exerting terrific pressure on the government to act; or a factional maneuver reflecting YAWF's misgivings about busing and its political opposition to the demand of wide layers of Black leaders for federal troops to enforce the law in Boston.

Following the announcement of the December 14 march, support groups came into existence, committees that brought together Black, Puerto Rican, and white students to build the action. In many cases these had been initiated by members of the Young Socialist Alliance, who throughout the fall had been urging the kind of demonstration December 14 had the potential to be.

On November 24, some eighty students from eighteen New England colleges met at Boston University, at the initiation of the Boston area campus support groups. The spirited gathering launched the Student Committee for the December 14 March. This body would seek to muster university support for the march, as well as reaching beyond the campus for broad national backing. It would publicize the coming action and seek to attract wider activist forces to make it a success. It would undertake all the things necessary to make December 14 a success—all the things the narrow Emergency Committee was unable or unwilling to do.

The students also proposed a teach-in at Harvard University the evening before the demonstration, to explain the busing controversy. While there had been many teach-ins in the area that fall, this would be a national student gathering, as befit an issue whose repercussions went far beyond Boston.

Among the leaders of the new organization were Ray Sherbill, the president of the Boston University Student Union; Willie McKinney, president of the Roxbury Community College Student Government, who, as the father of two small children, had a personal stake in the battle; Paul Mailhot, a student at Boston State College, a predominantly white school which trained many Boston teachers and where antibusing sentiment ran high; and Maceo Dixon, a newcomer to Boston.

Dixon had been a leader of the year-long struggle to abolish STRESS (Stop The Robberies, Enjoy Safe Streets), an elite "anticrime" unit of the Detroit police, whose decoy and entrapment practices had resulted in the deaths of twenty Blacks. Rising community anger and protest had forced the Detroit city government to eliminate the hated program. A national officer of the Young Socialist Alliance, Dixon had visited Boston in the fall of 1974 in the course of a national tour, speaking on the Detroit experience. When racist violence erupted in the Boston schools in September, he had emphasized the need to fight back. He had met with Black community leaders and discussed the possibility of calling a march to respond to the crisis, but nothing definite had resulted. Now, he was back in Boston to stay.

The Student Committee set up temporary operations in the

offices of the Boston University Student Union. At a November 27 news conference it announced its formation and emergency plans to rally the student movement nationally to the side of Boston's Black community, starting with a big turnout on November 30.

The "lull" initiated in mid-October, when the National Guard had been alerted, had begun to draw to a close—not only with the calls for the November 30 and December 14 marches, but in the schools. On the afternoon of November 21, South Boston High School exploded in fights. The next day, a special Thanksgiving boycott called by antibusing forces dropped citywide school attendance by ten thousand. And over the holiday weekend the fires of racist resistance would be stoked—literally—once more.

The turmoil and boycott at South Boston High had made it impossible to field a football team. But plans for the annual game between South Boston and East Boston went ahead with teams drawn from the neighborhoods. The game was to be a benefit for the antibusing movement. The night before, a motorcade honked its way across the city, drumming up support for the event with pom-pom girls and cheerleaders.

That day—crisp, sunny, and chill—six thousand supporters packed White Stadium in East Boston. It could have been the traditional game, save for the display of antibusing banners and placards. Then, at halftime, any such impression vanished.

A full-size replica of the hated yellow school bus was hauled onto the field, to a chorus of boos. Figures dressed as a pig and a donkey, representing Judge Garrity and Senator Kennedy, emerged, fleeing the bus. Louder boos. Then the plywood vehicle was set afire. Tremendous cheers, whistling, footstomping. David Duke and KKK crosses were unnecessary in Boston. This was a northern-style cross burning.

On November 29 Coretta Scott King came to Boston to address a news conference with Thomas Atkins, urging people to attend the November 30 demonstration. They were joined by Catholic, Protestant, and Jewish leaders. The news conference received wide publicity.

The next day, Mrs. King led the march from the steps of the State House, to which her martyred husband had brought fifteen thousand Bostonians a decade before. The weather was bitter cold and windy, but the marchers were spirited, singing "We Shall Overcome."

At the head of the march were Mrs. King and her children.

Grouped behind them were local Black leaders, including Tom Atkins and William Owens. The crowd swelled to twenty-five hundred after a short procession to nearby City Hall. On Tremont Street passersby either waved, cheering, or looked on in stunned, angry silence. Boston's streets were supposed to belong to the racists; *this was different.*

Indeed, the very sight of a probusing march was effective. Week after week, the racists had taken to the streets, dominating the media with their actions, their claims, their offensive. Now, a counterblow was being struck.

"There are those in Boston today who are unwilling to admit," Atkins told the rally, "that the cradle of liberty has been rocking a little monster called hate. It is time to save our children from the narcotic of racial superiority which leads grown men in the South to put on sheets and ride horses."

Rabbi Roland Gittlesohn, perhaps Boston's most widely esteemed Jewish leader, explained the logic of busing: "Given the segregated neighborhood patterns in which we live, given the failure of our society to eliminate bigotry and discrimination from employment, either there will be busing as a first step toward integration or there will be no integration of our schools."

Some of the speeches were short, their simplicity a telling refutation of the racists' torrents of demagogy which had made the situation seem "complex." Owen Reed, a Black high school student, capsulized it: "We are not trying to take over anyone's schools. We have a right to go to those schools our parents pay taxes for."

The December 1 *Boston Globe* termed the action "the largest rally in support of the federal court order." Organized and publicized on short notice, November 30 proved that what would be called "decent Boston" could respond to the crisis. It was a signal to the racists that, just as they had been opposed in the courts, they would be challenged in action in the streets. It was a step forward, evidence that there would be a fight to defend and implement desegregation.

"The issue in my view is not really busing," Mrs. King had told the crowd. "The conduct of certain opponents of busing has made the issue one of racism in its broadest forms." Those yellow buses could be anything; what counted was who was on them and where they went. November 30 was only a first step. "Your struggle," she said, "is just beginning."

That had been made amply clear a week before, when six

William Owens, Coretta Scott King, and Thomas Atkins (left to right) lead probusing march, November 30, 1974.

thousand bigots cheered the burning of the replica school bus in East Boston. On that occasion and at that moment, a challenge had been issued. The speaker had been Avi Nelson, a hero of the bigots—young, Harvard-educated, the son of a rabbi. A glib partisan of Ronald Reagan, he railed against the "social engineers" who "plan busing." He knew the titillating words and was skilled in the closed logic that could rip through the uninitiated on his four-hour radio talk show, which rated number one in Southie, Eastie, Hyde Park, and Charlestown. That was why the crowd chanted, "Here we go, Avi, here we go!" when he came to the podium.

He called for a big antibusing march on December 15, to answer State Senator William Owens and those who would march on the fourteenth in support of tyrannical Judge Garrity's order. To show the *real* Boston. As the mock-up school bus smoldered to a charred heap, a burnt remnant of the antibusing halftime show, Nelson had pulled this show stopper. The throng at White Stadium exulted over the challenge hurled by their boy Avi against December 14. That was how they liked it: eyeball to eyeball.

# 6

# The Siege of
# South Boston High

"I ain't gonna run."

That seemed to be what every Black student who rode the buses to South Boston said when asked why they continued to attend school.

"We got a right to go there."

It was that stubborn pride that rankled the bigots. Every day that the Black students came to school, the bigots grew more furious and more frustrated. The Black students were the living reality of the hated Garrity order. They would have to break the spirit of the Black students, difficult though that might be.

As rough and tumble a place as South Boston High School was, as hard as it was to learn anything, still there was a difference between it and the schools in Roxbury. "It's a dump, all right," a Black student said, early in the battle, "but I never saw a microscope until I went there."

The atmosphere was thick with foreboding as the warm weather of early fall turned bitter cold in December and the wind off the ocean whipped through the streets. On December 9, a crowd of a hundred—bigger than for several weeks, but smaller and less festively arrogant than the mobs two months prior—had gathered at the entrance to the high school. Mostly women, they were marching in a picket line, attempting to discourage teachers from entering the building. They turned only two away and screamed "scab" at the rest.

The buses roared up and the women began shouting epithets. As the Black students waited to depart, some would turn and stare at the bigots, trading gestures with them, grinning at and mimicking the whites. "Look at the fucking apes," a husky, greying woman shouted to her pals as the insults reached a peak.

That afternoon three white female students jumped a Black student in the girls' locker room. To meet the odds—which were typical—the Black woman grabbed a padlock and swung it like a mace, bloodying her assailants before she fled. Rumors spread: a "bonehead" had attacked three white innocents. It was starting.

The police force had been gradually pared down for several weeks as the mob presence diminished. Now, though something obviously was starting, something organized, there was no change in the deployment of police.

On Tuesday, December 10, a bigger crowd appeared at the school gates. More parents and boycotting students. The nonboycotting white students waited in a group as the Black students disembarked from the buses, mounted the stairs, and passed through the newly installed metal detector. Adult men wearing purple berets topped with blue pom-poms—the colors of the Mullens gang, a notorious group of toughs who frequented a bar on West Broadway and were now in league with ROAR—rapidly passed out buttons. Big green shamrocks and the words "Southie Pride" adorned the badges.

The white students had begun to put demands to South Boston High Headmaster William Reid. Squarely in the middle of the crisis, Reid looked haggard as he waited each day in the courtyard for the buses to arrive. A picture of despair, he had no great love for the local whites; neither had he taken the side of the Black students. He felt boxed in, dwarfed and dominated by a situation simply out of his control. There was nothing he could do. The violence was unstoppable, predictable, inevitable. Reid's face was deeply lined, eyes rimmed by defeat and exhaustion. He was weathering a storm that was sinking the ship.

The demands presented to him included one calling for the banning of Afro combs. The Blacks used them as weapons, the young bigots told him.

The organizers were busy on the street. They handed out buttons and gave the white students mimeographed "legal aid" forms telling them their rights if they were arrested. The sheets had probably been printed several blocks away in the South Boston Information Center. Staff members of this ROAR front organization circulated among the white students.

The collaboration of ROAR, the activist parents connected with the center, and the students was deepening. The kids were the shock troops. A year later, the organizational form of student opposition to desegregation would surface in Charlestown, South Boston, and East Boston with the debut of the "white student caucus." On December 10, 1974, it was more informal, based on student gangs, private discussions, the antibusing grapevine, and the momentum of hate.

It had been bedlam in the school for days. The white students had taken to using whistles as an instant communications system whenever a confrontation was sought. Across town, Hyde Park High School's white students utilized a similar method. Whistle blasts, in a coded system, would punctuate the classes. If a white was in trouble, if a fight broke out, if a Black student was down, piercing blasts would be heard. The Black students may have had the dreaded Afro combs (which would eventually be banned), but the whites had whistles. By December 10, the halls resounded with their shrill, ominous music.

That afternoon, the white students marched to the school auditorium for a "grievance session." It was an uproarious meeting. Sounds of the chanting at it echoed through the corridors and filtered into the classrooms in which the Black students sat alone. The session turned into a rally, which culminated with three hundred white students charging from the auditorium in what the *Boston Globe* termed a rampage.

They ran in gangs through the corridors, chanting, "Niggers eat shit!" The wild outburst caught the teachers and aides off guard. Some were thrown and knocked to the floor as they slammed doors and tried to physically block the white students from entering the classrooms. The frenzied rampagers bolted school early. They would return the next day, more hopped up than ever. The Black students, unintimidated, would ride the buses again.

It happened on the third floor, at 9:45 a.m. on December 11. Michael (Mikey) Faith, strong and handsome, was something of a leader. He had been at the frenzied rally the day before—everybody knew about the rally and rampage, knew what it meant. Now he was walking with a group of friends toward another group of students—smaller in number, and Black.

Michael Faith spotted James White in the group, a young Black who stuck up for himself and had been in his share of fights. (Later in the year, and into Phase II, it would be common for white racist students, the organizers and troublemakers, to seek out Black students for whom they had a special enmity. Conversely, the Black students came to look out for one another and to take note of particular tormentors. A Black Hyde Park High School student, for example, relates how when a riot broke out, she had "gotten" a white gang leader who had made life miserable for her. "I had to wait a year, but it was worth it," she said.) Michael Faith had been waiting for James White. His arm shot out, pointing at White. "That's the nigger I want," he shouted. It was a sucker ploy, a provocation. The young racists were ready for action, and the groups charged into each other.

Moments later, Michael Faith staggered down the hallway, bleeding from a deep knife wound. White was rushed from the school, under arrest. Word spread like wildfire through the building: "Michael Faith is going to die; a nigger tried to kill him."

Within minutes, not one white student remained in the building. G Street began to fill immediately, as the telephone network organized from the lists of the Home and School Association, the Information Center, and ROAR fairly burned with commotion. Men took off from work. Carloads of allies streamed in from across the city.

The first wave of buses that were to evacuate the 125 Black students now trapped in the building barely made it to the crest of G Street. The rumble of their engines was a dead giveaway. The mob surged forward, blocking the street and shattering the bus windows with a barrage of rocks. The bus drivers retreated, to huge cheering. The police, enormously outnumbered, blocked the school entrance to the horde, which had one thought: Get the Black students!

The crowd continued to grow, and after an initial skirmish a strange truce was called. Battle plans were being formulated—by the police and by the racists. Small groups of whites talked animatedly about routes, pickoff points, observation spots. Occasionally, a Black student would peer out of a window. "We're going to kill you!" a young mother screeched.

Slowly, police reinforcements from the Metropolitan District Commission and state troopers wearing riot gear began to arrive. The cops bristled at the obscenities shouted at them. One policeman took his place in the developing phalanx at the front of the school, his brown hair spilling over his shoulders. "Look," someone yelled, "a hippie pig." Other shouts of "motherfucking faggots" split the air.

A tense, drawn-looking Louise Day Hicks appeared and entered the building. She would try to speak to the mob from the steps. In the background was Senator William Bulger, a powerful orator and champion of the antibusing movement. He would not speak, but handed the bullhorn to Hicks.

She tried to begin. "My only concern is your safety," and her

Scene outside South Boston High during siege, December 11, 1974.

Louise Day Hicks

voice cracked as the boos began. "You must let the buses come and take the Black students back to Roxbury." Loud, angry boos and more than a thousand voices chanting in unison: "Bus 'em back to Africa, bus 'em back to Africa!" "I will not tell you to go home," Hicks stuttered, her voice rising. "Hell no, we won't go; hell no, we won't go!" Louder and louder.

Hicks would stop shortly, pointing out that the police had a job to do, that someone was going to get hurt, badly hurt, that Mikey's condition was stable, and that the buses should be let through. Then another big chant, angry and spirited: "Niggers eat shit, niggers eat shit"—the frightening words that had been on the lips of the white student rampagers the day before.

Hicks gave up. The big woman was shaken, unable to move the mob imbued with a lynch spirit, a mob that was there because of her painstaking efforts. This Frankenstein's monster was out of control.

Two hours had passed. There were hundreds of police on the scene, some of them on horseback. The buses had been positioned nearby. From one direction, a decoy bus would make its way to the school as the police parted the crowd. Then, from another direction, other buses would come and the Black students would be hustled out a side door, through a double line of cops, and into them as the decoy bus drew attention. At least, that was the plan.

The tension on G Street was palpable. The cold had ceased to matter. The sky was a neutral grey, eerie in its evenness. A nervous, exhilarating mood permeated the mob, now almost silent but only a second away from detonating.

Suddenly a brick from the center of the crowd slammed off the helmet of a policeman, knocking him to the ground. That was it, the signal, the spark, and all the pent-up force of the mob broke with fury. Shrieks and shouting tore the fragile quiet of the standoff. Bottles, rocks, cans, sticks, and bricks filled the air. A hail of debris showered the police.

The decoy bus rumbled up and was pelted with rocks, its windows flying out. The battle had begun. Mounted police rode into the mob, their nervous horses rearing and neighing in the crush. Rows of cops with clubs held at arm's length pushed against hostile faces and bodies, forcing the mob back. From the north side of G Street a caravan of buses cruised into place. The stunned mob was pushed back. The Black students ran from the side doors of the school, between police lines, onto these buses. It all happened with breakneck speed, as the split and swirling mob caught only glimpses of the Black evacuation.

"We ran down the hill—teachers, aides, students, everybody," Alma Carter, a Black South Boston High School teacher, would later tell Judge Garrity. "Aides were helping girls who fell. Some were in a poor mental state. One girl had a heart condition. There were two aides hurrying her along, but she couldn't run. One South Boston woman along the route yelled at us, 'Look at the dirty rats running out the back door.' Everybody Black ran."

The buses rushed to Freedom House. Percy Wilson was there, shaken, recounting the escape, the scene of a brush with death, as he picked glass fragments from his hair. He had been on the decoy bus.

The fighting continued in South Boston. Groups of cops chased the enraged bigots onto doorsteps, clearing a path for the buses, as scores of rock-hurling toughs leaped fences and ran up the big hill that the high school backs up on. The cops were angry. These Southies may have been their own kind, but the bricks and rocks hurt, and damned if they would take it lying down.

A big, long-haired young man had just knocked down a cop with a brick, and then, as police forced back and split the mob, he was alone and running frantically in an open space in the middle of G Street. Hundreds of Southies, aghast and scattered into small groups, watched the howling figure. Shouts of "No, no," and "Stop, my God, stop," echoed throughout the street as first one, then another policeman caught up with the runner, dealing him blows to the head and body. He ran like a halfback, zigzagging and ducking, but then he staggered and began to stumble awkwardly.

The long-haired "hippie pig" neared him as he was going down, reached across with his arm, and let go with an elbow drive that smashed the hooligan's head into the side of a parked car. The man bounced off the automobile as if he had received a blind-side body check in a frantic hockey game. He rolled onto his back, his hands in the air, pleading. Then the police were on him, making the arrest.

The skirmishing went on for hours, with groups of bigots backed up, then pushing forward on G Street and East Fifth Avenue. Bottles sailed into police lines as twilight settled on the city. A gang of teen-agers stoned an ambulance carrying an injured officer away. The windows of a police car were smashed out, and another cruiser was overturned.

The battle drew a line of blood between South Boston and the cops. The Tactical Patrol Force, which had carried the brunt of the action, was now an enemy.

South Boston High School was closed. It would not reopen until the new year.

Black leaders—Ellen Jackson for example—blamed the police for allowing the buildup of the mob. She had been on radio station WILD for hours attempting to reassure Black parents and protesting the treatment of the Black students. Indeed, by standing up to the mob, the police had prevented a bloody outcome for the Black students, but they had done that only at the last possible moment. This was the bitter fruit of Mayor White's school security policy.

The Black students were simply obeying the law, going to school, riding the buses. For that, 125 of them had been trapped in the school for hours, with a woefully thin blue line facing off a mob.

The media coverage of the event rocked the city. If the assault on André Yvon Jean-Louis had stunned and agonized Boston, the scene in Southie electrified the citizenry. News bulletins interrupted regular radio and television programs. The television images were startling: the white student rampage of the previous day, this day's mob fighting with the police, the clearly audible chanting—"Bus 'em back to Africa! Niggers eat shit!" Then the drama of the decoy buses; evacuation, an inch away from disaster; and Louise Day Hicks, the five-star general of the movement, booed down by her frenzied white legions.

What year was it? What city? This was like Selma and Little Rock. ROAR was the new White Citizens Council, animated by the spirit of Jim Crow. The bigots tried to recoup their battered prestige by dwelling on James White and his knife and protesting against police brutality. But the attempted diversion would not work beyond the antibusing enclaves. The events were too stark to be glossed over.

The conscience of the city, it seemed, had also been assaulted. It was time to respond, time for the opponents of bigotry to display some of what Ruth Batson called "clout." The whole nation would be watching Boston as the countdown to that eyeball-to-eyeball weekend in mid-December ticked away.

# 7

## The Racists Don't Own
## the Streets of Boston

In the cavernous old warehouse of a building whose second floor housed the offices of the Student Committee for the December 14 March, the heater was always breaking down. The staff of a dozen volunteers had expanded beyond the capacity of the Boston University Student Union offices and had moved down the block into the big, shabby room. Some were veterans of the antiwar and women's liberation movements. Others were getting their first taste of organizing mass protests. They had been working twelve to fourteen hours a day, functioning as a center for Boston-based student support committees and a coordinating office for student and community organizations across the country which were building the demonstration.

The pace of activity, and the constant financial pressure of organizing the demonstration and the teach-in that would kick it off, meant long hours and little pay—sometimes as low as twenty dollars a week. Yet the mood was one of exhilaration. The coming weekend of protest would be the biggest action in support of busing in recent memory. That was worth the extra, exhausting effort.

As the staff was settling into its regular 9 a.m. meeting to divide up the day's work on December 11, six miles away in South Boston Michael Faith and a gang of white students were going into corridor combat with a group of Blacks.

Radio station WEEI's bulletins about the stabbing of Michael Faith and the siege of the Black students at South Boston High School immediately broke the Student Committee's routine. It was now on alert status. Phone calls went out across the country: The crisis in Boston has reached new heights; double the effort; fill the doubtful bus; call local news conferences; bring more people. December 14 would be an emergency demonstration.

Some days previously, the Student Committee had scheduled a press conference for December 12. Its original purpose had been to get last-minute publicity for the December 13 teach-in and December 14 march, since the media had paid scant attention to them. Now the news conference became the vehicle for defenders of Black rights to respond to the racist mobs on G Street.

The press room at the State House was jammed with reporters. The usual cynicism and joking were missing; their mood was somber. Many of them had been in South Boston. Maceo Dixon, speaking for the Student Committee, was joined by Robert Harper, a Black student leader from Harvard; John Boone, whose defense of Black prisoners as commissioner of the State Department of Corrections had cost him his job but won him popular respect in Roxbury; Rev. Vernon Carter, who nine years back had vigiled for 114 days for the passage of the Racial Imbalance Law; and Jonathan Kozol, whose book on the Boston school system, *Death at an Early Age*, had put him high on the racists' hate list.

Kozol's appearance and statement were dramatic. He was in the course of a hunger strike protesting the racist violence and was obviously weakened and fatigued; he had to pause often during his statement. Since the school violence was a monster created by the foes of desegregation, "it was . . . Louise Day Hicks . . . who put that knife in Michael Faith," he told the reporters.

The high point of the press conference was the appearance of three Black students, fourteen and fifteen years old. Taken aback by the floodlights and cameras, they were almost too scared to answer the reporters' barrage of questions. What is it like in South Boston? "They hate us," a student replied. Who was to blame for the fighting? "We don't start things," one of the students said. Why? "We would get killed."

The Student Committee's teach-in at Harvard drew twelve hundred students, nearly half of them Black. This turnout and the action to follow the next day made the probusing point of view newsworthy. The city's leading newspaper, the *Globe*, devoted nearly all of page three to the teach-in, thus giving the march a last-minute shot in the arm.

Linked to the December 14 march, the teach-in paralleled the educational activities of the early days of the movement against the war in Vietnam. The speakers personified the connection of the old—the southern civil rights movement—and the new antiracist movement being forged to defend endangered Black rights in the first sharp test in the North.

Rev. Ralph D. Abernathy, the key aide of Dr. King, spoke about the Jim Crow buses of the deep South. Julian Bond, a Democratic state senator in Georgia and a former leader of the Student Nonviolent Coordinating Committee, evoked cheers as he told the audience that opponents of desegregation were not really opposed to busing. "For them it's not the bus, it's us," he said.

"From Little Rock's riots nearly twenty years ago to the Bay State's bigots of today, very little except the rhetoric of reaction has changed," said Bond. He described how the language of blatant racism had been replaced by code words, and listed some: "sanctity of the neighborhood school," "busing," and "quality education."

Rev. Vernon Carter sailed into those who "say the days of marches are over. The day we stop marching and singing with our minds fixed on freedom is the day America is doomed." The veteran of the 114-day vigil and picket was addressing new troops, the fresh forces of an embryonic movement, and his message was: "I say to you we must march again! We must never cease marching!"

Jonathan Kozol had been escorted to the auditorium by police because of threats on his life. He could barely stand. His speech was punctuated by applause. "A lot of you came here in *it* tonight," he intoned in mock seriousness. "I know, because I saw it outside. Something dangerous and strange, called a *bus*. Let's talk about that dangerous instrument of transportation. *Bus* was never a scare word in this land as long as it carried kids with freckles through New Hampshire. *Bus* becomes a scare word only when it means fair play in our home town," Kozol said, his voice shaking as he was interrupted by a long burst of applause.

"Let me just say that Mrs. Hicks was never very good at English spelling. Thus, in the spelling book of Mrs. Hicks, *bus* has always been a three letter word for 'nigger.'"

"Let me make one other point about the bus. A lot of people try to evade this issue. They say, 'It's quality that we want.' We've got to speak the truth about this matter. Quality education has become a euphemism in this city for perpetuation of segregated schools. There can be no quality education in a residentially divided city without riding a bus! There can't be quality education without equal use of funds. History proves there has never been equal use of funds so long as Boston has been racially divided. . . . There cannot be free, equal education without transportation."

December 13, 1974, teach-in: Black students speak out.

December 14, 1974, antiracist march.

Maceo Dixon spoke next. In a month and a half, he had gotten more than a taste of Boston. He was now a resident of the city, occupied with helping to lead the student committee. Soon he would move to Roxbury, and it would be home for the duration of the struggle.

Dixon introduced three Black students, two of them bused into South Boston. Richie Wallace, fifteen, a student at the Dean Junior High School, would speak for the three. Nervous (he had never made a speech before), at the last minute he balked. His companions, grinning, gave him a gentle push and he was on the stage, flanked by them. "My name," he began softly, "is Richard Wallace. I go to Dean Junior High School in South Boston," he continued, to shouted encouragement from the audience. "Every day we get off the bus and a crowd of white kids call us 'nigger' and 'bonehead.' They threaten us and tell us, 'Go back to Africa.' Inside the school, students call us names. Once, they sent little white kids with white sheets running through the school, saying, 'The Klansmen are coming!'

"The white teachers never explain the work to us. Sometimes they call us stupid. And they say we can't do the work. I don't think they care if we learn at all. You can't get a good education if you don't know what's going on behind your back.

"The white parents started the thing. They planned the walkouts. If the school opens Monday there will be big trouble. There's got to be more protection for the Black people that are being bused there. Instead of having the state police and the Boston police, they should," he paused, stretching out the words, "call out the . . . National Guard!" An ovation broke loose.

"I don't like South Boston High School," Wallace continued, firm and angry now. "I know some of you people out in the audience don't like it either. They say they'll never let niggers go in there. But we have the *right* to go to *any* school in Boston! You people here today must get the truth out about the racism that's been going on in South Boston. Everyone here should go to the march tomorrow. The Black students of Boston must have your support!" The hall reverberated with sustained, rhythmic applause.

At various points in the course of the teach-in, Dixon had read greetings sent by Black leaders throughout the country—from Detroit's Mayor Coleman Young, Gary's Richard Hatcher, the Congressional Black Caucus, Coretta King, and from a Black woman in Detroit whose brief message drew the biggest response:

"I wish to commend your march against racism in Boston . . . best wishes for a very successful program. Sincerely yours in the continuing struggle for freedom for oppressed people everywhere." It was sent by Rosa Parks, the heroine of the Montgomery bus boycott.

State Senator Owens came late. The rally was winding up, and the crowd had dwindled. He urged a big turnout for the next day. As he finished, he met Dixon on the stage. They had come to know each other, both directly and through Owens's aides and the Emergency Committee. It was a difficult and tense relationship, and Dixon, in the overall interests of the coming action, had deferred the central responsibilities to Owens through his senate office. Owens was friendly as he walked off the stage, saying that everything appeared solid for the march.

Then, he pulled Dixon aside. "We're going to get a couple of hundred people arrested tomorrow," he said, confiding that the march route had been changed. It would take an alternate route which the police had not approved, and which the participants did not know about. Taken aback, Dixon tried to set up an immediate meeting with Owens. But he said he was busy and walked out.

In general, civil disobedience implies a special set of political circumstances. In the South, the tactic of the sit-in had been utilized to challenge Jim Crow laws and force implementation of the Supreme Court ruling outlawing "separate but equal" facilities. Moreover, when these unjust laws were to be "broken," the protesters were prepared to be arrested—a foreknowledge required to ensure the integrity and discipline of the action. Furthermore, batteries of lawyers were present or arranged for. Even when the scene was shifted to some of the antiwar protests, where the efficacy of the tactic of civil disobedience itself was debatable, the participants were cognizant of the possible outcome—at least where there was a responsible leadership.

But in the case of the Boston march, a dramatic turn had taken place. Out of the blue, Owens—with the support of the Emergency Committee, to which he had assigned overall marshalling responsibility for the action—had arbitrarily and secretly decided to switch to a route which was certain to result in arrests.

The call for the action was for a legal, peaceful march. This had been repeatedly emphasized by the Student Committee in its publicity, and was motivated by both political and tactical considerations. In a Boston rent by racist violence, a legal, orderly march would make a powerful point as to where the responsibility for turmoil lay—on the bigots. Anything disruptive during the action would be seized upon to taint the emerging movement in support of busing. And to insure the largest possible turnout in support of Black rights, participants would have to come feeling confident that the march and rally would be secure and safe.

The Student Committee had assembled nearly five hundred marshals of its own to monitor and safeguard the big contingent of campus supporters. Determined to see a legal march come off, the leaders of the committee met that night and morning, trying to find Owens and convince him to follow the approved route—but to no avail. They also printed thousands of leaflets giving the original, approved march route, for distribution the morning of the event. Another matter worrying the Student Committee activists was the composition of the Emergency Committee's marshalling unit.

The Student Committee locally and nationally had given painstaking attention to the problem of marshals. Training sessions—in Boston, on campuses, with Black students and supporter groups—had provided its monitors with practice. This had been going on for two weeks, producing a team of marshals including many who were familiar with Boston and others who had built support for the action in their local areas. Many of these marshals had previous experience in monitoring the massive antiwar demonstrations of the 1960s and 1970s. Thus, among the Student Committee marshals there was a mixture of veteran experience and political training based on the perspective of organizing for a legal, peaceful march.

The Emergency Committee, however, was a shell set up by the Youth Against War and Fascism in the few cities where it existed. Virtually all its marshals were from out of town and shared a different political outlook—YAWF was well known among radicals for its confrontationist perspective. Because of their relationship with Owens at the start, they were now at the center of a situation with which they were totally unfamiliar; and they were supposed to secure the discipline of a march the building of which they had hampered.

December 14 was a cold, drizzling day. The monitors from the Student Committee, briefed on the problem, began arriving at 8 a.m., setting up a big, rectangular phalanx of monitors and distributing the flyers with the original march route.

The march was supposed to step off at noon; but by one o'clock, with nearly ten thousand people filling the assembly area, Owens had not yet arrived. Tension had mounted throughout the morning as Emergency Committee monitors tore up the march route leaflets and proclaimed that the alternate route—down the exclusive shopping district of Boylston Street—had been secured.

The opposite was the case. Police had refused Owens's request for a last-minute change, and the entrance to Boylston Street was packed with police vans and nearly two hundred officers, including mounted cops.

As Student Committee monitor leaders announced the legal march route, they were drowned out by the Emergency Committee marshals chanting, "We say no to racism." The longer the march was delayed, the greater became the confusion of the assembling demonstrators, who had no idea of the problem at hand. They had come to march.

By one o'clock a decision was reached among the Student Committee leaders: they would move out along the authorized route with their contingent, which now numbered some three thousand. The assemblage had been split by the Emergency Committee marshals, and thousands of marchers at the rear could not hear or see the Student Committee contingent at the front. Maceo Dixon turned to the front line of marshals. "Let's go!" he shouted, and the march had begun.

Thousands moved out, chanting loudly, "Stop the racist drive, keep the buses rolling!" The demonstrators—some from as far as Chicago and Saint Louis, Black and white, young and old—sang and cheered as they moved forward, calling on bystanders to join in. A wedge of monitors linked arms at Boylston Street, perhaps a hundred strong. Behind them, the police bristled.

The march turned the corner onto Commonwealth Avenue, chanting, moving steadily, bearing hundreds of Student Committee placards denouncing the racist attacks, supporting desegregation. The procession flowed on peacefully, without incident.

The Student Committee's act had done two things. First, it had started the march. Second, because it had taken the original, legal route—and because of its size—it had made clear the real line of action, and set a tone for the demonstrators behind. These were blocked by the Emergency Committee, which had yet to inform the remaining thousands about its intended confrontation with the police.

Twenty minutes later, Owens and his aides passed the Student Committee contingent marching out. "What are you doing?" he shouted. Dixon yelled back over the din, "We're marching!" The ultimate abdication had taken place. The students had acted in the vacuum created by the "official" leadership.

Owens moved the Emergency Committee out, and the crowd followed. The throng came to Boylston Street, face to face with the police. Marchers more than twenty feet back could not see the confrontation taking shape; many of them wondered what was happening. Why had the line stopped? Owens got on top of a car with a bullhorn. "We're going down Boylston Street at all costs!" he shouted. A handful of Emergency Committee monitors surged forward into the police. This was the moment they had been waiting for. A few scuffles broke out, and arrests were made.

Rev. Ralph Abernathy and John Boone, both scheduled to speak at the rally, were beside Owens as the fisticuffs started. The march was stalled, with virtually no one joining in the small foray. Abernathy and Boone, the former a veteran of civil rights actions which had included civil disobedience, saw the foolhardiness of the ploy. The police allowed Owens and a group of aides to pass through their lines; he would later rejoin the demonstration at the rally site. Abernathy and Boone then began waving the crowd past the police and the entrance to Boylston Street, down to Commonwealth Avenue, where the march resumed peacefully. The vast majority of the marchers would not know about Owens's attempt until the news broadcasts that evening.

As the second wave of the demonstration arrived on the Common, a huge cheer went up. A total of twelve thousand people filled the rally site, the majority from Boston. They had braved hours of delay, confusion, cold, and wetness and were tired, but spirited. They, the marchers, were the movement, and their discipline, in massive numbers, transcended the shenanigans of Owens and the Emergency Committee.

Banners were everywhere: the United Farm Workers, the Indochina Peace Campaign, District 65 of the Distributive Workers; delegations from the American Federation of State, County and Municipal Employees, the Meatcutters, Boston neighborhood and tenant organizations, the Puerto Rican Socialist Party, Black Economic Survival, the Attica Defense Committee, the Socialist Workers Party, and women's, gay liberation, teacher, and parent groups. There were marchers from Atlanta, Minneapolis, Cleveland, Saint Louis, Pittsburgh, Philadelphia, Baltimore, Washington, Birmingham, and Boston's suburbs.

"You will have to come back again and again to defeat segregation," Ralph Abernathy told the crowd.

High school students; Harvard's Nobel laureate George Wald; Amiri Baraka, of the Congress of Afrikan People; William Lucey, president of the Coalition of Black Trade Unionists; Dick Gregory; Ellen Moves Camp, of the American Indian Movement; and Owens were among the speakers.

Across the country, solidarity actions organized by the Student Committee took place in Pasadena, where a desegregation struggle had been churning for four years, 500 marched; in San Francisco, 500 rallied in the rain at the Federal Building; nearly 200 turned out in Portland, Oregon; in Minneapolis, 175 participated in a rally; in Denver, where busing had begun a year before, nearly 200 people; in Houston, 200; in San Antonio, 60; in Atlanta, 100 rallied while additional busloads had gone to Boston; 300 activists marched in Seattle; 40 picketed in faraway San Diego; and 70 in Saint Louis complemented the sending of a busload to Boston.

The December 14 march was front-page news in Boston and the lead story on television that evening. Predictably, the minor incident at Boylston Street was blown up: "Violence mars march" was the common media formulation. In reality, the "confrontation" had lasted only a couple of minutes. Perhaps thirty people had participated, while twelve thousand knew nothing about it or simply refused to participate in the stunt when it happened. If anything, the march and rally were models of responsibility and discipline. Owens's elitist move and the sectarianism of the Emergency Committee had placed them on the outside of the mobilization which they had brought to life, but could not bring to fruition.

As the new year came and passed, December 14 would be remembered as a pivotal and historic day of protest, the tiny fracas which marred it being generally forgotten. No racist march had come close to it in size that fall, nor would any in the future. Through the efforts of the Student Committee, the theme of the march had come through loud and clear: for Black rights, for busing, and against racist violence.

The action's greatest success would be in what grew out of it, for it inspired a process of education and action to continue the struggle. The two hundred and fifty Black, Puerto Rican, and white students who packed a classroom at the University of Massachusetts in downtown Boston on the night of December 14 sensed that. They were physically exhausted, some already wheezing from the chill, but the room was alive with energy. Something big had happened that day, something new and powerful.

At the teach-in and march they had been urged by the Student Committee to attend this meeting. Thirty-seven colleges and three high schools from the East and Midwest were represented. The proposal put before them was for a national student gathering in Boston on February 14 and 15 to map strategy to meet the racist offensive. After discussion the vote was unanimous. The students applauded, not so much for themselves as from a sense of the meaning of what was happening. A new movement, the *antiracist* movement, took a big step forward that bitter night in Boston.

December 15 was a cloudless day, sunny and fall-like. Motorcades came from South Boston and East Boston. Car caravans honked their way in from Roslindale, Hyde Park, and Dorchester. All converged on the bandshell in the Boston Common. The racists were rallying.

This was their promised answer to December 14. Given the wave of reaction to the South Boston blowup four days earlier, it should have been very big. But personality squabbles and political fights had begun to break out behind ROAR's closed doors. South Boston State Representative Raymond Flynn had played a principal role, with Avi Nelson, in the plans. Flynn was being touted as the "antibusing" mayoral candidate to oppose Kevin White, a move which challenged Hicks's supremacy in the movement. Hicks was an infighter when it came to that: *no one* shared her throne.

The rumors of potential violence at the rally that circulated within the antibusing movement, Flynn thought, were coming from Hicks. She opposed the march. Leaders like Albert "Dapper" O'Neill and John Kerrigan were present—perennials wherever such a crowd gathered. Nelson and Flynn had created a patchwork of unity in last-minute negotiations. The demonstration could be considered a rough gauge of the antibusing movement's ability to mobilize under fire. Slightly over three thousand racists came to the Common.

The theme of the march and rally was uninspiring to the throng: a constitutional amendment against the use of busing for desegregation. It seemed too legalistic, time-consuming, and impractical, but it was Nelson's pet project and the cheering was polite. The crowd displayed a certain spirit, but something was lacking—confidence.

The mother of Michael Faith, who had been stabbed on December 11 at South Boston High School, addressed the crowd, becoming hysterical. Nelson produced a Black speaker, a Birchite type from Texas named Clay Smothers, who pontificates in his radio program in the Dallas area on the evils of welfare, abortion, fluoridated water, sex education, and forced busing. Prior warning had gone out to the crowd via marshals to put on their best behavior for this unique speaker. But even Smothers's thirty-minute self-abasement—"You can call me colored"—failed to rouse them.

When Nelson claimed thirty thousand people had turned out, a burly bigot sporting half a dozen buttons and an American flag turned to his friend: "Now *that* is really bullshit."

Nelson was able to evoke a cheer when he contrasted this "peaceful" antibusing rally with the "violence" of December 14. But the comparison was flat and phoney. The memory of December 11 was real and lingering; this crowd knew the taste of combat with the police in South Boston. If anything, Owens, to their minds, had backed down to police with whom they would fight it out for hours any day of the week.

Considering the course of events from the march organized by the clergymen on November 30 to the present, it was clear that something was happening. Slowly, surely, despite difficulties and problems, the racists were being answered. As the antibusing rally participants trudged home, upset by the small size of their demonstration, critical now of Nelson's rash challenge for a public contrasting of support, the whole city could assess the result of the weekend. The bigots had lost. But their machine remained, and they were still strong and tenacious. They had not fought for a decade to give up over one bad inning of struggle.

The Student Committee for the December 14 March had coined a slogan. It had been emblazoned on the banner that draped the stage at the Harvard teach-in. It had been chanted by thousands the next day. It was taken up by the Blacks and whites, the students and parents, the busloads of people from out of town who had marched. It was a rallying cry: "The racists don't own the streets of Boston."

# 8

# Labor Allies
# —and Enemies

Rexford Weng—Black, handsome, a union man from head to toe—was not used to being scared. A vice-president of Local 575 of the Amalgamated Meatcutters and Butcher Workmen and an at-large vice-president of the Massachusetts State Labor Council of the AFL-CIO, he worked an eight-hour day in a local packing house. Watching the news, seeing the racists batter the school buses and the Black students, made him angry.

What concerned him most that tumultuous fall was that whenever he and his fellow Black union members went to their union hall near Andrew Square in South Boston, they took their lives in their hands. Three locals of the meatcutters met in the brick building in South Boston. Two had a large Black membership, and the leaders of those locals spoke out in support of desegregation. Black members and statements in favor of busing met with terror that autumn in South Boston.

"White kids who are out of high school hang around waiting to do something," Weng explained. "They've set fires to the garbage cans in back of the hall." They also attacked lone Black unionists, vandalized cars belonging to outspoken meatcutter officials, and smashed the office windows. Police showed no enthusiasm to take action. The attacks continued. Windows were boarded up, a watchdog was brought to the office, the front door was fortified and always kept locked. By mid-October the meatcutters were meeting at a Howard Johnson's in "neutral territory." They would never return to their old headquarters, putting it up for sale in 1976.

Weng heads the civil rights committee of the state labor council. Early in the school year, he helped organize a news conference to show labor support for desegregation and to voice opposition to the violence of the racists. The statement Weng read was endorsed by locals of the United Auto Workers, the United Electrical Workers, and the Distributive Workers, and by a handful of officials of other unions. Weng pushed to have affiliates of the state labor council speak out for busing—a position long held by the national AFL-CIO. He ran into a brick wall and was told to "cool it." He was rocking the boat.

The state labor council did nothing. That was typical of the labor movement in Boston and Massachusetts. Antibusing bureaucrats at the top of the unions paid respects to the racist movement.

Rexford Weng's greatest anxiety, however, was not about physical assault, but the abandonment of the Black community in its hour of need—a worry that the unions' accommodation to the antibusing movement would strengthen the bosses' greatest weapon against labor unity: racism. "We have to stop this division," Weng said. "The labor movement, I believe, is the most powerful movement in this country. The AFL-CIO leadership have to make a clear stand for integration in the crisis in Boston."

The racists were assaulting a union headquarters in Boston, ganging up on union members, driving them out of their offices. That alone, Weng thought, should make you get up and shout. He himself had shouted, marched, and picketed.

At the November 30 rally in City Hall Plaza he sat between Thomas Atkins and Coretta Scott King and was nervous as he took his turn to address the twenty-five hundred listeners. But his short, crisp speech brought cheers. "Anything we have ever gotten from the bosses we have to get by doing as you're doing now," he said. "Go to the streets and demonstrate—that was the only way." His efforts stood out almost alone in Boston as an example of what the union movement should have done.

The civil rights struggle of the 1960s had arisen outside the AFL-CIO because of the latter's abstention from the burgeoning fight against Jim Crow. The independent power of the civil rights struggle had forced the unions to act, strengthening the drive for Black rights and infusing new energy into the labor movement. But for several decades it had been the exception, not the rule, for labor unions to defend Black rights effectively; this was one of the factors that had weakened labor in the constant conflict with the employers.

Racism focuses the attention of white workers on Blacks as their "enemy"—not the employers who lay them off and worsen working conditions. The old labor maxim "an injury to one is an injury to all" indeed applied to Boston, but was not and would not be put into practice by the unions. A narrow-minded, conservative caste, bent on maintaining the relative privileges of white workers, has a strong grip on the Boston union movement. Politically, it is in the tow of the Democratic Party, "labor's friend."

The union movement stood aside as goons assaulted Black students, just as it had kept silent during the years of struggle to overturn the segregationist policies of the school committee. In those years, the school committee had pitted whites against Blacks while education and school facilities deteriorated for all. Small crumbs of privilege were thrown to whites to reinforce their opposition to Black parents seeking equal access to the better schools their children were kept out of. All the while, the school department became bloated with patronage and graft-seeking careerists. The reading level of *all* students sank to among the lowest in the nation, and all-white schools bulged with overcrowding produced by the dual school system.

The union at the center of the issue is the Boston Teachers Union, an affiliate of the American Federation of Teachers. (The National Education Association, the nation's largest teachers' union, backed the Garrity order, but it had no local in Boston. The NEA collaborated with the antiracist movement from the beginning. Its statements for busing were a step towards an action policy of the union movement.)

The BTU, as school opened in the fall of 1974, had an official position of support to integration. In practice, the all-white leadership of the local had opposed the state Racial Imbalance Law as "educationally disruptive."

Now the BTU opposed the section of Judge Garrity's broad desegregation order challenging racial discrimination in teacher hiring and school assignment, a keystone of the segregated system. Garrity had ordered parity hiring of Black teachers with whites until 20 percent of the teacher force was Black—a figure based on school department statistics of Black enrollment in the schools. This hiring policy would redress years of discrimination.

The BTU launched an appeal that would eventually go to the Supreme Court. Its opposition was based on preserving teacher employment as a virtually all-white job trust. The theme of opposition to desegregation ran through the BTU ranks as well. It was a position that fostered enmity toward the union in the Black community, a potentially substantial ally of the teachers in the fight for a better education had their union but reached out.

The BTU's racist response to the crisis in Boston was a cue to unions throughout the city and the nation. A visible, affirmative stand by the BTU behind the Garrity order would have exerted moral and political pressure on other AFL-CIO affiliates to stand up to the racists and could have brought the weight of the national union movement behind the Black community. This did not happen. The refusal of the unions to act deepened the isolation of the Black community. The results of this policy became alarming as the crisis grew.

In the summer of 1975 the national convention of the American Federation of Teachers would be highlighted by a debate on desegregation. AFT national President Albert Shanker, the leader of the United Federation of Teachers in New York City, personally took the floor to oppose busing, demagogically calling for federal aid to improve "quality education for all." The reversal of the AFT's position in support of busing to achieve desegregation would signal greater opposition to busing in the union movement.

Shanker's opposition to busing to achieve desegregation reflected his determination to gut the educational rights of minorities in New York City. There, the struggle for equal educational opportunity had taken the form of a heated confrontation over community control of the schools. Struggles in the 1960s by Blacks and Puerto Ricans had won significant educational reforms, including parent supervision of schools, teacher hiring, and curriculum. New York City's teacher force is overwhelmingly white; the schools are predominantly Black, Puerto Rican, and other nonwhite minorities.

Under Shanker's leadership, the AFT fought—and fights—a tooth-and-nail battle against minority parents who demanded increased hiring of Black, bilingual, and Chinese teachers and school supervisors, and curricula suitable to the needs of their children. Boston, for the Shanker-led union, was another side of the New York City battle. The BTU followed Shanker's lead.

Generalized governmental cutbacks in public education require a united movement to prevent a decline in the quality of education. Teacher layoffs, slashes in aid, the cutting of programs, and the raising of public college tuition are part of an across-the-board federal and state campaign against the rights and needs of working people. Starting with the teachers' unions, all organized labor faces the test of organizing a social and political response to such a strategy of "austerity." In Boston, the point of departure for a campaign in support of public education should have been a rallying of teachers behind the improvement of Black students' education and the scrapping of the segregated school system.

The irony of the union movement's abdication of its responsibility toward the Black community is pointed up by the character of the forces attracted to the antibusing drive: the John Birch Society, the Ku Klux Klan, the Nazis. All of these retrograde elements are mortally opposed to the rights of labor. In Louisville in the fall of 1975, racism would be the cement between the Klan—which would lead mass protests against desegregation—and union leaders and members who answered their antibusing call.

As Louisville became the second front in the struggle for school desegregation, the racist actions of local unions compelled AFL-CIO President George Meany to reaffirm the labor federation's support for court-ordered busing. The Kentucky unionists had attempted unsuccessfully to overturn national AFL-CIO policy at the federation's national convention in the summer prior to the opening of school.

Meany would be forced to act again in Boston, this time threatening to revoke the charter of the Massachusetts State Labor Council for approving, on November 7, 1975, a statement opposing desegregation in Boston. The state body backed down before Meany's challenge. Over the months of the school desegregation battle in Boston, however, it would become clear this was not enough. The racist movement overlapped the union leadership, pushing the labor officialdom to act against Black rights. Speaking out more and more for "white rights," the unions faced the economic crisis cut off from Black support in their own ranks and the community, increasingly conned by the demagogy of such "labor allies" as Louise Day Hicks and Albert "Dapper" O'Neill. The common interest linking the labor movement and Blacks was doomed by antibusing frenzy.

It was divide and rule, the oldest and most successful strategy of the employers: white against Black, man against woman, skilled against unskilled. Boston brought the divisions to the surface.

The strongest labor backing for desegregation would come from Black unionists—the Coalition of Black Trade Unionists, the Black caucus of the American Federation of Teachers, and individual Black unionists like Rexford Weng. Their stance would challenge the unions to act, for all the reasons that the unions came into being.

The unions that capitulated to the racists did not speak for their Black members. Nor did they speak for many of their white members, who supported Black rights but had no means of being heard. It would be a matter of strategy for ROAR to curry the favor of the unions, to try to make the word "labor" synonymous with the antibusing drive. ROAR in Boston sought to create an image of united white opposition to desegregation, and for this the unions were a prime target.

Yet behind the impression of white solidarity against busing there was a story to be told. For all its window dressing of union support, for all the energy of its resistance, the antibusing movement did not speak for white Boston. That was true in several neighborhoods where racist defiance and organization did not exist. It was also true in the very heart of the enclaves of opposition to busing. It was there that ROAR's method of "organizing" was a well-kept secret. It was there that terror was truly color blind.

# 9

# Cracks in the Racist Monolith

*"If my husband knew I was talking to you, he would kill me . . ."*

Louise Day Hicks often spoke of "the people of Boston," and no doubt, in her own way, meant to include Blacks. But her view of the city's Black residents was only a modernized version of the Jim Crow politeness of a bygone era in which southern Bourbons avowed concern for "our nigras." And when the matriarch of the antibusing movement spoke of *her* Boston, it was a view of that special *white* Boston, the city of neighborhoods—excluding the liberals of Beacon Hill and the students of Allston.

ROAR's rhetoric sought to portray a solid front of white resistance to desegregation—a front for which it spoke. To make credible this image of a monolithic reaction, discipline was necessary, a discipline that would enforce "unanimous" consent to ROAR's leadership in the key antibusing communities.

Social pressure was powerful in forcing compliance. Tightly knit South Boston was a prime example of this. Ostracism, the "silent treatment," gossip, and peer tension created a menacing pressure on individuals and families who either supported the court order or—more likely—were at least willing to comply with it. The mood of resistance propagated by ROAR created an atmosphere hostile to debate. There could be no discussion. The point of departure was opposition to busing, hatred of Garrity, period.

From the very start, however, there were cracks in the wall. These were small groups of parents who wanted to send their children on buses when they were assigned out of the district. Also there were the brave parents who sat on the biracial councils, mothers and fathers who despised ROAR. Their own version of Southie pride recoiled from the image of a garrison of anti-Black hysteria that was fast being fashioned by events.

This potentially powerful sentiment faced tremendous odds.

Publicity attached to speaking out, however modestly, invited reprisals. Because of the depth of resistance in South Boston and the constant pressure from the antibusing forces, secrecy rapidly became the mode of organization for these small bands of parents.

Police protection for *whites* against the racists in the lair of antibusing hostility was hard to come by. The very act of seeking law enforcement aid only made the target of racist vengeance more conspicuous. For these white parents—in South Boston and, to a degree, in East Boston, Charlestown, Hyde Park, and parts of Dorchester—a new word was introduced into their vocabulary: *terror.*

Some were well-known community figures, such as James O'Sullivan, a 1940 graduate of South Boston High School, a devout Catholic and pillar of the church. He was a foe of busing like, he thought, everybody else. Tall and greying, he spoke with a sharp, nasal Boston accent. He had gone to G Street for the first couple of days of school and had seen the ugly spectacle of neighbors assaulting the Black students with words, spit, and rocks. He had been to an early Home and School Association meeting, which had been turned into a howling antibusing rally by ROAR leaders and activists. He had had no idea it would be like this. And, he would tell the U.S. Commission on Civil Rights at its June 1975 hearing, it had turned his stomach. It was racism. "It made me ashamed to be from South Boston, ashamed to be a Catholic," he said, staring down a gallery packed with ROAR members.

O'Sullivan had never known a Black. But he rapidly became embroiled in the school busing controversy, serving on the Roxbury–South Boston Parents' Biracial Council, braving hate letters and phone calls, as well as physical harassment.

The numbers involved in the council were tiny, he recalled for the commission, and the initial meetings verged on walkouts by both sides. But they settled down, forging a link between Black and white parents determined to see the law implemented. The experience loomed large in his life. Deeply religious, he was appalled by the hate and violence generated by the bigots, and, in his strong Southie brogue, he called them racists. O'Sullivan publicly took his stand against the stream. "We are so small," a Black woman had said to him at one of the meetings. "Well," O'Sullivan countered, "Christ began with only twelve."

Tracy Amalfitano, a strong-looking blonde woman, was

identified with sentiment in favor of busing in South Boston. An activist, she was perhaps the most outspoken foe of racism in the community. Her children did not honor the boycott. She was backed by her husband, strengthened by white friends across the city who had known and worked with her, and by Blacks like Ellen Jackson, who admired and respected her. Her house came under attack. Windows were smashed out as bricks and bottles broke against the walls. The family car was repeatedly torched. Phone threats were common. There was hate mail, harassment, and, finally, pariah status. But Amalfitano would not buckle. Relatives moved in to provide support. Then the beauty parlor owned by her sister was wrecked and the tires of her car slashed. The sister was politically uninvolved.

Once Amalfitano was visited by a known supporter of desegregation from Dorchester. How the racists found out about the visitor is not known. But as the Dorchester woman rose to leave, she looked outside. A mob of one hundred had gathered, surrounding the front of the house and blocking her car. They waited an hour for police to arrive and disperse the mob.

Tracy Amalfitano and her family remained in South Boston, living in the nightmare. She had the courage to stay, continuing her work for implementation of the law through the second year of school desegregation. But the price was nonstop fear.

If O'Sullivan and Amalfitano had been public and suffered for it as individuals, the Catholic Laboure Centre became a target as a building. The priests and nuns there were not in favor of busing; if anything, they wished it would go away. They offered service to the community. That was all. But the scope of the violence and racism compelled them to act. They coupled modest statements for an end to the anti-Black graffiti and for peace with low-profile attempts to counsel and aid parents who complied with the law.

Phase I would be a rough year for the Laboure Centre. It became the butt of jokes from ROAR bigots, who warned the priests and nuns to keep their noses out of the busing issue if they knew what was good for them. Windows in the center were broken. A van used by its daycare center was firebombed. Priests were roughed up; some of them transfered out of the center. Finally, the quietly organized meetings for parents complying with the order were, according to a co-worker at the center, "infiltrated by ROAR members . . . who physically broke them up, shouting, throwing chairs, whatever. . . ."

The violence drove home ROAR's message to those Southie parents who were willing to comply with or submit to Judge Garrity's order. The neighborhood had been thoroughly canvassed by ROAR prior to the opening of school. Door-to-door recruitment had gone on in the projects. Store and home windows sported big placards proclaiming, "We support the South Boston School Boycott," and not displaying one caused the raising of more than a few eyebrows. The *South Boston Tribune* printed news, editorial, and feature pieces raging against busing. And galvanizing all this was the surging momentum of the movement—the motorcades and rallies, the Home and School Association meetings in the neighborhood, and the ROAR meetings in the city council chambers, the walkouts, fights, stonings, and battles with police.

It is against this backdrop that the actions of anti-ROAR parents can be best judged. Many of them, in one way or another, opposed busing; but it was an opposition not motivated by racial hatred as much as by a terrified confusion of the issues. It was here that the code words of bigotry could least be challenged. It was here that blood and friendship ties were snapped by differences over the order. It was a father beating the drums for ROAR and a mother agonizing against the boycott, whole families splitting over the issue. "You hear the word *Judas* a lot," one community worker said, describing the process.

Only a handful of parents would momentarily allow reporters to talk with them. The danger of exposure was too great, and police protection was a mirage. At the same time, the media backed off from in-depth investigation of the situation, even though it would have made "good copy." More than once, Black leaders personally urged editors of the *Herald* and *Globe* to go after such news. Here was the most obvious way to expose the demagogy of the racists: white parents faced terror for merely attempting to comply with the desegregation order. Hardly rabble-rousers or ideologues, they were ordinary working people who wanted their kids to go to school. But to go after these stories of harassment would be opening a big can of worms: Who was behind the harassment? What were the police doing? Where was the protection? Weren't federal civil rights statutes being violated? The media magnates were not willing to do their job and thus break their pact of deference to the bigots.

For every parent whose stand was publicized, there were scores, even hundreds, whose protests were silent. There were the dozen or so parents who gathered every morning on Day Boulevard, watching out for hooligans as their children boarded buses leaving South Boston. Among them was a mother who lived on the second floor of a three-decker house, who had trouble sleeping. The upstairs residents jumped and pounded on the floor at midnight to let her know that they knew.

There was the Charlestown mother, a lifelong resident, who repeatedly called friends in the police department to tell them she knew who was threatening to break the arms of her nine-year-old son, who rode the buses out of the neighborhood.

Or the Hyde Park mother, a busing foe until school opened in September 1974. She was repelled by the violence and decided to send her children to school. Gangs drove up on her lawn on motorcycles, ripping the grass to shreds in the middle of the night—and in broad daylight.

"They met in little bands of parents, maybe four or five, and moved from one house to another each week," said a community agency staff member, describing the informal gatherings of these parents. Utmost secrecy. No publicity. For some mothers, it would be on a husband's bowling night. Some would never tell their spouses, their relatives, their children. Meeting places would sometimes be arranged by word of mouth. "You never knew about the phones," one woman said.

Kathleen S. from South Boston attended such meetings. "I never knew what it was like to live in fear," she confided, "Now I do." Some of her friends found out about her. "Now, when they see me, they turn their backs. . . . When you get criticized or asked questions, you just clam up or talk double-talk. It may be cowardly, but it's the only way for a lot of us. You don't know what will happen to you."

Some friends who shared her attitude had learned the cost. "Signs were painted on their houses, shots fired through windows, and cars have been ruined," Kathleen said. "You hear stories of threats, like 'We'll find you wherever you are. We'll get your kids. You'll have to get your kid back on a stretcher.'"

She, like other parents, did not favor the busing plan. "But people don't have the right to keep their children out of school. I was raised to obey the law, and this is the law." Kathleen fears—and loathes—ROAR. Her readiness to comply with the order put her informally into contact with Blacks, and the experience led her to new conclusions. "The Black students face quite a bit of abuse," she said, "but they have as much right to go to school here as my kids do. I've learned about the Black community. I can feel what the Black parents are going through now, and I know we have the same concern for our children. I have grown up considerably in the past year and a half from this all."

Kathleen is not alone. Young, red-haired, pug-nosed, she is Southie to her bones. But ROAR did not speak for her, "because ROAR doesn't represent all white people. That is just not true when they say that." Kathleen's husband does not know her views, does not know of the meetings she went to. With them, busing is the issue they have agreed to disagree about—silently. They go to church together, to movies, to restaurants, and, together, they feel the tension in the neighborhood. When he leaves for work, she is on the phone, with friends he has never heard of.

Parents like Kathleen have no way of knowing the ideas of a college boy like Kevin L. They could have bumped into each other in the Broadway supermarket or been within yards of one another at Carson Beach. But there was—and is—no vehicle for their meeting in South Boston. It is too dangerous, too fraught with problems.

Kevin L. is a second generation Southie. His grandparents came from Ireland. His father is a tough, semiskilled worker and a union man. Kevin holds down a job and goes to college at night. He thinks ROAR is racist and that busing is good. He keeps his opinions quiet. A friend's car had a bumper sticker favoring desegregation, and it was torched. His father tells him to "keep my mouth shut or we won't have a house."

"I can see people being against busing, I can respect that opinion," he said, "but I can't see them shouting obscenities and throwing stones at Black students. I'm against that kind of intimidation and the people who go out of their way to do it. I took buses to go to school and no one ever called it busing. These people just don't want their Johnny or Mary to go to school with Black kids, or have their kids make friends with Blacks."

It is the rude, primitive fear that he talked about, a product of the community's extreme insularity, a backwardness fostered and preyed upon by the racist politicians who head the antibusing movement. "It really is a racist movement," he noted. "If it isn't, why are people throwing stones and shouting obscenities?" The violence made him think about the issue. Like many South Boston residents, he would oppose the disruption, but something bigger was at stake. Busing is "one more step, a key element leading to quality education," he said.

"I'm for it, it's part of a process that I think could have been much more gradual if the school committee hadn't been so opposed and had begun to desegregate ten years ago when it was supposed to. They just built up more and more segregation. I put the blame on the school committee, on people like Louise Day Hicks."

His support for busing was not reversed by the resentment that the order had inspired in the neighborhood. "When schools are desegregated, when white students go to formerly all-Black schools, it just starts to happen that the all-white school committees and city councils start spending more money for teachers and books and education in those schools. Desegregation means equalizing funds so there can be better education," Kevin said.

Kevin's comments have the ring of truth, and coming from South Boston gives them added power. How deep such sentiments may run there is impossible to estimate because, as he says, "People can't speak out in South Boston. Not if you want to live."

There is, however, one woman who, despite harassment and persecution, continues to speak out in defense of school desegregation. Evelyn Morash has lived in East Boston for more than two decades. She and her husband have five children, the two youngest attending magnet, i.e., voluntarily desegregated, schools. Short and stocky, pleasant-faced, she is a person whose calm, easygoing manner might be mistaken by her adversaries as a sign of weakness.

Phase I had drawn a line of blood in Eastie, and Morash would cross it. She helped initiate East Boston for Quality Education (EBQUE), a parent group, which undertook to prepare the neighborhood for whatever Phase II desegregation would mean the next year. There were small meetings with school department officials, community agents, and parents in anticipation of the order. Leaflets and flyers were circulated. Morash herself had first hand experience with the desegregation issue as a member of the state board of education, a community worker for the Greater Boston Catholic Charities, and a parent. She would later be appointed to the Citywide Coordinating Council, a body set up by Judge Garrity to monitor the process of school desegregation in its second year.

If there was any one person who spoke for and symbolized East Boston's antibusing movement, it was Elvira "Pixie" Palladino, the local head of ROAR. Palladino, in the fall of 1974, was preparing the resistance for combat in the coming year, when the plan was expected to include Eastie. Her strong-arm tactics had caused early splits in the antibusing organization. In East Boston, a widespread rumor was the danger of rape awaiting white girls in Roxbury. That fitted Palladino's rough-and-tumble style. A ward heeler for the Democrats, she had long been involved in opposing progressive movements in the neighborhood.

Palladino is not an orator capable of crowd-rousing stemwinders. There is, though, a stunning fierceness about her. It is in her face, pursed in barely restrained tension, and in her eyes, burning, intense, almost glazed with anger when busing is the topic of discussion. That is her obsession.

She was at a private meeting in Mayor White's office with other racist leaders summoned to discuss the crisis with Black leaders on October 8, just after the mob beating of André Yvon Jean-Louis in South Boston. The incident was brought up by Melnea Cass. Palladino looked her in the eye. "That nigger got just what he deserved," she shouted. "What was he doing there, anyhow?" The already tense meeting fell apart. In that instant, she was ROAR's rising star.

Palladino was in the center of the fight, and she spoke the words common on the street. The violence of the bigots would be her constant promise, and she would make no excuses for it. On a table in her living room is a framed portrait of Benito Mussolini, which she describes as an heirloom.

She and Evelyn Morash had previously crossed swords over other issues. To Palladino, Morash was a turncoat, the enemy. Morash's work in support of desegregation had put her at the top of the bigots' hate list. Throughout 1974 and into 1975 the animosity simmered. In May 1975, with the announcement of Phase II desegregation plans—which included modest busing plans at the elementary and middle school levels—the hostility took the form of action.

The windows of the Morash home became targets for nighttime hooligans. Red paint was splattered on the house. Morash's eighty-five-year-old mother, who lived on the building's first floor, would be rousted from bed, terrified by shattering glass. Then,

Albert "Dapper" O'Neill

Elvira "Pixie" Palladino

William "Billy" Bulger

Avi Nelson

John "Bigga" Kerrigan

James Kelly

there were the phone calls—obscene phone calls, racist epithets, and death threats.

Morash refused to take the abuse passively. She campaigned to defend her rights and push the East Boston police into action. The *East Boston Community News,* a weekly paper with a decided dislike of ROAR and Palladino, editorialized in support of desegregation. It publicized the Morash situation. In turn it faced harassment. Threats were made, paint was splashed on the paper's storefront, and a fire was set.

For the two years of desegregation, the *Community News* would be a conscience of East Boston. With a circulation of five thousand in a community of forty thousand, it would go behind the scenes of the antibusing opposition, provide valuable news on the plight of the handful of Blacks in the area, and serve as a beacon of progressive attitudes on the desegregation issue.

The lengthy police investigation of phone harassment of the Morash family resulted in two arrests, which had a chilling effect on the hostility which directed it. Evelyn Morash had pressed recalcitrant officials and continued to speak out, and it had paid off. Michael Renici, a young nephew of Palladino, was arrested along with Thomas Johnson, Jr., whose father was the president of the Charlestown Home and School Association, a member of ROAR's secret executive board, and the central leader of the Powderkeg Information Center. But the wheels of justice ground to a halt with the initial court proceedings: the case of the racist duo was bound over for a year and at this writing has yet to come to adjudication.

"I think we've been left alone," Morash recounted, "because we decided to fight it out in the open." Indeed, though the antibusing machine rumbled along in East Boston, the neighborhood itself was not swept into motion because Phase I had not touched the area, and Phase II would only begin to erode the segregated character of the schools. At the same time, an important nucleus of intransigent foes of ROAR was organized. It served as a pole of attraction which countered Palladino and her team—whose roughshod methods had precipitated a wave of splits in the antibusing ranks. In the spring of 1976, in a wild, brawling neighborhood meeting on administrative control of a community school project, pro-Palladino forces were narrowly defeated by more moderate elements.

For Evelyn Morash, the decision to send her young children on the buses had not been particularly hard. She was a proponent of desegregation in principle, and, if anything, the challenge of the bigots stiffened her determination.

EBQUE members had leafleted the community for Phase II. "Busing will not go away," was the headline of the flyer. "For years," it stated, "antibusing leaders told us it would never happen here. But since 1954 the U.S. Supreme Court has said that segregated schools like those in Boston are unconstitutional. *Segregation is against the law*. And that law won't be changed."

Under the heading "The right to go to school," EBQUE took dead aim at the disrupters. "Last September several East Boston parents received phone calls warning them to keep their children out of school. Other parents became afraid and pulled their children out of school when protest marches were held. . . . Those who want to send their children to school should be able to do so without being afraid."

For East Boston parents who made such a decision, busing "out" meant students being sent to formerly predominantly Black schools, where, the racists intoned, the whites would be educationally shortchanged. These were the schools to which the Morash children went. "I was amazed at how much better the education is that they're getting," Morash recalled.

"I believe a desegregated education is best for both Blacks and whites," she continued. "In Phase II, it wasn't simply a question of manipulating numbers to achieve balance. The plan includes increased parent involvement, expanded curriculum, new programs, and so on. It's an educational experience. The school one of my children is going to was a mess before it opened. That is the way it probably was kept when it was segregated. . . . But with the parents coming around, with busing opening it up, it has been all cleaned up. There is a teacher-pupil ratio there that has meant more time for individual attention. It's a better school than the comparable middle school in East Boston."

News of the experience of the Morash children trickled back to parents who had succumbed to the pressure of the racists. Slowly, quietly, they would talk to Evelyn Morash and ask how to get their kids into the schools. "Once in a while, someone comes up to me and says, 'When it's all over, your side is going to win because you're right.' So I ask them to do something about it if they feel that way. . . . You cannot be silent on this issue. Silence gives your consent to the antibusers. That is why," Evelyn Morash says, "people have to stand up."

It is certain that the majority of white parents of Boston reject the physical violence, the anti-Black terror, and such victimization as was suffered by the Morashes in East Boston and the Amalfitanos and Kathleens and countless unnamed in South Boston and Charlestown. The right to send children to school, to board buses, to engage in the simplest kinds of activity to smooth the workings of the court order, became an obstacle to the ROAR machine. Such acts constituted practical opposition to the boycott and possibly signified support for desegregation.

The basis of ROAR's argument—indeed the common denominator of President Ford, Louise Day Hicks, and the rock throwers they jointly inspired—is "white rights." The rhetoric might be for "quality education" or opposition to "forced busing," but the single-minded concern was the sentiment of whites who regarded neighborhood and school segregation as a privilege. Equalization of access through busing peeled the verbiage away to reveal a neanderthal prejudice against Blacks.

"You know," Evelyn Morash says, "I would bet 99 percent of the women of East Boston have never been to Roxbury. There is great fear and ignorance. Everything was unknown." For a decade, that backwardness and isolation had been solidified by the school committee, heated into a frenzy by the city's politicians, and galvanized into militant resistance by ROAR.

A monolith—the united white face of the "people of Boston"—was ROAR's goal, the aim of its demagogy. But such unity was a fiction imposed on the public, as is proved by the justified fear of those opposed to ROAR though living in its strongholds. And these are more than a handful. They include mothers, longshoremen, secretaries, nurses, community college students, Irish and Italian families, churchgoers, parents, and students.

"You people," one Black parent told a South Boston mother at a secret meeting late one night, "have it worse than us. At least we can go home at night and be safe." The South Boston woman to whom this had been said laughed as she recounted it. Then her voice dropped to a sudden, soft hush on the phone. "I have to go now," she said, "I think my husband's coming home."

He would not know.

# 10

# A Call to Action

There was no Christmas spirit in Boston for Colly Seaborn as 1974 drew to a chilly close. He had not been able to shake off the terrifying memory of being dragged from his delivery truck by a gang of whites in South Boston two months earlier. Black and beaten for it, he was one of many. His story made the news media—a holiday vignette.

"For twenty-one years I walked the streets of the city of Boston without fear," the Black man said. "Now I'm afraid of this city. I'm almost afraid to go out of the house. I wake up in the middle of the night and I think about it. I have to sit on the edge of my bed, shaking, until I can fall back asleep."

Colly Seaborn left Boston and moved back to his native Virginia. He did not remain in the city to the end of 1974. Happy New Year.

On December 18 the racists sustained a setback some of them had not expected. Garrity, the antibusing leadership had been boasting, had overstepped himself with his sweeping June 21, 1974, desegregation decision. They would do their best to make the implementation of busing rocky, and finally the courts were bound to come their way. A week before Christmas, a three-judge federal appeals court dashed that hope. The unanimous decision backed Garrity to the hilt, and in strong language. "We do not see how the Garrity court could arrive at any other decision," the judges stated. The Boston School Committee, they affirmed, has "systematically" maintained and expanded school segregation. Garrity's order was proper "in light of the ample precedents in the Supreme Court."

School committee Chairman John Kerrigan promptly announced an appeal to the Supreme Court. Mayor White promised city funding for the legal legwork to overturn desegregation.

The first semester of Phase I had ended. Even as it had been announced in the summer of 1974, however, speculation was focused on the broader plan in preparation, covering the entire city. Garrity's initial decision had said that every classroom in the school system would have to be desegregated. This was required to remove the stigma of the heinous dual structure "root and branch." The Phase I plan had been a first, admittedly rough, step towards that.

On December 16 the Boston School Committee voted three to two to refuse to submit to Judge Garrity a plan for Phase II. Four days later, Garrity found the three in civil contempt of court. He gave the school committee until January 8 to present to him their proposal for Phase II. On that day, the schools were set to reopen.

In South Boston, more than five hundred local and state police massed on G Street, near the L Street Annex, at the Dean Junior High School. They patrolled the bus routes. They were inside the schools.

It was a frigid, windy day. The streets were bare. No crowds. No mobs. The white student boycott remained steady. Less than a tenth of the Black students assigned to South Boston boarded the buses that morning. It was "wait and see" in the Black community. Bitter as the day was, weather did not explain the empty streets bordering the schools in South Boston. Behind the windows of houses past which the buses rolled were the angry faces of South Boston residents. They could not march on the school. They could not get at the buses. The police were out in force. The next day, Black enrollment swelled.

In his chambers that day, Judge Garrity accepted the Boston School Committee's plan for the second phase of desegregation. It was a work of evasion, counterfeit on its face. The school committee, for years the center of "legal" opposition to desegregation, in contempt for refusing to submit a plan, had merely changed its style.

Masterminded by Kerrigan, the committee's offering to Garrity was based on the concept of "voluntary integration." Mandatory busing was eliminated. It was a bogus plan—nothing more than a slightly refurbished version of the "open enrollment" scheme which the school committee had used to reinforce segregation. That Judge Garrity would implement the plan was highly unlikely; that would sabotage the decision he had made seven months earlier. Yet his acceptance of it was surprisingly cordial considering the committee's intransigent opposition to any real measure of relief for the Black students.

The judge lifted the contempt citations. Kerrigan, his mortal enemy, termed Garrity's action "a sign of reasonableness and . . . a personal victory." Garrity would move only as far and as fast against the bigots as he felt was demanded of him; he was seeking to avoid confrontation once the desegregation plan was—however shakily—operative. There was a flaw in his method. Any and every modicum of credibility granted to the bigots' maneuvers emboldened them, raising anew the question on the mind of every racist in Boston: Can we force Garrity to back down?

The real question was not Garrity the man or Garrity the judge. His order was a product of the struggles of Blacks for equality—from Selma to Boston, from the 1950s to December 14, 1974. The racists' real question was, Can we force the Black community to back down?

On January 9, a day after the contempt citation had been lifted from the three school committee members, a day after "voluntary integration" had become worthy of the judge's consideration, the racists went back to what they did best. Hyde Park High School was closed for the day, after a small police riot capping a fight between Black and white students. Thirteen Blacks and one white were arrested.

Thomas Atkins, more than any other Black leader in Boston, had been on the hot seat in the fall of 1974. He had become president of the Boston NAACP that July, and in a few months the branch had become functional again. Atkins drew the fire directed at the organization. The NAACP and the Freedom House Coalition together were the organizational center of the Black community's response to the racists. Sometimes contact was regular and agreement on what to do next was easy. Sometimes there were disagreements, arguments, debates, but always cooperation in the end.

It had been assumed, Atkins recalled, "that I would be the major spokesperson." He would be the most exposed to public view, to questions, to controversy. The arrangement seemed to suit the young lawyer, who, as Ruth Batson would later remark, is "something of a loner."

Sometimes cautious, other times hot tempered, Atkins is confident, even headstrong. His views reflect a sentiment widely prevalent in the NAACP—an unflinching belief in the inevitable victory of the Constitution over the bigots. The NAACP's persistence in pursuit of Black equality through the courts for more than half a century is at the foundation of this belief. It meshes with Atkins's own personal self-confidence and his lawyer's belief in the duty of judges fairly to define and pronounce the law.

He had watched the unfolding of the South Boston drama with the gnawing sense of impending explosion. For a while he was prepared to support the December 14 march. But then, he said, "it got too hot in South Boston." Atkins drew back, despite his belief that William Owens, the state senator who had called the demonstration, "is a good man." Atkins did not trust "the people he had gotten involved with"—the Emergency Committee—and doubted that the march could come off properly. Atkins had, however, endorsed the teach-in sponsored by the Student Committee. And he was impressed by the Student Committee members' presence of mind at the march, their responsibility and discipline in the face of potential confrontation.

A component of the Student Committee coalition had been the Socialist Workers Party. Its candidate for governor, Donald Gurewitz, had run a hard-hitting, well-publicized campaign with defense of school desegregation as its main theme. Atkins had met and worked with Gurewitz in support of the November 30 march, which Atkins had helped organize.

That Christmas holiday, Atkins conceived the idea of another demonstration, a special kind of demonstration that would "have an impact" in Boston. It would commemorate the historic *Brown* v. *Topeka Board of Education* decision, whose anniversary was May 17.

Atkins called Gurewitz to discuss the idea. But Gurewitz was out in Saint Louis, where over a thousand activists were gathered at the national convention of the Young Socialist Alliance. In Boston and throughout the country, that organization had plunged into the desegregation battle, and the convention's high point was a report on the subject by newly elected National Chairperson Malik Miah. He had been a political activist in the Black high school movement in Detroit. The YSA, he urged, should help launch the new antiracist movement demanded by the Boston crisis; for in that city, Miah said, "a victory for the racists would set in motion other racists across the country to try to do what Nixon's rhetoric about law and order couldn't—beat back gains won by Blacks over the last two decades."

"The struggle in Boston," he continued, "is around a simple, basic democratic right: the right to an equal education . . . around whether or not the buses keep rolling to South Boston schools. If the racist boycott is victorious and the court desegregation order rescinded—that is, the buses stop rolling—that would be a defeat for Black rights. . . . The issue in Boston is *equal* education for Blacks. That's it—plain and simple. The racists say no! We say yes! The racists say no buses. We say the buses must roll. The line is drawn: for or against busing."

The delegates unanimously approved plans for a campaign of education—teach-ins, debates, forums, all methods of getting the issue out, publicizing and popularizing it—as well as action. The latter meant pursuing a policy to bring about the broadest possible alliance of forces, starting with Boston's Black leaders, the clergy, the unions, the student movement—all the foes of racism. Such an alliance could mobilize the widespread sentiment for Black rights that existed, make it visible in the streets, and defeat the bigots.

Though small in numbers these socialists were experienced in such efforts. They had been among the leaders of the antiwar movement and the women's liberation struggles that had spanned the country. They had acquired new training in Boston, in building and participating in the December 14 demonstrations. And they were ready to go to work.

Upon Gurewitz's return to Boston, he and Atkins discussed the May 17 idea. Further deliberations would be held with the leaders of the Student Committee, which, in anticipation of the February 14-15 meeting of activists it had scheduled, had renamed itself the National Student Conference Against Racism.

Early in January, Student Committee leader Maceo Dixon and Atkins met. They saw eye to eye on the main issues. The National Student Conference Against Racism, Dixon told Atkins, would start off with a teach-in, an ideal setting in which to announce the May 17 demonstration. The following day would be for discussion and debate. Hundreds of activists would be ready to go with the idea. Dixon was certain because the new organization, with its emphasis on the need for action, was evoking considerable interest on campuses, especially in Black organizations. Meanwhile, Atkins would promote the idea of the march within the NAACP. Dixon was excited and optimistic as the discussion concluded. "It was clear May 17 was real," he recalled. "It was a matter of time, more discussion. And, yes, it had a ring to it. . . ."

On January 10 Kenneth Edelin, a Black doctor at Boston City Hospital, went on trial. He had been indicted in April 1974 for manslaughter, for performing a *legal* abortion on a seventeen-year-old Black woman. The charges specified that he had killed a fetus. Separate indictments had also been returned against four others for research on fetuses, under an 1814 statute against "grave robbing" and "illegal dissection."

The opponents of abortion rights—organized in the Massachusetts Citizens for Life—had been after Edelin and the other doctors since the appearance of an article on fetal research in the *New England Journal of Medicine* in June 1973. The "right-to-life" forces had enlisted the aid of Raymond Flynn, South Boston's state representative, a leader of the antibusing movement. "I share your views," he wrote in response to their request for help, "and the views of all right-thinking people that abortion should not be permitted under any circumstances despite the decision of the United States Supreme Court.

In September 1973 Albert "Dapper" O'Neill convoked a city council public hearing for the benefit of his "right-to-life" allies. O'Neill, one of the antibusing crowd's favorite pols, was joined by Patrick McDonough, another antibusing city council member, whose brother was a member of the Boston School Committee. Edelin spoke out in defense of abortion rights at the hearing. The proceedings turned into an election-year gold mine for Suffolk County District Attorney Garret Byrne, who called the grand jury which indicted Edelin and the four other doctors.

The combined weight of the antibusing and "right-to-life" movements were now brought to bear on the Black doctor. The prosecuting attorney was Newman Flannagan, an ardent Catholic foe of abortion and a lawyer who would go for the jugular to win a verdict of guilty. As he returned to his seat from questioning witnesses, Flannagan would mutter insults to Edelin. The jury was all white.

On Friday, February 14, more than twelve hundred students, many of them from Boston, arrived at Boston University's Hayden Hall for the National Student Conference Against Racism. Over eight hundred more activists would come in by bus, plane, train, and car the next day. All together they represented 113 different organizations, including 50 Black student groups, and came from 147 colleges and 58 high schools from California to New York. It was the largest gathering of student activists in more than half a decade.

Thomas Atkins, the keynote speaker at the evening rally, was greeted with a standing ovation. He launched into a history of the campaign for Black rights, linking the early civil rights movement and its fight against Jim Crow with the tasks confronting supporters of the Black movement in the Boston crisis.

"We must resist the dedicated racists who know what they are doing. We must resist the ignorant racists who are told what to do. We must resist the little racists who are being trained how to be big racists. We must resist the good people who aren't racists at all, but who are allowing themselves to be led by racists. . . . Because the forces of racism in this country have from time to time achieved tremendous strength, those of us who recognize the incalculable harm it has done must organize to oppose it."

Continuing with the proposal for action, Atkins said: "The Boston NAACP calls upon this conference to join with us in organizing against those forces which could drag our country back to 'separate but equal.' We call upon this conference to support us in our effort to commemorate the historic *Brown* decision on May 17."

The room exploded with cheers and clapping. For the next two days, in workshops and plenary sessions, the conference would hammer out the fine points. Most of the workshops were on the Boston situation, some conducted by teachers and Black students. Other topics included affirmative action; Black, Puerto Rican, and Chicano community control of the schools; the need for bilingual education; and support to victims of racist political frame-ups.

The conference voted overwhelmingly to support the call for May 17. They also set April 4—the anniversary of Martin Luther King's assassination—and April 19 as the dates for actions across the country leading up to the Boston demonstration. The unity and commitment of the gathering was marred only by a small Maoist organization which opposed busing and desegregation. It led a brief walkout of about a hundred Black students—a minority of the Blacks at the conference—most of whom later returned.

The Maoists and other leftist sects which had come to the gathering disagreed with its central theme: the fight for Black equal rights through busing. As their opponents in debate charged, they substituted ultraradical rhetoric for concrete work in defense of the rights jeopardized by the antibusing offensive. The debate was heated and sharp, dismaying many of those new to such conferences with the spectacle of division. But the sects proved to be of little significance, and the dominant mood was one of deep solidarity.

This was reflected in the discussion on the structure of the new organization being launched. The National Student Coalition Against Racism (NSCAR) would have its headquarters in Boston and would be led on a day-to-day basis by elected coordinators. A national steering committee composed of representatives from each chapter would hold periodic meetings open to all. Special emphasis was placed on the participation of Black student organizations. NSCAR's highest body was to be its national conference, open to all, with each person having voice and vote.

The new organization belonged to its membership, the activists in the struggle against racism. It would democratically discuss issues, debate them out, and decide what to do. And, with its geographical scope, its multiracial compositon, its ranks composed of members from scores of different organizations and groups, and its participation in the struggle against racism, it has lived up to its name.

Fundamentally, it was the commitment to mass action—first and foremost that proposed for May 17—which cemented the new organization. A feature of this unity in action was the participation of the country's two largest radical youth organizations, the Young Socialist Alliance and the Young Workers Liberation League. This was quite unusual. The YWLL, which is in political solidarity with the Communist Party, seldom functioned in coalitions, particularly when they included the YSA. It had many sharp disagreements with the socialists.

In Boston, the YWLL and the CP had participated unevenly in the school desegregation struggle. In 1971 and 1973, the YWLL had run Patricia Bonner-Lyons, an articulate young Black woman, for school committee. In the fall of 1974, the two organizations had helped to build support for the November 30 march sponsored by the Committee for Quality, Integrated Education. However, the YWLL had refused to support the December 14 demonstration. Its national chairman, James Steele, had branded that march a "routine exercise in left sectarianism."

The source of this inconsistency was the YWLL's belief that social change could come through the liberal wing of the Democratic Party, a position long held by the Communist Party. As the struggle intensified in Boston, it became clear that mass actions, regardless of who called them, were aimed at the

Democratic Party, which controlled the city and state governments—and a sector of which had organized and led the antibusing movement. Consequently, as the crisis sharpened and took on national proportions, the busing issue had become a hot potato within the Democratic Party, with its elected officials retreating on Black rights.

Massive mobilizations in defense of those rights exposed the two-party system and were helping to forge a new, militant leadership capable of leading the Black community out of the grip of the Democrats. The YWLL and CP opposed such a perspective, holding firm in their belief that the Democratic Party's liberals—Black and white—are a "lesser evil" than conservative Democrats and Republicans. With the national presidential campaign beginning, the YWLL and CP would back away even more from united, militant struggles that pointed to the need for a break from the two parties. They would engage in protests, but seek to blunt their edge and their source of strength—the independent mobilization of those fighting for social change.

The NAACP, however, had called an action which symbolized the fight of the Black community nationally and in Boston. Furthermore, the YWLL supported busing. At the conference, the YWLL disagreed with a number of aspects of the policy adopted, but it stated its agreement on the necessity of the May 17 action. It was *in* NSCAR; in fact, it proposed the name of the new organization. Though it was not used to coalitions, to the freewheeling give and take of a mass movement, the YWLL's participation was important. Its presence underscored the unity required to defeat the racists. It would have to learn to work with those with whom it deeply disagreed, to help achieve the biggest possible turnout on May 17. That was the most important thing.

The students who had traveled across the country to Boston had participated not only in a conference but in a protest. Two thousand desegregation activists in the center of conflict over busing was—or should have been—big news in Boston. But the Boston, media, bound by the lingering pact, denied the conference any significant coverage. Reporters from the *Globe* attended the two-day affair only after pressure had been put on the editors. Their copy never saw the light of day. Promises of coverage by local television and radio, whose news directors had received notices well in advance, followed by updates and phone calls, never were carried out.

The only publicity given was to a *denial* by the conference of any connection with a proposed picket line at the South Boston home of Louise Day Hicks. The call for this picketing had been issued by the Committee Against Racism. CAR, a small antiracist group, opposed mass demonstrations, maintaining that the best way to combat racism was through physical fights and confrontations. It was led by the Progressive Labor Party. Together, the PL and CAR supporters at the conference numbered twenty. They announced the action as the gathering ended, after being roundly opposed by the other activists. However, their proposed provocative stunt caught the media's attention. In South Boston, a crowd of two hundred whites, mobilized in a few hours by a shadowy organization called the South Boston Defense League, gathered at Hicks's home. A picket line there would have been a bloodbath. CAR's action was cancelled after the police refused them an escort. But the media's refusal to cover the NSCAR conference, coupled with its sudden interest in CAR, was indicative of things to come.

On February 15, while the students were founding NSCAR, the all-white jury convicted Dr. Kenneth Edelin of manslaughter. The news traveled through the conference like electricity. It had been assumed that Edelin would be acquitted. A hung jury was the least that many activists felt was in store. For the women at the gathering, the verdict was doubly stunning. Here they were, mapping out a campaign to defeat the anti-Black bigots, and Edelin had been railroaded by antibusing officials who had no love for women's liberation.

Now, starkly, the mood of reaction in Boston had been defined. Racism would brook no reform. The connection between the foes of Black rights *and* women's rights was clear. That Edelin was a target of a mentality spurred by the segregationist campaign was unmistakable. Michael Ciano, a white alternate juror from East Boston, related typical comments by the jurors, creating a furor with his disclosures. "That nigger," one white juror had said, for example, "is as guilty as sin."

Forty-eight hours later, a hastily organized protest called by Boston women's liberation activists brought more than two thousand angry, shouting demonstrators into the streets. For many of them, such code words as "neighborhood schools" and "forced busing" were no longer deceptive or confusing. They realized that those phrases were being used to mask racism, just

Dr. Kenneth Edelin

as the bogus concept of "the right to life" was a cover for denying women their democratic rights.

The battle of Boston was over desegregation, to be sure, but the social terrain of the battlefield had suddenly expanded. And for many of the undecided and unsure, the question: "Whose side are you on?" had become painfully immediate. The stakes were getting higher.

Despite irritating incidentals, the student gathering had been a tonic for those attending. As they prepared to leave for their various destinations they had something tangible to take home—to Chicago, New York, Atlanta, Cleveland, and a hundred other localities—a plan for action on May 17, something to work on, something to build. It would be an action linking the struggles of the past and the present—a commemoration of the historic *Brown* school decision and the current fight to defend it. These young activists were the products of a generation of social protest: from the fight against Jim Crow, the draft, and the Vietnam War to women's liberation. The new organization they had founded would combat racism in *all* its forms. As they left the conference hall their rhythmic chant was "Keep the buses rolling, desegregate the schools."

# 11

# Skirmishes
# on a Widening Front

Phase II was the name given to Judge Garrity's final desegregation order for the Boston public school system. Such white neighborhoods as Charlestown, West Roxbury, the North End, and East Boston had been relatively untouched by the Phase I dismantling of the dual school system. Now schools in those districts faced inclusion in the overall desegregation process.

On February 4, Garrity appointed four "masters" to prepare a plan for him. He would not be bound by their advice; but what they produced, many thought, would frame his decision. One of the masters, Francis Keppel, a former dean of the Harvard Graduate School of Education and the late President John F. Kennedy's Commissioner of Education, indicated the intent of the four-member panel: "Desegregate and defuse." It sounded calming, but what if these were incompatible? Which then took precedence—desegregation or the reduction of tension?

The antibusing forces had only one price for being "defused"— the complete ending of desegregation. Concessions were an incentive to them to keep the city tense. And with a mayor, city council, and school committee involved in an unstinting campaign to overturn the law, they already had confidence in their muscle.

"We have the responsibility of keeping this city from being torn apart," Boston attorney Edward McCormack, one of the masters, said. South Boston born and raised, McCormack had been a city council member and state attorney general and was well known in Massachusetts. His uncle John had been the Speaker of the U.S. House of Representatives. Both were opposed to "forced busing." On March 4 the masters began to crystallize their concept of "desegregate and defuse." They rejected the NAACP's recommendations, which called for an increase in busing to achieve full abolition of the dual school system.

The same day, in Washington, D.C., lawyer John Doogan,

executive director of the usually low-profile Massachusetts Citizens Against Forced Busing, headed a lobbying effort for a constitutional amendment against desegregation-related busing. Doogan received a pledge of support from Democratic House Majority Leader Thomas "Tip" O'Neill. "If you could get it on the floor," O'Neill told him, "there is no question in my mind it would pass overwhelmingly." The proposed constitutional amendment was a frontal attack on *Brown* and the equal protection provisions of the Fourteenth Amendment. It was a deadly serious threat, and the Black community would not take it lightly. O'Neill later recanted his support.

Senator Edward Brooke of Massachusetts was backed down by the lobbying racists. Yes, he believed in desegregation, he said, but, "I am not wedded to the concept of busing. . . . I would like to search for that other way." Brooke's hedging encouraged Doogan.

On March 19, thirteen hundred antibusing partisans rallied in a cold drizzle on the steps of the Capitol in Washington. The demonstration, called by Boston ROAR, capped a weekend strategy session attended by representatives of thirty right-wing groups. The rally supported the proposed constitutional amendment. The demonstration fell far short of the forty-five thousand that ROAR had predicted.

During the march towards the Capitol, a section of the demonstrators broke away to pursue a Black motorist. "That nigger gave us the finger," one bigot yelled, triggering the chase amidst shouts of "Hey, nigger, get out of the car and do that." The Black man escaped.

The Klan was there, along with a small group of uniformed Nazis. Louise Day Hicks spoke. It was a good, old-fashioned, Boston-type rally. The next demonstration, she announced, would be back home and would follow ROAR's first national convention. The bigots were going beyond Boston, going national. The date set was particularly significant. It would be on May 18. Thus the two sides in the busing battle were to lock horns again on the day of, and the day after, the anniversary of the *Brown* decision, in the city where the principle of that historic ruling was facing its stiffest challenge in more than a decade.

On March 21 the masters announced their version of Phase II. Their weeks of work had produced a smorgasbord of ideas for desegregation, including greater parent participation in the schools, university and college "pairing" with school districts, and involvement of the business community. At the center of the plan, however, were a downgrading of busing and a division of the school system into carefully defined districts. Student assignments in terms of mandatory busing were strictly limited. A central theme of the plan was "voluntary busing" to an array of "magnet schools."

The masters' plan meant, in cold figures, that fully two thirds of the city's schools would remain *outside* of Judge Garrity's general guidelines for desegregation. The burden of busing was on Blacks; the majority of school closings recommended were in the Black community; and all-white or predominantly white schools in affluent West Roxbury and in East Boston would remain so.

The media editorialized in unison for the masters' plan, urging Garrity to implement it. The reaction of the bigots varied. Pixie Palladino hardnosed the recommendations: "It's a rotten plan because it still requires mandatory busing." South Boston State Senator "Billy" Bulger analyzed the plan more shrewdly, realizing concessions in it: "The first plan was horrendous and this is an attempt to retreat from it. Implicit in that attempt is an admission that the original plan was wrong."

Thomas Atkins's statement reflected widespread sentiment in the Black community. He termed the masters' plan "a massive capitulation to violence or the threat of violence. . . . The plan would have the federal court itself order into existence permanent segregation in Boston. . . . For the federal court to issue such an order would be tantamount to the court's becoming an instrument of *de jure* segregation." The NAACP pressed its own, genuine desegregation plan in court.

The hint of retreat on desegregation spurred the racists. While the legal debates went on, they chafed for action. On April 9, they found a favorite target.

The ROAR crowd was angry and shouting, maybe as many as two hundred, mostly women. Senator Edward Kennedy was wrapping up a speech at Atlantic Junior High School in Quincy, a city south of Boston. In general, vague terms, Kennedy had continued to support Garrity. But nearly a year of abuse had made the senator an infrequent visitor to Boston, and he would rarely speak about busing, let alone criticize the perpetrators of the anti-Black violence. The racists felt a special venom for Kennedy—a traitor to them, by God. They were also aware of his power and authority. He could not be persuaded, so he had to be shoved. The Kennedy mystique no longer had its one-time potency.

"There he is," someone shrieked, as the uncomfortable senator, draped in aides, tried to pass through the crowd. Obscenities. Insults. The antibusing jibes. Then the women, who had brought little American flags along, began poking him, swarming in, jostling. Kennedy made it out of the mob but was so shaken that he went to the subway rather than to his car. It was a wise decision. The tires had been slashed. But he still would not rebuke ROAR.

The next day, the scene shifted, but the tactics were still the same. Faneuil Hall, the stately old brick meeting house where Sam Adams and Joseph Warren had discussed strategy for the American revolution before a gallery packed with patriots, had a reputation in Boston. It belonged to everybody. It was a free speech center. For a few dollars for maintenance one could rent the hall, no matter what the issue. Faneuil Hall was special, preserved, protected, hallowed in the traditions of liberty.

The three hundred supporters of the Equal Rights Amendment were mostly women office workers. They had come to Faneuil Hall at noon for a rally sponsored by the Governor's Commission on the Status of Women. Something was wrong, however. Throughout the crowd were ROAR members—big, tough-looking men, and women holding signs: "Feminist Domination Equals Communism," "Abortion Is Murder." Some sported ROAR vests and buttons; others carried pictures of fetuses; and then there were the antibusing placards. It was menacing.

Elaine Noble, the nation's first elected gay state legislator, rose to start the rally. Noble supported busing, had endorsed the December 13-14 protest weekend, and had helped the organizers of the National Student Conference Against Racism. In January she had been embroiled in a bitter confrontation with ROAR women who had attempted to break up a ceremony inaugurating International Women's Year, at City Hall—ROAR's turf. The situation had turned into a heated debate over desegregation. ROAR vowed to be present at every women's meeting from then on, to press the "issue of forced busing as a women's issue." Kitty Dukakis, the governor's wife and a supporter of the Equal Rights Amendment, had beaten a hasty retreat from City Hall on that occasion to avoid what might be, for her and Governor Michael Dukakis, a messy confrontation.

Now at Faneuil Hall, Noble attempted to calm the bigots. "I will listen to you, just let me talk," she said. But the "dialogue" was ugly, rife with antigay insults. Kitty Dukakis was now on the stage, and Noble, facing the mob, attempted to open the rally. A chant went up, directed at the lesbian legislator, who was not unfamiliar with similar snide remarks in the State House corridors. "We like men! We like men!" Then, their men joined in, singing "Southie Is My Home Town," the neighborhood song. It was chaos. Noble pleaded for order. Boos, catcalls, more chants.

Florence Luscomb rose and walked to the podium. At eighty-seven, she, not unlike Faneuil Hall, is something of a Boston institution. Luscomb had been a suffragist and was a revered heroine of the Boston feminist movement. Her voice was high pitched but strong. She was small, frail looking, but carried herself with vigor and determination. An emeritus leader of Boston Women's International League for Peace and Freedom, Luscomb was a rock-hard backer of desegregation, representing WILPF at numerous news conferences supporting the Garrity order.

She had an unblemished reputation for integrity as a supporter of civil liberties for oppressed nationalities, women, radical parties. It was a moral authority based on nearly eight decades of commitment to social change. And Florence Luscomb had spunk. If *she* could not calm them down, no one could. The television cameras whirred as Luscomb reprimanded the bigots: "You have no right—no right!—to do this." But the hooligans kept shouting, chanting, waving their signs. The din was terrific. Luscomb finally sat down, shaking her head. Noble took the podium to cancel the meeting.

One of the hecklers shouted that neighborhood schools had to be preserved. "That's the issue," she yelled. Noble looked at the mob. Enraged, she shouted back, "The real issue is racism in Boston!" The ERA rally was over.

Prospects for the NAACP march on May 17 looked promising. In March the NAACP's national board of directors gave its backing, the first time they had endorsed a national demonstration since the civil rights March on Washington in 1963. Chapters of NSCAR had sprouted across the country, and many were working closely with local branches of the NAACP. Added impetus to the coming demonstration was given by the fact that ROAR had chosen that same weekend for a national push and hoped to top the NAACP march with an even bigger rally. This would redeem it in its followers' eyes for the poor showing it had made against the December 14 demonstration in support of desegregation.

On April 12, 125 Black, Puerto Rican, and white student leaders came to Boston for the first meeting of NSCAR's national steering committee. Thomas Atkins addressed them, giving the strongest tongue-lashing yet to the masters' Phase II plan. Moreover, like many other Black leaders, he had lost confidence in Mayor White in the course of a year. He confessed that he had not trusted White from the start. Now he believed that Garrity would reverse the masters' scheme but was having doubts. May 17 could be a demonstrative sign that the Black community would not tolerate a retreat.

"The local media write editorials that say, 'Why doesn't the NAACP get reasonable and accept the masters' plan,'" he said. "They think there's no reason why there shouldn't be permanently segregated schools in Boston. There's nothing inconsistent with the federal judge, operating on the basis of the Fourteenth Amendment, ordering schools in Boston to be segregated, they think. 'If only the NAACP would accept this,' they say, 'peace and harmony would come to Boston.' I'm here to tell you, as I've told them, that they can shove their peace and harmony! Despite the pressure that is being put on the community, and there is enormous pressure, I can tell you that this community is not going to buckle, it is not going to crack. We are mobilizing to go forward."

On May 3 a thousand supporters of Dr. Kenneth Edelin rallied at the Massachusetts State House, chanting "Defend Dr. Edelin, defend abortion rights." The march there had been ringed by two hundred marshals to secure the event against ROAR disruptions. Unlike with previous events, the Coalition for the Defense of Abortion Rights had widely publicized statements noting its preparations against ROAR. Lawyers, police, photographers, and Justice Department officials, the coalition leaders had promised, would be on hand.

ROAR did not show up. It could have been that they were detained five miles away, where a spectacular confrontation had erupted between hundreds of racists and nearly twenty-five hundred demonstrators called to Boston by the Progressive Labor Party.

The PL march, whose theme was "death to the fascists," had begun on the fringe of South Boston. PL and the small organization CAR (Committee Against Racism), which it led, were notorious and resented in the antiracist movement for their brash, confrontationist tactics. The size of the march was attributed to the presence of many youths from out of town, who had been promised a serious antiracist demonstration and a free trip to Boston. They were unprepared for what they met.

PL has a long record of trying to make a name for itself through wild brawls. Its publicized boast of marching on South Boston stirred up a hornets' nest in Southie. The PL monitors, wearing thick leather belts, some carrying chains and bats, formed the vanguard of the march. They were ready for the kamikaze mission. But before the march could begin, gangs of racists—probably organized by the clandestine South Boston Defense League—attacked the demonstrators, showering them with rocks. The racists carried ROAR's flag. A battle ensued, with police wading into the mostly unprepared demonstrators led by PL. Eight people were injured and ten arrested. The racists also attacked Blacks walking or driving by.

Sensational media coverage followed the riot, and South Boston was teeming with rumors of a "communist invasion." It didn't matter that the attack on the PL-led marchers was premeditated and illegal. Whatever may have been the marchers' good intentions to demonstrate against racism, the foolishly provocative action and posture of the participants had opened the door to victimization and heated up an already tense Boston.

The spectacle of "out of towners" picking a fight with Southie had given the bigots a means of portraying the antiracist movement as a violent aggressor. It also enabled the media to pelt May 17 organizers with questions about the legal and peaceful character of their upcoming march, dwelling on the subject and thus associating it in public thinking with disorder. Louise Day Hicks seized the opportunity to write Atkins a carefully worded "Dear Tom" letter—released to the media before he received it—asking him to close the May 17 demonstration to "communist terrorists."

The foray had repercussions inside the schools as well. On May 7 and 8, fights broke out in South Boston High School as gangs of white students beat Blacks. One Black youth, rescued from a corridor mob, had been set up for allegedly unfurling a Progressive Labor Party banner—a neat trick, given the search students were subjected to on entrance and the great preponderance of white students in the school. The hotlines of the antibusing phone network spread the news, as did ROAR sound trucks, which roamed South Boston streets calling for an early morning rally to "keep communists out of South Boston."

Hyde Park High School was rocked by fights on May 7 and 8. On May 9 nearly three hundred police pushed back a South Boston mob of five hundred to keep them from the buses. Garbage cans were hurled at the cops. In early May, a Puerto Rican family moving into predominantly white Orient Heights was firebombed out of their apartment. A crowd of a hundred cheered as the blaze drove the family into the street.

In East Boston, South Boston, Charlestown, and Hyde Park—in fact, throughout the whole city except for Roxbury—posters for the ROAR national convention were going up. This was the first time the bigots had felt compelled to really *build* an event, especially the May 18 rally which was to be the culmination of their weekend gathering. To advertise the racist conference, city council members Hicks and O'Neill posted huge red letters, spelling out ROAR, in the windows of their City Hall offices for all to see. They were bragging to the world as to who ruled Boston.

# 12

# The NAACP March
# for Desegregation

Events broke swiftly in May. Thomas Atkins's pledge that the Black community would not buckle under to the masters' plan had been kept. This had brought the sharpest criticism from the Boston establishment, but its effect on the morale of the forces favoring Black rights and the accelerating activity for the May 17 demonstration were reassuring.

On May 10 Judge Garrity announced his Phase II plan. He had overhauled the masters' recommendations. Busing was increased to achieve greater citywide desegregation. Certain aspects of the masters' plan which could assist overall desegregation were adopted—a few magnet schools and the involvement of parents, universities, and businesses. But the essence of Phase II lay in the force necessary to break down the legacy of the dual school system. Garrity, however, exempted East Boston—a concession to the feared opposition from the community where Pixie Palladino was the tough ROAR boss.

Speaking for the NAACP at a news conference, Thomas Atkins noted that while he was not satisfied with everything in the Phase II plan, he thought that in general it went "far toward eliminating the vestiges of segregation and discrimination which have afflicted Boston schools." Beaming, he pointed out that major concessions to the racists, such as acceptance of the sham "voluntary" concept of desegregation, had been averted.

The antibusing forces were stung by the decision. They howled in reaction. Phase II, Hicks said, "Will trigger rising tensions and chaos and disorder in the schools, followed by a mass white exodus from Boston." Palladino concurred: "The plan is a prescription for chaos and violence." Mayor Kevin White was "bitterly disappointed." There would be appeals from the school committee, the Home and School Association, and—as he hit the campaign trail for reelection—from Mayor White.

Two days later, the U.S. Supreme Court refused to hear the

Boston School Committee's appeal against Garrity's initial decision. The blow was stunning to the antibusing elements. The federal court order and the busing it mandated in Phase I were uncontestable in the courts. Now, attention was riveted on the streets, on the forces in motion there. The weekend for ROAR's founding national convention and the NAACP march had arrived.

May 17 was a perfect day for a demonstration. A bright sun shone from a cloudless blue sky. The NAACP march, as it moved out of the Fenway, would pass within a hundred yards of the John B. Hines Auditorium, where ROAR was meeting.

Nearly ten thousand people had massed at the assembly point by 12:30. It was a coalition of forces, some of them coming from old, established organizations such as the Urban League and the Americans for Democratic Action. Middle-aged Blacks mingled with young whites; Roxbury parents pushed babies in strollers. There was the Boston chapter of the National Organization for Women, along with a contingent of supporters of Dr. Edelin; rows and rows of members of the American Federation of State, County and Municipal Employees (AFSCME) and of smaller unions; priests and clergypeople; gays; African foreign students. It was the young and the old, the veterans of Selma and Montgomery and high school and college students who had only been able to read about the fight against Jim Crow. The black, red, and green colors of Pan-Africanism rippled in the wind, as banners from the radical New American Movement, Democratic Socialist Organizing Committee, Young Workers Liberation League, and Young Socialist Alliance were raised.

Thousands of yellow brochures announcing the campaign of Norman Oliver, the Black activist running for mayor on the Socialist Workers Party ticket, were distributed.

At the head of the march a street-wide banner proclaimed the "NAACP march for quality desegregated education and the Constitution."

It was that kind of mix—the tradition and history of the civil rights movement blending with the energy of Black and radical-minded militants in a spirit of good nature and camaraderie. NSCAR marshals, some of them young Blacks knowledgeable about Africa and students of socialist politics, wearing dashikis and Afro cuts, teamed up with conservatively dressed Black workers, members of the Roxbury lodges of the Masons and the

Elks. The issue spanned the generations, and the feeling of solidarity was apparent.

A drum and bugle corps sponsored by the Syria Arab Patrol—the Black Shriners—wearing red and gold uniforms and fezes, some astride huge Harley-Davidson motorcycles, trumpeted the start of the march. The chants grew loud as the seemingly endless ranks of marchers passed the Hines Auditorium, where ROAR was laying its plans. "Keep the buses rolling, desegregate the schools!" "Two, four, six, eight, Boston must desegregate!" It was a mile-long stream with placards and banners, the composition of the marchers evenly divided between Black and white. Disciplined, orderly, chanting and singing, it caused heads to turn as it flowed down Commonwealth Avenue. Thousands joined in.

The marchers had come from as far as Oregon and Birmingham. Volma Overton, the president of the Austin, Texas, NAACP, had driven for forty hours. His reason for coming was the same as that of thousands of others, but a bit more immediate: Austin was embroiled in a desegregation suit. "If we don't show a force and only just pass it off, they [Austin bigots] are watching and will see us," he explained.

The president of the Delaware NAACP was there, worried that a city-suburban plan for Wilmington would be overturned as a similar Detroit plan had been a year earlier in the Supreme Court.

That day, in a show of solidarity with the Boston march, NAACP/NSCAR-supported demonstrations and rallies were held with 350 participating in Los Angeles; 400 in Oakland; 150 in Seattle; 300 in Salt Lake City; 250 in Portland, Oregon; and a dozen of smaller size in other places. The several thousand marchers, pickets, and protesters who took to the streets outside of Boston, along with those in the Boston march, constituted the front line troops of a new movement.

"I implore you," Samuel Sheats, a former Pasadena School Board member, told the Los Angeles rally, "to take more action in the future. The time for segregation is passed." The Pasadena case, not widely known, was on the Supreme Court docket following an appeal by local racists. The implications of that verdict would carry far beyond the Rose Bowl City.

Thomas Atkins surveyed the growing crowd, as the marchers thronged onto the Boston Common. "We welcome you," he repeated over and over, listing the cities from which contingents had come. Following NAACP tradition, the rally opened with the national anthem, followed by the "Negro National Anthem," whose moving words were written by Black poet James Weldon Johnson.

Then the speakers of the day were introduced. "We will not yield one word or one bit of our constitutional rights to hypocrites, who talk about law and order and desecrate the law and order they don't like," Joseph Rauh told the crowd. Rauh, a noted labor and civil liberties lawyer and vice-president of the Americans for Democratic Action, was a pillar of the old, liberal wing of the civil rights coalition. "George Wallace stood in the schoolhouse door in Alabama to bar Blacks from entering," he said. "Those who bar the schoolhouse door here are not different from George Wallace just because they speak with a Boston accent. Bigotry with a Boston accent is still bigotry."

Roy Wilkins, the elder statesman of the NAACP, came forward for a brief speech. "I pledge to you that we will be here as long as it is necessary. We're not going out of business. We've been here sixty-six years. And if the Boston bigots can last that long—I doubt it—we'll be here sixty-six more years."

Hearkening back to the *Brown* decision being commemorated, Thomas Atkins declared: "We took that ruling and carried it all over the South. We used it to brush away the crowds gathered outside Little Rock High School to prevent a handful of Black children from going to school, and we used it to remove obstructors from the doorways at 'Old Miss.' We used that decision to reverse the entire system of Jim Crow laws across the South. Not just in education. But in voting rights. In housing. In public services. And in employment. And we're going to use it in Boston."

If Wilkins personified the traditional and conservative at the rally, NSCAR Coordinator Maceo Dixon personified the rebel. His speech drew the warmest response; he emphasized that the antibusing forces were racists and that they had to be fought, and the rally concurred. "Today's is the kind of answer we have to give—massive countermobilization to secure and extend Black democratic rights . . . the only method of struggle to successfully end the injustices we suffer as an oppressed people."

"If President Ford can send bombers, troops, and ships to Cambodia in violation of the Cambodian people's human and political rights, he should be able to send troops and tanks to Boston to enforce the law. Send those troops to Boston to enforce

the law and to protect Black children from racist lynch mobs."
Dixon's point hit home with the audience, which responded with
a shout of "Troops!" It was only days before this that President
Ford had ordered the military incursion into Cambodia to seize
the S.S. *Mayaguez,* a merchant vessel detained by the Cambodi-
ans.

Estimates of the number participating in the commemoration
ranged from the NAACP's high figure of fifty thousand to
NSCAR's conservative fifteen thousand; the police department
gave a tally of fifteen to twenty thousand. In any case it was the
biggest such march in Boston in a decade.

For a change the media gave the coverage the event deserved.
The *Globe,* for example, featured the march on the front page,
with all of page two for further coverage. The NAACP march
made a great impression on the public. No antibusing demonstration up till then had come close to matching it. Now it was
ROAR's turn to stage its rally.

"Look at poor old Tom Atkins," Dapper O'Neill quipped to two
thousand ROAR faithful in the bunting-draped Commonwealth
Pier exhibition hall. "He works all this time and he only gets five
thousand people. We can snap our fingers and get that many—"
He paused as the bigots' cheering echoed through the cavernous,
unfilled hall. Then, lamely, the final words, ". . . if we wanted
to." Dapper, the racists' top showman, clown, con artist, pol of
pols, and rumbling baritone of the "little people," was shaken by
the May 17 demonstration.

The ROAR rally climaxed a much smaller working conference,
which had elected Louise Day Hicks its national president and
pledged a lobbying campaign to pass the constitutional amendment against busing. The presidential election campaign was
also seen as an arena for the offensive against Black rights.

The conference and rally made clearer than ever ROAR's links
with the extreme right. Indeed, John Birchers had done
considerable recruiting among ROAR's rank and file with their
line against communism, abortion, the ERA, etc. Hicks presented
a plaque of appreciation to John Rarick, the Birchite congressman from Louisiana. Long known as a last-ditch defender of Jim
Crow, Rarick has also been branded by Jewish organizations as a
"notorious anti-Semite."

There was a procession of local Democrats—members of the

school committee, the city council, the state legislature—to the podium. In addition there were Ray Wells, a racist leader from Prince Georges County, Maryland; some veteran race-haters from Georgia and Virginia; and a newer breed—"up South" bigots from New York and Chicago.

Two ministers, sporting coonskin caps, recounted their battle with "atheistic, communistic, white-hating" books in Charleston, West Virginia, where they had made bonfires of the "offensive" material. Kanawha County's school book controversy had captured the nation's attention months earlier, as whites mobilized by fundamentalist preachers and right-wingers had forced closing of the schools. Rifle fire had shattered the school windows, and teachers had been too afraid for their own and their pupils' safety to teach.

The leaders of this crusade against the school books in West Virginia told the rally that they found the ROAR atmosphere "a lot like home." One of the preachers shouted, "And when we get home, we are going to take to the streets of Charleston and burn the red flag of communism!" The crowd broke into cheers.

They were not beaten, not for a minute. ROAR's members were a resilient bunch that could pick itself up and dust itself off, ready for the next round of action. "Boston's on the war path, ooh-ahh" was the repeated chant. Avi Nelson took the mike. He was exultant over the seizure of the S.S. *Mayaguez*. "Between what we did in Cambodia last week and today's rally," he proclaimed, "it feels good to be an American." More chants, neighborhood fight songs, ROAR's anthem—"We'll Do It RO-AR's Waaay" to the tune of Frank Sinatra's song. Chester Broderick, the head of the Boston Police Patrolmen's Association, promised, "I'll make sure you get the truth no matter what you hear from [Police Commissioner] diGrazia. "Cut his Afro," came a shout from the crowd in reference to the longish hair of the police commissioner detested by the bigots.

There were ROAR buttons for sale, showing a huge lion clawing a school bus. Louise Day Hicks, smiling, on the stage with an enormous stuffed lion, archly asked in a cloying voice, "And what does a lion do?" Responding on cue, the audience made a rumbling, growling noise—"Rrroarrrr!" It was all done in dead seriousness.

Four hundred and fifty activists who had taken part in the NAACP march attended a special NSCAR steering committee afterward in the basement auditorium of the University of Massachusetts, Boston Campus. The multiracial student organization had reason to be proud of its contributions to building the march itself and in organizing the marshalling of it. In charge of the latter was Boston SCAR leader Mac Warren, who, like Dixon, had come to Boston to be part of the struggle. Warren had been a Black community activist in Atlanta, organizing support there for the Boston struggle, until he pulled up roots and moved to Boston early in 1975.

But the NSCAR picture was not one of unrelieved success. Three weeks before the May 17 demonstration, the Young Workers Liberation League had left NSCAR. Foreshadowing that had been a series of scathing articles against NSCAR, written by the YWLL national secretary, in the *Daily World*, the newspaper reflecting the views of the Communist Party. Unfortunately, although it had participated in founding NSCAR, the YWLL had not been active within it. Nor had its commitment to May 17 enabled it to rise above its disagreements with some NSCAR positions—as had been done by other groups and individuals. Consequently, the YWLL had marched alone, in a small contingent, during the demonstration.

Their political opposition was to NSCAR's perspectives—the building of a massive, independent antiracist movement led by those most victimized by racism: Blacks, Puerto Ricans, and Chicanos. To this concept of militant, multiracial action the YWLL counterposed support to liberal Democrats. Governed by such an outlook, they were not prone to jump into May 17, because the implications of it meant a constant pressure on those forces, despite the support that many different kinds of people, including liberals and Democrats, had given to the action.

Moreover, its long-term hostility to the YSA resurfaced. Unused to working in coalitions, the YWLL had gotten into a coalition where the socialists were part of the leadership. The untimely and divisive departure of the YWLL from NSCAR and the tapering off of support from the Communist Party to May 17 were a blow to the action. Thereafter, this leftist current became generally inactive in the Boston struggle.

Despite YWLL's withdrawal, the mood at the NSCAR steering committee was buoyant. It would launch a national defense effort for Joanne Little, a young Black woman in North Carolina, whose trial would become an international issue. Summer would also be a time to work in preparation for the fall, when Phase II would begin.

Dixon mentioned to Warren that it might be possible to ease the tempo of activity somewhat. The two young Black activists, however, did not foresee that Boston's summer of 1975 would offer little respite.

Perhaps at the very moment on the Sunday afternoon that Louise Day Hicks was holding up the stuffed lion, it was happening. A Black student from Utah State University and several white friends were tired. They had marched. They had slept on floors. They ached. The sun was bright, and it was warm for a spring day. It was a beach kind of day.

They saw the ocean from their car window, people in the water. They parked, walked onto the sand. Suddenly, a gang was on them. *Get out, nigger!* Sand and feet and fists, everywhere. They ran. Made it to the car. Safe. The Black student was shaken, terrified, a little cut. The place was Carson Beach—a name that would sound like *Anzio* before the summer ended.

# 13

## Racist Terror
## at Carson Beach

Summer vacation closed the schools. Antibusing frustrations would now be vented in ways other than protests within and around the schools and rock-throwing at the buses. It was not a methodically organized campaign. A mood of racial hatred provided the motive force. An epidemic of anti-Black violence began to spread throughout the city.

On June 10 it had been the East Boston apartment of the Perry family that was firebombed. On June 19 an unsuspecting Jamaican family, the Daleys, bought a home in predominantly white Hyde Park. As they moved in, gangs threw rocks and bottles, shouting "niggers get out." When Mrs. Daley and a younger brother attempted to walk to a local grocery store they were showered with rocks, and she suffered a broken cheekbone.

When police arrived on the scene they questioned forty nearby hooligans. They left upon being satisfied that the Daleys had "provoked" the incident by "shouting racial slurs at the whites," as one sergeant put it. That night, the house was assaulted by the same hooligans. Windows were smashed and the fence uprooted. It was a siege that made the front page of the *Globe*. The next day, a round-the-clock patrol by the police was set up, but no arrests were made.

On June 20—Father's Day—Benjamin Hollis was driving with his family on Day Boulevard, which borders Carson Beach. The vehicle was stoned by a gang of whites. "The rock just missed my wife's head," Hollis said. "There was glass all over my kids."

From June 21 to June 23 a dozen incidents were reported to police by Blacks who had attempted to drive to Carson Beach in South Boston. Young racist toughs had devised a new tactic. They waited on overpasses on Old Colony Road, at the edge of South Boston, for Black motorists to drive beneath. Then rocks, bottles, and bricks were dropped, shattering windows and bouncing off trunks and hoods.

Verna Staples, a Black woman, and her ten-year-old son and thirteen-year-old daughter were caught in traffic in South Boston. A roaming gang of youths wielding bats attacked her car, spraying glass on her and the children as they smashed the windows. They surrounded the car until, finally, the traffic moved and she could push the gas pedal down and roar out. "My son was terrified," she said. "He had never experienced anything like this." By the end of the summer, hundreds of Black victims would experience that baptism of fire.

In East Boston, Blacks fought back desperately. Outnumbered Black youth repelled a gang of whites on June 18, but at midnight a hundred racists returned, armed with chains and clubs, clashing for an hour with forty Blacks in hand-to-hand combat. The news barely trickled out of Eastie.

The issue of personal safety had transcended the school struggle. The Perrys, the Daleys, Verna Staples, the Black motorists, were not students or activists in the desegregation movement. But they were Black, and, to the racist gangs, that made them the enemy.

The antibusers were grasping at straws to halt Phase II. On May 22 Garrity had rejected the school committee's prompt appeal for a year's delay, and, with rare speed, the U.S. Supreme Court on June 23 denied a similar appeal by the Home and School Association. As the Supreme Court released its decision, Garrity reprimanded the Boston School Committee for its technical obstruction of the Phase II plans.

Pupil assignment was all-important and required painstaking, detailed work to ensure balance. Seating capacities had to correspond to assignments, busing plans, and school pairing. Moreover, parents had certain choices. All this called for a large number of mailings. While the school committee had sought to delay implementation of Phase II, it had refused to start the task of pupil assignment. It was dragging its feet, as if to make good its claim that not enough time existed to implement Phase II.

In announcing Phase II, Garrity had urged broader community participation in implementing the plan. Subsequently he appointed forty-two members to a Citywide Coordinating Council (CCC) to serve as his "eyes and ears" in "monitoring" the implementation. This body itself would be rent by internal division—hamstrung by antibusing partisans appointed by the judge to "balance" the body and by moderates intimidated by the scope of resistance. But now the CCC was new and gave at least the appearance of a force that would facilitate implementation of the order.

The school committee had bucked Garrity's order to meet with the CCC for weeks, and now Garrity was angry. "Where the busing plan makes a specific provision, the power of the school committee is superseded," he noted in court on June 23. This meant that, without formally saying so, Garrity was beginning, this time through appointed "experts," to administer the school system. To make the decision clearer, he stated: "It is not just in the matter of assignments, it is across the board . . . there are all sorts of things which the school committee has simply lost power to do."

Many Black leaders had felt the school committee should have been stripped of all power from the start. The original decision by Judge Garrity paving the way for Phase I had actually enjoined the school committee from discriminating against Black and other minority students. But despite the mild civil contempt rebuke of its three members in December 1974, the school committee remained committed to overturning or sabotaging the order. As one Black leader put it, it was like leaving the fox in charge of the chickens.

The carrying out of Garrity's June 23 ruling effectively removing the school committee from "planning" at least part of Phase II could mean another blow at segregation. Predictably, the howl of protest went up: "Garrity is a dictator!" "When," Louise Day Hicks asked bitterly, "will he take over Boston?"

Throughout the first year of Phase I Ruth Batson had been worried and dissatisfied with the Black community's inadequate preparation. She continually asked herself what should be done in preparation for the coming fall. A member of the Freedom House Coalition, Batson said, "We had to do more than just answer phone calls."

The community agencies that had staffed the hot line of the Freedom House Institute for Schools and Education could be more formally organized, brought into the planning and monitoring work. The "debriefing" sessions at the Freedom House could be expanded and regularized. Feedback could be gathered on a range of topics, from safety and security and the situation in the schools to various educational aspects of the plan itself.

This work would come under the Coordinated Social Services Council, which, with the opening of school, would gather every

Wednesday morning at Freedom House. The regular CSSC meetings became the principal vehicle for community and leadership discussion of the workings of the plan. Eric Van Loon, the confident young lawyer from the Center for Law and Education at Harvard who had assumed the central role as counsel for the Black plaintiffs in the desegregation suit, would give weekly court reports on Judge Garrity's proceedings and answer questions from concerned Black parents.

Actually the CSSC would come to function as Garrity's "eyes and ears" as the image of the highly touted but ineffectual CCC wore thin. Ruth Batson and Ellen Jackson served as the CSSC cochairpersons.

But Batson felt even more was necessary. "I felt," she said, "that somehow the mental health profession had to be drawn in." This was her field. She was an associate professor of community mental health at the Boston University School of Medicine. It was not therapy that Batson had in mind. What she doggedly pursued was the formation of groups of community activists, white and Black, who could offer a range of support—counseling, parent aid, monitoring—for the Black students and their families. She secured funding for this from the National Institute for Mental Health—"the first time something like this ever happened," she points out. What resulted was the Boston Public School Crisis Intervention Teams.

All summer long, an expanding nucleus of members met in the sixth-floor offices of the Doctors Building at the Boston University School of Medicine. The discussions dealt with the philosophy of desegregation, its psychological impact on Black students, the relationship with the police, and community involvement. Crisis team members were trained in marshalling by NSCAR's Mac Warren. He and Maceo Dixon emphasized to them methods for "cooling" hot situations. A key task of the teams was to instill a sense of discipline among the Black students, to urge them to refuse to be drawn into no-win fights with bigots over racial epithets.

Team members would ride the buses, monitor bus departure and arrival centers, serve as intermediaries in the South Boston district police station, and in some cases be allowed into the schools. They would form a network of visible, citywide support for Black students—not "neutral" observers, but trained people aware of the psychological stress on the Black students and sympathetic to them.

Dixon and Warren were team captains in Dudley Station in

Roxbury where, Batson felt, racist attacks might provoke retaliation against white students who traveled through the stop. Black retaliation to racist violence was a constant concern of community leaders. Spontaneous, angry outbursts could bring on, as Percy Wilson warned, "a military occupation of the Black community." That, he thought, was what some of the more clever bigots were counting on. Then the police would move—against Roxbury.

The crisis teams met through the summer, preparing for the fall. But the summer had to be gotten through, and as June merged into July it was evident that that would be a hurdle. By July the "Relate" program on WILD, a radio station geared to the Black community, had turned into a sound-off program for reporting racist attacks. The police were covering up, the media were covering up, and James Rowe, the soft-spoken program moderator, was getting nervous.

On July 15, two hundred fifty racists blocked the entrance to South Boston High School, attempting to sabotage an election of the white component of the South Boston–Roxbury Parents' Biracial Council, which had functioned clandestinely the year before. Only days before, the newly purchased home of Katherine Thomas in Hyde Park was stoned by a white gang after nearby Blacks had been beaten up. A cross had been burned on the porch and the words "nigger go home" scrawled on a wall. No arrests. The Thomases moved out.

The upsurge of violence had not been met by police force, and repeated Black demands for a law enforcement presence near Carson Beach had been rejected. The hands-off attitude toward hooliganism had encouraged it. Now, a summer of boredom and frustration based on high unemployment of white youth (no doubt exacerbated by a fear of the future compounded by a year's boycott of school by several thousand) combined with rising race hatred to find expression. The chaos and violence predicted by Hicks and Palladino as the reception for Phase II became a reality.

July 27 was one of those days that made Boston summers particularly oppressive. A hot sky, sweltering heat that soaked your clothes. It had been that kind of week: smoldering heat, simmering tension. For six Black Bible salesmen from South Carolina, hitting the bricks in Roxbury was hard, exhausting work. They had climbed into their car and begun to search for a beach. There it was, packed with people sprawled on the sand, the water glistening in the sun. They parked the car and walked over to the shore.

"We'd been working all week, and we just wanted to come to the beach and enjoy ourselves," James Barrowright later explained. So they stretched out on Carson Beach. "Next thing we know, all we see is white faces calling us niggers and telling us to get out of here," Barrowright recounted. They bolted for the car, as a mob now numbering a hundred, some holding pipes and clubs, screamed after them. They had forgotten that *the car doors were locked.* Now, fumbling for the keys, there was no time. Before they could split up, the mob got Robert Jackson, jammed him against a chain-link fence, and beat him to the ground. The police arrived, peeling into the crowd. Jackson, bleeding, dazed, was hospitalized with head, rib, and leg injuries.

The police combed Southie, looking for the other five Black men, eventually finding and evacuating them. Their car was in ruins, its windows smashed, reeking of the garbage that had been dumped inside.

Robert Bumpers, a longtime employee of the Greyhound Bus Company, was leaving the garage on the edge of South Boston. It was quitting time. As he left, he was grabbed by thugs who had been part of the Carson Beach mob. They beat him with sticks and pipes. He broke away and locked himself in a bus. The police arrived, and his assailants fled. No arrests.

And for all the violence, excitement, and sirens occasioned by the beating of the Bible salesmen, only two arrests. "I'm thirty-two," Major Lawson, the supervisor of the Black South Carolinians said, "and I've never heard of a racial situation like this. I mean, maybe in Mississippi or Alabama, but here? . . . We'll get the hell out of here. There is a much more serious problem here than I thought there was."

Two days later, at a news conference called by the Boston Student Coalition Against Racism, BSCAR coordinator Mac Warren and Boston NAACP Youth Council Director Leon Rock blasted police inaction, laying the blame on Mayor Kevin White. They announced a Black community "Commission of Inquiry on Racist Violence," to be held August 2 at the National Center for Afro-American Artists. Its purpose, Warren said, would be to offer "a forum for all Black and Puerto Rican residents of Boston who have been victims of racist attacks to come forward and testify for the first time—to tell their story of the day-to-day racist violence that they face in Boston."

The Commission of Inquiry was heated and angry, as high school students and parents came forward to document the terror in Boston. Those testifying were community people, some awkward in front of television cameras, others fearful of talking—especially those who, living in predominantly white areas, might be identified for retaliation.

Reginald Budd, a young father trying to make a life in Hyde Park, told of the kerosene torch that had smashed through a window in his home forty-eight hours before, setting fire to several rooms and ruining his car, which had caught fire from the debris. Two years of torment, he said, then this. "The police told me there is nothing we can do."

Brenda Franklin, seventeen, a recent high school graduate, testified. Her family lived in a section of Dorchester whose racial composition was beginning to change. "Me and my sister were down to Fields Corner [subway] station," she began, almost shyly. "There was a group of white youth who came up to us. They started throwing rocks. We didn't know what to do so we ran to the station. A policeman was there. We told him we'd been attacked. He refused to go down to where the attack took place, refused to even acknowledge," her voice rose, as if she were reliving the scene, "there had been an attack!"

"We're afraid to even leave our own community," Dorothy Plummer, a Roxbury mother said, trembling. "I know I am. But I refuse to just stay and not go anywhere."

Beatings. Firebombings. In homes. On subways. It was everywhere. The whole Black community, it seemed, had been affected, through family, friends, acquaintances. "What are we going to do in September?" one witness asked. Another, nervous, angry: "I don't want anything happening to *my baby* on that bus!"

Benjamin Hollis told of his frightening Father's Day drive near Carson Beach. "They could have that beach over there. I really wouldn't care. But the fact is it's *my* beach too. If I want to go there, I feel like I should be able to go over there." Another speaker concurred. "I think I've got all the right I need to take my weary feet and put them in the Atlantic Ocean."

Carson Beach! It was becoming a symbol. It had been almost twenty years since the famous "wade-ins" in the South, where Black "freedom swimmers" and their white allies had braved cattle prods, dogs, mobs, and racist police to swim in theretofore lily-white waters. Now, as if it had reversed the newsreel of history, the antibusing movement was reproducing the situation. The white lettering had been splashed on a shed at the beach: "Niggers keep out."

Obalajii Rest, director of the Columbia Point community task force and one of the commissioners at the inquiry, announced as the anger rose on the subject that a Black family day was being planned for Carson Beach on August 16. Though the date and title of the event would be changed, there would be a protest.

A week later, after gathering a second round of information, the commission presented to law enforcement officials and Mayor Kevin White its findings: a systematic pattern of racist harassment of Black citizens and the gross default of Boston police.

On August 3, groups of white men—some teen-agers, others burly adults—had begun to gather early. They were drinking beer in the sun, sauntering down to Carson Beach along Day Boulevard. The rumor was everywhere: *a Black invasion.*

This was perhaps the first "public" display of organizational capacity by the clandestine South Boston Defense League. ROAR was the public face of the antibusing movement, its image carefully cultivated by Louise Day Hicks. Within ROAR, however, under cover of secrecy, were partisans of bolder action. As antibusing fervor and desperation mixed, the logic of racist opposition pointed towards the evolution of terrorist formations. Such secretive groups were relieved of the burdensome tasks of public relations, publications, and dealings with elected officials in the glare of the spotlight. The Ku Klux Klan had been an example and mentor for this. But the real thing would come from their grass roots, the housing projects and three-decker houses of Southie: the home-grown toughs.

Simultaneously with the introduction of Phase II, new leaders had begun to emerge in ROAR, hardly as diplomatic as Hicks. But she would back them all the way. The social groupings and bar-based gangs that had convivially supported ROAR at the start had since been steeled in combat. The South Boston Defense League made no bones about it. It was for a white South Boston and it would fight to keep it that way, period.

There were three hundred of these guardians of the community massed at Carson Beach, awaiting the invasion with bats, clubs, chains, and table legs. No invaders showed up. Surly and disappointed, the mob broke up, but not before a carload of Puerto Ricans which had come within throwing range of a section of the departing toughs was bombarded with rocks.

In the period of a few weeks, Carson Beach had become a test case, a *public beach* turned into a fortress, sealed off to Blacks by white vigilantes—without police interference.

A member of the Boston NAACP executive board told Thomas Atkins of proposed plans for a march on Carson Beach. Atkins opposed it. The subject cropped up a second time when Atkins was informed that an increasing number of residents of the Columbia Point housing project wanted to use the beach but feared attack. Atkins met with local law enforcement officials and representatives of the Justice Department. From them came the view that protection of Blacks there was "impossible." Increasingly disturbed but still opposed to a protest march, Atkins went to "one of the broader meetings [ever] held" among Black community leaders.

At this gathering, Atkins learned of a number of racist attacks on Blacks "that were not reported in the media." Also, he became convinced that some sort of protest would occur, based on the action of the Columbia Point residents. Without support from the Black community as a whole, he realized, such a protest was certain to end in a "massacre." Consequently, he changed his mind. The NAACP would participate in the protest, he said, on the condition that it be nonviolent and "rigidly controlled" to assure maximum security. At the same time, Atkins pressed for complete collaboration with the police on all security matters. The meeting agreed.

Atkins assumed the NAACP's participation—"we were the last group in"—would be modest. But as rumors of the impending protest grew, he recalled, "immense pressure" was brought to bear on key forces that had brought together the action. Leaders began to drop away. Conservative religious leaders urged the Black ministers involved to withdraw their support. Through "his people," Mayor White brought the weight of the city government down on the ad hoc sponsoring group. The police, Atkins said, "thought [the protest] was a bad idea," but seemed ready to cooperate. On August 6, Atkins appointed Maceo Dixon, the NSCAR coordinator, to head the marshalling of the event. Dixon and Mac Warren joined in the rush job of assembling monitors for it.

On August 8, a major news conference publicized the Carson Beach Community Picnic, a protest designed to "exercise the fundamental right of every citizen to use public facilities." The action was only forty-eight hours away. Why the haste? Atkins would later note that unavoidable schedule conflicts required central leaders to be out of town the following weekend. He, himself, would have to be away then. He was convinced that pressure to cancel the action had become so great "that had I not been there, it would not have happened." He felt committed. "Everything I stood for was offended by what was happening to the people from Columbia Point."

In the Black community there was a will to protest. The attacks during the summer had stretched Roxbury's patience to the breaking point. This spiraling anger was the basis for mobilizing a healthy turnout, even on short notice. With the protest about to take place despite all the pressure that had been brought to stop it, Mayor White issued a statement: "I will use all the powers at my disposal to ensure the safety of our fellow citizens [and] . . . the right of any person to travel unmolested in any section of this city." Governor Dukakis followed suit: "Anybody should be able to walk and ride through the community without fear of injury," he declared. "If people want to swim on a public beach, he or she ought to be able to do so."

Louise Day Hicks wasted no time. The picnic was "a provocation. . . . Thomas Atkins yelled fire in a crowded theater." Another South Boston community leader proclaimed, "We don't see how violence can be avoided . . . an invitation like this invites retaliation." If such rhetoric inspired attacks, still a confrontation was not desirable for ROAR and the antibusing movement. The racism of such violence would be simply too flagrant for the bigots' public image. South Boston State Senator Raymond Flynn hastily called a "Southie pride rally" for Farragut Point, more than a mile from the beach, urging residents to steer clear of the beach. But Carson Beach was "their beach." For the cadres of the racist movement, steeled in action over the past year, Southie pride was a rock in hand.

Atkins had spent a year in the hurricane of events. As he was driven by a police bodyguard to start the motorcade from Roxbury to the beach, he was ready. Dixon and Warren were in command of a solid marshalling team, and a strong sense of discipline pervaded the protest picnickers. Atkins had not wanted the bodyguard. But that morning there was no choice. It was a police order. He was accustomed to threats from the bigots, but the police were especially alarmed that day. Phone calls to them had specified the intersection where racist snipers had vowed to cut him down.

# 14

# A Picnic Becomes
# a Battleground

It looked like Omaha Beach in wartime Normandy. More than eight hundred uniformed police were on hand. A police helicopter circled above. Two Coast Guard launches patrolled the water. Justice Department observers and FBI agents were present.

Stern rules had been announced to the picnickers as they assembled in Roxbury on August 10. Nonviolence was the discipline of the day. They were to follow the lead of the marshals. If any trouble broke out, they were to leave.

Problems began before the motorcade of picnickers arrived. An early detachment of Blacks from Columbia Point was met by gangs of whites who had gathered at the L Street Bathhouse. The Blacks were taunted and shouted at by the racists. White toughs grew bolder as police made no move to disperse them. A Black man attempting to take a picture of a racist wearing a "white power" T-shirt was spat upon. More jeers. Then a short flurry of rocks and debris. No arrests.

The police radio blared information as Atkins was driven to the beach. The report was ominous. Twenty carloads of members of the Committee Against Racism and the Progressive Labor Party had also arrived early. Most of the group was white. They had started in with the Southies. Fighting was breaking out. CAR and PL were not part of the community picnic. They had come wih rocks and bats. "They had come to fight," Atkins recalled. It was a provocation, a breach of the discipline of the protest. The marshals forced the confrontationists to shed the "equipment" they had brought. But the damage had been done.

The police, breaking a prior agreement with Atkins, cordoned the beach into zones—one for the picnickers, one a "no man's land," and the third for the gathering crowd of whites. The Black community picnic occupied about 15 percent of the beach.

The Blacks began piling out of their cars. The crowd swelled to fifteen hundred. They had come to picnic, to protest by so doing.

It was a sparkling, sunny day: blue sky, blue water, warm and clear—a perfect beach day. Some picnickers had brought food. Others had come with frisbees, footballs. Soon blankets were spread out on the beach.

In their zone the gangs of racists swelled. Epithets were shouted louder and more rapidly.

Blacks splashed in the water which so far that summer had been reserved by racists for whites only. Behind the invisible boundary marked by the Coast Guard boats, a nautical protest was taking place. A bigot had strung a bedsheet banner over the side of his craft: "Please God, Stop Forced Busing." It was a tense, strained situation that soon would break.

A rock flew from the crowd of bigots. It was like a signal. The Blacks groaned. Then a shower of rocks and bottles burst from the white side. Suddenly, a ten-year-old boy was on his back, knocked down by a pop bottle that caught him on the hip. A rock to the head flattened an older woman. A middle-aged man stood dazed, his head dripping blood. War whoops went up from the Southies. They had been stocking piles of rocks, bottles, debris. Volley after volley descended among the Blacks.

The police began to move—against the picnickers. "Move the Blacks back, move them back," was the command that snapped out of the police radio. Back. Towards the water.

Some young Blacks, angry, some stung by the missiles, tossed the rocks back, and the police moved in, arresting them, pummelling others with clubs. Melvin King, a Black legislator, was furious. He corralled a group of police, berating them. King is tall, husky, and unmistakable. The police pushed him, shoving him back. King kept yelling. He was surrounded by white police and, in a second, disappeared as they swarmed over him, wrestling him to the ground.

In the midst of the frantic scene, Atkins was arguing with police officials. The picnickers had no room, he pointed out, they were being boxed into a corner. The pushing by the police was adding to the rage. He demanded more space. The police refused. Atkins left them, returning to the milling crowd. The picnic was over. Maceo Dixon and Mac Warren readied the marshals to pass the word and organize the move to the parked cars. A downpour of rocks, bottles, and debris was pelting the Blacks.

The PL and CAR members would not leave. Among the most unrestrained when it had come to starting fights early in the day, they now were in the kind of situation they liked best. They were

Picnickers gather at Carson Beach.

PL and CAR ultralefts taunt racists.

Police trap demonstrators.

joined by a smaller group from the Maoist October League, which had also come to Carson Beach prepared to violate the nonviolent spirit of the picnic. Between them they mustered about two hundred people. While physically obstructing the departure of the Blacks, they began a chant: "Hell no, we won't go!" It was bizarre, suicidal.

Their provocation enabled the police and the racists to continue the assault on the crowd. Police on motorcycles roared to within inches of the mass of Blacks, trying to speed the confused, frenzied departure. One marshal was rammed by a motorcycle and thrown to the ground. Another cop drove his big Harley-Davidson cycle at the crowd, spinning at the last moment so it fell over on a woman, pinning her underneath. A fight broke out. Police rushed in, their clubs flailing. As the Blacks made it to their cars, the police, keeping off a mob of screaming, rock-hurling racists, blocked the exit road. Then it was over.

Later, Melvin King, still smarting over the beating he had received from the police, denounced the law enforcement officials. Black leader Percy Wilson, who had been on the beach, also placed the blame for the fracas on the cops. "The police have to make up their minds that we must be able to move freely and that when people try to prevent that, they must be arrested. . . . [The police] deliberately put up barricades for us and the whites, but our group hadn't done anything. They didn't deal with the folk who were infringing on our right to use the beach," he angrily told reporters.

"The policy of the police from the very beginning was to give the racists a free hand and continue to push us into the water and off the beach," Maceo Dixon told the media. "Cops who attacked our people must be arrested and prosecuted for brutality. The mayor and governor must call on President Ford to send federal troops into South Boston and other racist strongholds in the city to uphold the democratic rights of Blacks and Puerto Ricans to go anywhere in the city free of physical attacks."

Atkins, however, blamed CAR for the violence: "They came to fight, not to picnic." In his view, they had provoked the skirmishing and were responsible for a police response that was a "catastrophe."

News of the Carson Beach melee spread like wildfire through Roxbury by word of mouth from victims and on television. There had been a few instances of Black retaliation in the past year. The assault on André Yvon Jean-Louis and similar explosions of white violence had sparked sporadic stonings of white motorists in Roxbury. But these had been short-lived. Roxbury had been tense but relatively cool over the summer, though tempers had risen in the last few weeks. Now, with the Carson Beach attack, all the frustration and bitterness built up over the past year simply burst.

White motorists driving near Columbia Point and Roxbury's Mission Hill were stoned by Black youth. Perhaps thirty cars were pelted. No serious injuries were reported. Several autos were set afire. The streets were swarming with young Blacks. The cops moved swiftly and brutally. The kid gloves worn on G Street for a year and at Carson Beach that day were taken off.

Columbia Point was occupied, along with the Mission Hill and Orchard Park projects. The dogs were brought out, and the cops let them loose in Mission Hill, where the crowds were biggest. One child was bitten by a police German shepherd that night. A pregnant woman, unable to move, was mauled by a dog utilized by his uniformed handler in a ruthless version of "crowd control." The turmoil continued for several nights, with scrambling knots of youth foraying against the police and occasionally setting up roadblocks to head off white motorists.

A bar on Mission Hill was invaded by cops, who maced and beat patrons and wrecked the inside of the establishment. "They couldn't catch those wild kids throwing at the cars and they wanted to beat up on somebody," the manager of the taproom recounted. "They said nothing to me. They just hit me in the mouth with clubs and then on the head." Police denied the incident had taken place. Months later a board of inquiry reprimanded the officers identified in the incident. "The cops stayed for a few minutes," the manager said, "beating on people, and, as they were leaving, they took their clubs and knocked out the cigarette machine and knocked drinks and bottles off the bar." The kids, the police said, had run into the bar.

In an August 15 meeting with Police Commissioner diGrazia, Black leaders protested the occupation. Senator Edward Brooke was there, weary looking. He had been unusually quiet during the past year, sometimes bending to the pressure of the racists. Now he had been stunned by the spectacle at Carson Beach. The Black community, he told reporters, "is disturbed and very concerned and has lost its faith in not only the ability, but the desire of the police department [to protect Blacks]. . . . Racism is deep-seated and deep-rooted here. This has to change."

The next day, two hundred Blacks picketed downtown stores at the call of Melvin King and Robert Fortes, a young Black Democratic state legislator, demanding that downtown businesses pressure the city administration to remove the police garrisoned in Roxbury. "Kevin White, have you ever had a dog trained to kill and attack your kids?" one placard asked.

The Carson Beach protest sparked discussion and debate in the leadership of the Black community that still goes on. Characterizations of the event spanned the spectrum. For Ruth Batson, it was "a fiasco." For Percy Wilson, "a frustrating failure." To him, the police had flunked a key test, a major reason for the picnic—to see if they would protect Blacks. However, he thought, "the fact that there was a call for people to go, and people turned out and people went, that was a success." For Wilson, the protest was incomplete because "there should have been a return to Carson Beach . . . to keep the pressure up, to keep returning until such a time that people could go in to that beach when they wanted to." The provocations on the beach loomed large in his view. The picnic, he said, "was infiltrated."

Thomas Atkins later evaluated it as "neither a rout nor a victory," and an event which had a "sobering impact on the city." "Carson Beach is, at best, a battle in what is still a war. It was not the first battle. It was by no means the last battle. . . . We don't concede that there is an inch to this city that can be walled off to Blacks. There could be another Carson Beach, in two days, two months, or two years—we might still have to go back." Subsequent protests, Atkins observed, would have to be prepared differently. That day, he said, marked the end of the ability of "organizations like CAR" to play any role "in our community."

Maceo Dixon regarded Carson Beach as a powerful, if flawed, Black response to the summer of racist harassment. "The Black community stood up for itself and protested on short notice. That in itself was a victory. The police, the city government were exposed in their complicity with the bigots. What was necessary then, what was necessary the first day of school, what was necessary throughout the crisis was a united, militant community struggle to compel the government to enforce our right to go to any school, any beach, any public facility in Boston. Carson Beach was part of that. But what tended to happen, because of the victimization, because of the outbursts in Roxbury afterwards, was a withdrawal from street protests by the community leadership. I think Carson Beach showed a hint of our power. Other people thought it was a defeat. But the community was ready to move, more than ever."

On August 20, the U.S. Commission on Civil Rights issued a 223-page report on the Boston school situation. The commission has no legislative or law enforcement power and serves largely to monitor the progress of remedying racial discrimination. It periodically holds hearings, on the basis of which it publishes reports and recommends congressional action. Under the Ford administration it had been reduced to impotence.

In June 1975 the commission, headed by Arthur Fleming, a former Kennedy administration secretary of health, education, and welfare, had conducted a lengthy hearing in Boston. Its report chided President Ford for his antibusing statement and for contributing to the "obstruction" of desegregation. The Boston Police Department was blasted for having "no effective mobilization and operation plan for potential disorders" and for assigning a "low priority" to enforcement of the school desegregation order. Mayor White's antibusing rhetoric, it said, had "confused the public and constituted a disservice to the rule of law."

As to the Boston School Committee, it had carried out "a deliberate policy of minimal compliance" with the desegregation order. "The effect of its statements, policy and inaction was to foster within the community outright resistance to school desegregation." If the committee persisted in its course, the commission said, it should be stripped "of all authority."

Finally, the "lack of initiative by most federal agencies [and] the absence of coordinated federal strategy [served] to bolster the opponents of school desegregation," the commission declared. The sweeping charges made the picture unmistakably clear. From the White House to the mayor's office to the streets of South Boston, there was a pattern of sabotage of the Garrity order. It was a conspiracy of obstruction, noncompliance, and disruption. Boston was the test case, where racist resistance had boldly surfaced.

In June of 1974 the U.S. Supreme Court had reversed a federal court order for city-suburban busing in Detroit. This high court blow against desegregation exempted suburban school systems from inclusion in busing plans if such districts were not found to be deliberately involved in the discriminatory educational practices of the inner city. The right to equal educational opportunity and the bus routes that implemented that right now stopped at city limits.

The Detroit NAACP had filed a second plan for school desegregation, involving only inner-city busing. In view of a racial composition of the schools that was slightly less than three-quarters Black and other minorities, it was a step towards equality. But Federal District Judge Robert DeMascio rejected this plan on August 16, 1975, along with an even more modest proposal announced by the Detroit Board of Education. He thereupon issued a bogus desegregation plan.

The Detroit NAACP announced an immediate appeal. The DeMascio plan meant only minimal, one-way busing for a handful of Black students. The very meaning of desegregation had been redefined. "There was Boston in that decision," Detroit NAACP executive director Joe Madison commented. The turn in the Detroit situation was not lost upon the city which had so much influenced that court order. "Judge DeMascio," Louise Day Hicks proclaimed, "faced reality and was not swayed by sociological hogwash." Detroit's Black community, whose majority favored busing according to local polls, had been dealt a double blow.

Soon, another city would make headlines in relation to desegregation. On July 30, the federal district court in Louisville had ordered busing to dismantle the dual school system based on predominantly Black inner-city schools and the all-white school system of the Jefferson County suburban belt. Here segregation had been deliberately fostered. White resistance to the court order had been organized beforehand in Louisville. In Boston, where the buses mandated by Phase II would start rolling on September 10, ROAR was awaiting the first day of busing in the Kentucky city. School would begin there on September 4. And ROAR was hoping for a second front in the war against Black rights.

# 15

# The Beginning
# of Phase II

Louisville exploded. A rally of ten thousand whites cheered the call for an opening day boycott of the schools. Sue Connor, the leader of Concerned Parents, the Louisville variant of ROAR, told the angry throng, "If Martin Luther King were here tonight . . . I'd say move over, buddy, here comes Sue Connor and her people." A representative of Boston ROAR gave greetings from the podium.

The boycott was huge and by no means peaceful. Black students faced physical and verbal harassment as they boarded and rode the buses. Then on September 6 a rally of 10,000 bigots at Valley High School turned into a nighttime mob, blocking traffic on the Dixie Highway and Valley Station Road. Police arrested 135 as the rioters threw bricks and cinder blocks at them. Two houses and a car were torched by a mob of 300 at Fairdale High School. Southern High School, where many buses had been parked for the weekend, was the scene of a rampage of 2,000. They burned two vehicles and smashed the windows of twenty more before police dispersed them at 2 a.m. Then they scattered down Preston Highway, shattering store windows.

Antibusing Governor Julian Carroll ordered the National Guard into Louisville. Federal District Judge James Gordon assigned many of the eight hundred guardsmen, armed with rifles and bayonets, to ride the buses with Black students.

It had been a spectacular eruption, enthusing the Boston antibusers. But the massive deployment of armed force had a chilling effect. Over the volcanic weekend more than four hundred bigots had been arrested. Parades and demonstrations were banned. The buses rolled the following Monday.

The leaders of the Concerned Parents were untouched by the law. The name was deceptive; behind the facade lurked the Ku Klux Klan. This border city had southern traditions. The painted word "nigger" had been added to stop signs in Jefferson County.

On September 5 in the downtown area Louisville cops attempted to block an illegal demonstration. The cops were attacked, and store windows were shattered in the melee. At the front of the march were Walter Groves, the Exalted Cyclops of the Louisville Klan, and Phillip Chopper, the Kentucky Grand Dragon. A gang had darted out from the march and beaten a lone Black man, who had not joined an earlier exodus of Blacks from the street as the march approached. Only ten arrests were made, and the modesty of this police response emboldened the bigots to bigger things that evening.

Louisville had become Boston's blood brother. But here, too, the Black students had been valiant. They were *for* busing. One tenth-grader compared her new school to the segregated Shawnee High School which she had gone to. "Better gyms, better lunches," she said, "better than anything Shawnee ever had." Curtis Harris, a Black student not being assigned to a new school, complained: "I think I should have been bused. I would like to volunteer to be bused because I'm not learning too much right here. I could go out to another school and learn out there where the white schools are, because they teach more and have better equipment and stuff. I want to learn more, because this is my last year and I've got to learn more."

Louisville's racists had had only a few months in which to prepare, and the explosion subsided after it was met with force. The Klan-led bigots lacked the decade of preparation of their Boston counterparts. The roots were there, the racist conscious-ness, but not the battle readiness, the sense of the long haul, the citywide apparatus.

A new factor had been introduced in Louisville, however. The white ranks of the union movement had been mobilized, and the big General Electric plants had been shut tight by racist walkouts called by local officials of the International Union of Electrical Workers. Soon, United Labor Against Busing would form, attempting to rally white workers in a conscious anti-Black effort.

If the spotlight had been on Boston before, now the glare was blinding. Louisville had stoked the furnaces of white resistance. Now, it was up to Boston racists to deliver.

For all the tension of the first year of desegregation, the Black community had rallied behind it. In the first days of Phase I, the racists had attempted to portray the Black community as at least divided, if not opposed to busing. A survey published by the *Boston Globe* noted an increase in Black support for busing from

57 percent prior to the beginning of Phase I—a figure conditioned by the understandable fears of the day—to 65 percent at the end of the year. Moreover, 77 percent of those polled were for busing at the high school level, reflecting a belief that the older students were more able to defend themselves and thus would be safer than young children.

The Black community was increasingly behind the desegregation plan. The fiction of "Black opposition" was dropped by the bigots. And, because of racist violence, Black pride had been sharpened. It was no longer busing and racial balance in the abstract, but the dignity of an oppressed community that was being challenged.

Summer preparation for Phase II had been intense. Community involvement was greater. The Crisis Teams were ready—although they would not be permitted to enter some important schools—especially in South Boston and Charlestown. The Coordinated Social Services Council meetings were set. Volunteers had been mobilized at Freedom House, and agencies across the city had set up special programs for the Black students. "We were much more prepared this time," Ruth Batson recalled. "We were ready."

So was ROAR. The white boycott was extended to Charlestown, where Black students were to be bused.

School opening was preceded by a war of nerves waged by the Boston police. Chester Broderick, head of the Boston Police Benevolent Association and a favorite of ROAR, promised a "sick-out" if a contract dispute could not be settled. The economic issues hardly veiled the daring threat: a police strike against desegregation. Mayor Kevin White, whose national reputation was now on the line, called on Governor Dukakis to send in the National Guard. Already on alert, the troops droned into Boston in green army trucks. Broderick backed down under threat of fines and imprisonment.

On September 7, ROAR rallied in City Hall Plaza. In the same place almost a year before to the day, there had been eight thousand whites. Now, despite the presence of a Charlestown contingent chanting "Here we go Townies, here we go!" there were only three thousand. Boston ROAR President Rita Graul led the chants. "What are ROAR's words?" she would ask. "Resist!" "Never!" Then, a long, bellowed "Boycott!" "Boston's on the warpath, ooh-ahh." John Kerrigan beamed down from the speakers' platform. "Louisville is resisting," he crowed to the bigots. They cheered, and "Long Live Louisville" signs were waved in the breeze. "But remember this," the school committee member and city council candidate said, "Louisville is Boston's farm club. So let's show this to the world!"

The whole world was watching Boston. There could no longer be any "media pact." More than eight hundred out-of-town reporters—some from as far as London, Berlin, and Tokyo—were in the city. ABC Television had assigned more personnel to Boston than it had to Vietnam during the peak of its war coverage. Bunker Hill, overlooking Charlestown High School, was jammed with journalists. The penetrating glare of publicity placed added pressure on a city administration that had been challenged by more than thirty thousand antiracist demonstrators over the past year. It still felt the sting of the Carson Beach episode. Atkins was in direct contact with the mayor and the Justice Department. But despite provocative directions given by the antibusing leadership and their clear intention to disrupt, no measures had been taken against them individually.

The test would be at and in the schools. Judge Garrity's prohibitions of demonstrations near school grounds continued. Two dozen federal marshals would be on hand to observe. They, along with Justice Department officials, complemented a mobilization of nineteen hundred city and state police, deployed across Boston. Six hundred national guardsmen were on alert at the Fargo Building in the warehouse district of South Boston.

As the guardsmen settled into the mammoth old building, two hundred enraged South Boston racists attacked police lines assigned to guard the facility. The battle raged into the night as police cars were stoned and cops were driven back by rocks and bottles. The hooligans were stopped by the police, and several were arrested. Hours later, on a sparkling, cloudless morning, Phase II began.

In the North End, it was serene. The Michaelangelo Middle School enrolled Black students. The police surveyed the crowd of sixty who had gathered, many of them middle-aged. The North End was an antibusing area, but few, if any, of the neighborhood students had been bused out. Now, Black children trooped off the buses. Some of the adults muttered under their breath. Then it was over. The buses rolled out. "Ah, what's the fuss?" one white was heard to say.

But within view of the North End were the bridges leading to Charlestown, which bristled with police. They had cordoned off the bus routes, which had not been disclosed beforehand, and backed away the crowds that attempted to march on the high school. Early, well before the buses rolled out at 7:30 a.m., two police helicopters circled over the neighborhood, waking residents. A police sharpshooter in a bulletproof vest was visible on the roof of the high school. Mounted police patrolled the streets leading to the high school, and swarms of motorcycle cops and plainclothesmen choked the arteries.

Four blocks away, a hooting, frustrated mob had gathered at the Bunker Hill housing projects. They cheered as the burning effigy of a Black man was tossed from the roof of one of the squat, yellow brick buildings. It bore a smoldering sign: "Nigger beware."

Later, they converged along Bunker Hill Street, testing police lines. Two blocks up the hill was the high school. Chants and shouts rang out. The police were showered with firecrackers, bottles, bricks, and stones, but the lines held. As the mob was repelled, groups broke away and overturned parked cars, setting two afire. As the afternoon wore on, the tension and desperation of the bigots intensified. Only a handful of arrests had been made. The cops did not clear the crowds that packed the sidewalks and street on Bunker Hill Street. Knots of young racists roamed the side streets. Then, a group broke off on the run, and others joined. Something was going to happen. They bolted through the neighborhood, bursting into Bunker Hill Community College.

Harvey Fisher, a Black student, was strolling in the campus lounge. The mob flung open the doors and surged into the room. Fisher tried to run but was cornered, kicked, and beaten to the ground; his arm was twisted until it snapped.

In South Boston, the crowds were smaller. The police presence was enormous, and they surrounded the buses as they rolled in. No mobs, no stonings. Day Boulevard teemed with mounted police and motorcycle cops. On that day a year before, hundreds of racists had lined the route, bombarding the buses with rocks. Today, the street was virtually deserted.

Michael Alexander, a Black reporter from *Newsday*, Long Island's major daily paper, had not been lucky enough to drive in that quiet area. As his car made its way through South Boston, a gang spotted him. In a second, glass was shattering around him. He veered to the curb, stunned. Another mistake. The hooligans rushed his car, jumping inside and beating him.

But on G Street, at the high school, the crowd had been tamer, as the police cordons held. The bigots for the most part stayed inside, as the helicopter engines roared above. Those who did come out kept their distance. Small groups walked up the hill, only to be ordered sternly by the police to move back. Spit and catcalls filled the air as the buses rolled up, but there were no rocks, no pounding on the buses.

At Hyde Park, the streets were almost empty save for hundreds of police. Roslindale was calm. The buses were off limits.

That first night of Phase II, the police would be the targets. The temper for combat was aroused by a blaring motorcade winding its way out of South Boston, past South Station, and onto the expressway to Charlestown. There had not been a car caravan for months. This one was markedly smaller than those of the previous fall, which had been composed of up to a thousand automobiles. This night the cars were adorned with placards and bunting, some with flyers and pinwheels—a parade. But the chants were brash and ugly. It had been a bitter, frustrating day. They could not deliver a Louisville. And their enraged war cries startled passersby. "Kill the niggers!" "Niggers eat shit!"

The motorcade broke up late in the evening, as fighting erupted in South Boston and Charlestown. Upwards of two hundred skirmished with police at the edges of Bunker Hill until midnight. Firemen braved rocks while attempting to douse a blaze ignited by a firebomb at the Prescott Middle School. No arrests were made. Guerrillalike attacks on police punctuated the night in South Boston and Charlestown as bigots shot metal-tipped darts at all-night patrols.

Across the city in Brookline, the historic home of John F. Kennedy was set afire. The damage was put at $75,000. Sprayed on the sidewalk was the arsonists' message: "Bus Teddy." There was no comment from Massachusetts' senior senator.

On the first day only small numbers of Black students had embarked on the buses. Others had been detained by anxious parents. But on September 11, Black students packed the buses journeying to South Boston and Charlestown. It was apparent that the police had deterred potential mobs, though with a rare restraint when showered with bricks and bottles—and the deadly metal-tipped darts.

The federal marshals, present not as police but as observers, had made a dent as well. "The U.S. marshals had an impact well beyond their number," the *Boston Globe* noted. "In South Boston, for example, they took motion pictures and stills and made notes. When they came near State Police squads, the squads often felt it was time to make a sweep of whatever spectators were nearby."

Gangs of young whites that day again challenged the police. Day and nighttime strikes continued for the week.

A new twist was introduced on September 11. Obviously aimed at the media, it attempted to portray the bigots as grievously wronged. Mothers' marches were staged, first in Charlestown, then in South Boston, and, for good measure, in Hyde Park and again in the North End. The women of the antibusing movement came forward, led at times by neighborhood figures and, at others, by Louise Day Hicks. They trooped through the side and main streets to church, intoning Hail Marys or Our Fathers, and ended with prayers to "deliver us from forced busing and the TPF [Tactical Police Force]."

For two days, the army of reporters had watched the police fend off the small mobs. They had heard the anti-Black chants. And they had seen new graffiti splashed up on the walls. In Charlestown these were particularly bright and vivid on the main drag, Bunker Hill Street: "Kill Zulus." "KKK." "Busing is for niggers." In South Boston, the faded epithets had been refreshed with new advertisements of hate: "Tom Atkins is a nigger lover," "Niggers smell like apes."

For many of the reporters the violence and the rage of the bigots was mind-boggling. At the same time, the Black students had carried themselves with singular dignity, braving taunts and insults, occasionally smiling at the huge gatherings of reporters as they made their way through police lines. The contrast between them (in hostile territory, outnumbered by the whites, ordered about by nervous police) and the racist students (who blithely told the media "We just don't like niggers") was striking. That difference would be communicated on television news across the country.

That made the bigots mad. If police lines caved, it was when the antibusing crowds came face to face with the reporters, yelling at them for favoring the Blacks. "You always tell their side," one bitter woman shrieked. "What about us, what about us?" The vituperation turned to physical harassment, as some reporters seeking a cup of coffee would be shoved, pushed, insulted, and spat upon. This anger and abuse did little to win converts among the media.

The "mothers' prayer marches" were indeed bizarre. They were duly reported by the media, but their crude contrivance brought grimaces to the faces of even the most hard-boiled journalists. As one such demonstration trickled by the far side of Bunker Hill, a short, red-haired woman marcher bellowed, "Garrity, suck your mother's ass!" Friends moved to her side to quiet her, but the distinct shift from the sacred to the profane was heard by all within earshot. "Jesus," one weary reporter mumbled, "I think I'm going to vomit."

Kevin White was not comfortable with Phase II. Opposed to busing, he had appealed the order. Embroiled in an election contest with Mattapan State Senator Joseph Timilty, whose ambiguous relationship to ROAR had enabled him to be viewed as more antibusing than White, the mayor was in a box. As the city's chief official he was duty bound to enforce the law. And, with a national audience watching and with a Black leadership which had taken an increasing distance from him, he was under pressure to continue a heavy police presence. But doing that in turn meant losing votes to Timilty. White had to throw some bones to the bigots.

As the second school day of Phase II ended, the first morsel was tossed out. "The sooner we get the police off the streets the better I'll feel," White declared. He offered a unique explanation why. "When it reaches the point where [there is] an overemphasis on law enforcement, physical presence becomes, in a way, debilitating, psychologically speaking." Whose psyches were being damaged was not specified.

Black school attendance climbed rapidly. But on September 15, half of the six hundred national guardsmen on call in Boston were relieved of duty. Although Judge Garrity's permission would be required for a similar police demobilization, their lines began to diminish in size with the beginning of the second week of school.

That day the crowds at South Boston High School were tiny. But four blocks away, a group of toughs stoned a city bus. The Black driver was injured by flying glass. The bigots' frustration had deepened with their inability to penetrate police lines. The random violence against individual Blacks that had wounded the city over the summer was not slackening.

For Blacks and Puerto Ricans, safety required nothing less than a broadening of police presence at tense subway stations, on bus routes, in "neutral territory." As to the security problems at the school sites themselves, Justice Department official Stanley Pottinger made a keen prediction at a news briefing. Challenges to safety now, he said, "would arise *in* the schools, and not outside."

White enrollment in South Boston had risen above that of the previous year—sometimes as much as 50 percent of projected white enrollment was being attained, a figure that was matched in Charlestown. Black students were more than ever outnumbered at these schools now. And, while the majority of white students were not formally organized into racist groups, gangs and a cadre of tough, pugnacious, anti-Black youth had been prepared for combat within the school.

The nighttime assaults on the police continued. Now, gasoline bombs were being hurled in South Boston. The numerical reduction of the police force was a signal for racist advances. It had been the *number* of the police, not their attitude, which had made the buses secure. The police resented the situation into which they had been thrust. The beat cops, the majority of the police mobilization, were now targets of community hatred, pelted with bricks, darts, and rocks, even though they themselves opposed the law they were under pressure to enforce. The federal marshals were a burden to them. Any Black student who made the mistake of crossing the police found little sympathy and, more often than not, a club or shove.

On September 13, 180 leaders of the National Student Coalition Against Racism—assembled at a steering committee meeting in Boston—issued the call for the second National Student Conference Against Racism to be held October 10-12 at Northeastern University. The steering committee meeting began with a picket line at City Hall, demanding increased law enforcement presence at schools in the all-white neighborhoods. It was the first picket of the fall in support of busing.

On September 22, the Boston Teachers Union struck the school system, as a long-simmering dispute between it and the school committee came to a head. The strike vote had been overwhelming, but the union leadership postponed the deadline until two weeks after school opening lest it disrupt the inauguration of Phase II and thus run afoul of Judge Garrity, who was rumored ready to enjoin the strike.

The predominantly white union did not enjoy widespread

support in the Black community. Though its reputation was not as bad as that of its counterpart in New York City, it nonetheless had remained officially "neutral" in the busing controversy. In Boston such a position was tantamount to support of the status quo—the racism of the dual school system. The BTU also had appealed Garrity's order for parity hiring—designed to increase Black teacher rolls to reflect the makeup of the student population.

The school committee had the BTU in a bind. It seized the opportunity to cripple the union, and by adopting an intransigent negotiating stance it prolonged the strike and halted Phase II.

The city's Black leadership was alarmed by the implications of the strike, but few would oppose it publicly. Atkins, however, opposed it openly and was prepared to ask Garrity for an injunction. He was joined in this stance by John O'Bryant, a former teacher and a candidate for school committee. O'Bryant headed the Black Educators Association of Massachusetts (BEAM) and urged its members to cross BTU picket lines at schools in the Black community.

The BTU's rallies galvanized rank-and-file support for the strike, and picket lines were large. But the desegregation issue was carefully avoided by the union leadership, and no real overtures were made to its principal potential ally—the Black community. Within the union there was a beginning of ferment. A new Black caucus of BTU members emerged. It supported the strike and would press the union to support Black rights. White teachers who were against busing and had theretofore given their loyalty to school committee members became disillusioned with them because of their strikebreaking stand. Kerrigan's name, for example, was booed at union meetings.

The strike was for *quality education,* better-trained teachers, more remedial programs, more time for classroom preparation, and the putting into effect of an arbitration award more than a year old. Money was almost incidental. The true face of the school committee was revealed for many white teachers for the first time when it forced a strike on these issues.

The two-week strike ended with a partial victory for the BTU. The year-old arbitration award would be implemented and wages increased 6 percent (the cost of living in Boston had risen 9.7 percent). The suspension of school attendance caused by the strike seemed to some Black leaders a blessing in disguise, a relief from the tension of Phase II.

On September 18, snipers fired at police in Charlestown, after a gang had stoned the police station and unsuccessfully attempted to firebomb it.

The following day a South Boston mothers' march turned unruly close to the bus routes, as white youth milled near the police and taunted them. They made their biggest effort to date to penetrate the lines of the state police. One sixteen-year-old was arrested for attacking a federal marshal.

Twenty-four hours later, the Summer Street Bridge leading into South Boston was set ablaze, and police began a round-the-clock patrol of seven bridge arteries connecting the peninsula to Boston.

Pottinger's prediction was beginning to come true. The schools were heating up inside. A special "emphasis" boycott at Charlestown and Hyde Park high schools caused a plunge in white attendance.

On the first day of Phase II, Charlestown ROAR leader Thomas Johnson—who had invoked the Fifth Amendment more than twenty times before the U.S. Commission on Civil Rights in June—had been arrested at the high school. He was back the next day. Johnson, a husky man, presided over the Powderkeg Information Center and the Charlestown Home and School Association. Because of his latter position, he could gain entrance to the school and was conspicuous in the corridors, in his windbreaker emblazoned with the ROAR symbol and initials.

On September 22, Charlestown antibusing leader Pat Russell led a delegation of fifteen through police lines to demand a meeting with Frank Powers, the school's headmaster. Powers, an outspoken opponent of busing, had refused the "crisis teams" admittance to the building. It was a seemingly small incident, but the meaning was great. Garrity's prohibition on gatherings near the school was being flouted. A double standard was clearly in effect, as Thomas Johnson circulated through the corridors and antibusing delegations aired "white grievances" in the troubled school.

On September 21, the eve of the teachers' strike, two hundred white youth mounted bicycles for an antibusing "bike-athon" from Charlestown through the North End—a good-natured protest in a driving rain, until an adult chaperon drove into a police officer, hospitalizing him.

The racists in Charlestown were drawing on Southie's year of experience. And in South Boston, school incidents had begun slowly to spiral upward since the first day of classes. The crisis promised to reach new proportions in the coming month. However, it was not against the police cordons in Boston that racist pressure was having most effect, but on the political front in Washington.

On September 17, the Senate passed the Biden Amendment, named after Delaware Democratic Senator Joseph Biden. The fifty-to-forty-three vote signaled the first antibusing victory in the hundred-member body. The amendment, attached to a funding appropriation for the Department of Health, Education and Welfare, would have no application in Boston, but it did hearten resistance. It was immediately acclaimed by the bigots, whose leaders gloated that the "message is getting to Washington."

The amendment would prohibit HEW from withholding funds from districts which refused to implement desegregation plans—a prime method used in the past to crack down on derelict city governments and school committees. The Biden amendment was "unquestionably the most sweeping attack on a civil rights act passed by the Senate in recent years," according to the U.S. Commission on Civil Rights.

A week later, the Senate passed the Byrd Amendment, which prohibited HEW from utilizing its funds to require the busing of any student "to a school other than the school nearest to the student's home" *only* for purposes of desegregation. The amendment—sponsored by Robert Byrd of West Virginia, the Democratic majority whip in the Senate—outraged the U.S. Civil Rights Commission, which described it as "little more than an effort to reinstate the separate but equal doctrine." The commission declared the measure would "lock minority students to attendance only at unconstitutionally segregated schools inasmuch as many school districts have deliberately constructed and maintain schools in such a way as to create and perpetuate segregation."

Though still requiring final approval from the joint Senate-House conference committee, the passage of the Biden and Byrd amendments was the harvest reaped by the Louisville resistance and a year of sustained opposition in Boston.

President Ford again attacked court-ordered busing. And Vice-President Rockefeller, "speaking for himself," soon afterwards announced his support for the constitutional amendment against busing. The effort to undercut desegregation was bipartisan.

# 16

# The Madhouse
# in the Schools

The mood of the Black students had changed in that first year of desegregation. Nervous and edgy at the beginning, unprepared for and stunned by the hostility, the Black students in South Boston had risen to the challenge, riding the buses daily. There was no amity between them and the police, not an ounce of it; but the wall of blue had stood off the awful mobs of the year before. Confidence was up. They were digging in. They would respond to the catcalls, mimicking the bigots' antics to amuse themselves on the buses and to defy the Southies.

One grey September morning at the school, a metal detector had broken down, and a busload of Black students was delayed from disembarking. They were animated, chatting, joking, as the police let a group of white students pass a barricade into the schoolyard. It was a typical scene.

In the back of the bus a young woman, a big smile on her face, began clapping her hands and broke out in a sing-song chant: "Here we go Southie, here we go!" This was the cry that had spurred the football, hockey, and basketball teams in the past, and now was heard at every antibusing rally. It ran through the bus like a shot, and in a second, the Black students had picked it up. They were chanting, louder and louder, serious and laughing at the same time. "Here we go Southie, here we go!" The bus rocked with the rhythmic words as the white students passed the vehicle. Headmaster William Reid rushed to the bus, climbed aboard and angrily lectured the Black students. The chanting stopped.

It was a brief episode, lasting perhaps a minute. But the singing from the bus, the chant that had belonged to *them*, had, in a moment of delicious mockery, taken on a new meaning: *We are here to stay. This is our school.*

On September 30 and October 3 fifty white students staged

walkouts at Charlestown High School. On October 3 in South
Boston a hundred racists tried unsuccessfully to break police
lines at the Gavin Middle School.

Inside South Boston High School the mood was deteriorating
rapidly. Fights and brawls were breaking out. Classrooms had
segregated seating patterns. Police harassment of Blacks was
increasing, along with fraternization with whites by the recently
assigned state troopers. The overwhelmingly white administrative, teaching, and aide staffs had lined up against the Blacks.
Racism was a festering, open sore. Education had broken down.

The Black students' story had not gotten out. Rumors were rife,
however, and, when asked, the young Blacks would respond, "It's
a war." Though hardly peaceful, the school appeared outwardly
calm. Charlestown seemed to be the place of most tension. That
was where the walkouts and protests had been most prominent.

Then on October 8 virtually all of the ninety-two Black South
Boston High School students who got off the buses that day—a
figure which reflected a decrease in attendance—refused to enter
the building. They demanded increased protection within the
school and protested the withdrawal of police. They were all
suspended. It was the lead story in the Boston news media. The
South Boston High School Black student caucus had dramatically emerged.

On October 10 Charlestown High School was rocked with
fights, one of them "a major disturbance," according to police.
Headmaster Frank Powers, usually icy and noncommunicative
with reporters, was tight-lipped on the incidents. Two whites and
one Black had been arrested. The same day three hundred white
students walked out of South Boston High School, protesting
"preferential treatment of Blacks." No suspensions.

For the ninety-two Blacks to return to the school and be
relieved of a three-day suspension, they had to come accompanied
by parents, which, for security reasons, was virtually impossible.
Ruth Batson put the crisis teams into emergency gear. With
Percy Wilson and Ellen Jackson, she assembled a team of
support, assuring the Black students of readmittance based on
the consent the parents had given. Batson, Wilson, and Jackson,
with team captains Maceo Dixon and Mac Warren and ten other
Black team members, were able for the first time to gain entry to
the school as they brought back the suspended students. Dixon
and Warren spent the day in the building.

"That convinced me," Batson recalled. "All the hate and fear

Louisville explodes.

ROAR rally at City Hall, September, 1975.

Buses line up for first day of school, September 1975.

Antibusing mob in Charlestown, September 1975.

Students disembark from buses at South Boston High.

and frustration packed into the cafeteria. Something had to be done." She had never seen anything like it. Ellen Jackson was aghast at the racism she saw, and exhausted by the experience.

"Just as we got into the school," Dixon related, "in full view of the police, administrators, and students, a big white student came up to a Black student and called him a nigger. The Black student said, 'What did you say?' So the white student said, 'I called you a nigger.' The Black student knocked him down with one punch, and then he not only got suspended but arrested for assault and battery."

Dixon described the school as "a madhouse" because of the terrific din of fighting, name calling, and swarming of the students in corridors during breaks between classes.

Warren witnessed a group of Black students walking to class, accompanied by a Black teacher's aide, all being jumped by a gang of whites. "You have to remember these aides wear yellow shirts that say 'teacher's aide' on the back," Warren said. "But the cops came and led the white students away while one cop pulled the Black aide up by the neck and slammed her into a locker and whacked her with a club. Luckily, the Black students got away.

"The white students wait at the top of the stairs and spit on Blacks," Warren added. "That kind of harassment and name calling and shoving is constant. But the cops, almost all of whom are white, assume the Blacks are at fault, even though the Black students are outnumbered and in hostile territory."

Percy Wilson was infuriated. He wanted South Boston High School, the symbol of "their turf," shut tight and the students dispersed throughout the school system.

For weeks, the Coordinated Social Services Council was occupied with animated discussion over what should be done about the school. Ellen Jackson was undecided. Would demanding that the school be closed to rescue the Black students from their daily ordeal there be seen as a sign of weakness or strength? Ruth Batson made up her mind the day she visited the school. She wrote a personal letter to Judge Garrity, urging that he place the school under his control—in receivership, as she put it. South Boston should not be allowed to view the school as its own.

The situation was heating up again. The breathing spell was over. The debate was now public. The future of South Boston High School was at stake.

Mac Warren met with Eric Van Loon, the attorney for the

Black plaintiffs, and provided him with names of Black students willing to testify before Judge Garrity about the situation in the school. Van Loon and his fellow lawyers rapidly went to work preparing a powerful brief detailing the harassment in the school.

Meanwhile, on October 14, 175 white students walked out of Charlestown High School. No suspensions.

The next several days, mimeographed flyers inciting anti-Black violence were given out in South Boston High School. "Wake up, will you?" the handbill urged. "Don't be scared by the federal offense threats. A fight in the school isn't a federal offense. . . ." On October 16, 250 white students bolted out of the school after issuing demands including the reciting of the "Pledge of Allegiance" in every homeroom, the placing of American flags in every classroom, and the flying of a large American flag on the school's unused flagpole. The "white student caucus" had officially emerged. Also demanded was the unconditional right for white students to leave the school whenever they felt their safety was jeopardized by Blacks. There were no suspensions.

The next day there was a near riot. Nearly two hundred white students blocked the school steps. Twenty-five conducted a sit-in on the lobby floor. Tension increased as lines of Black students pushed against the whites in the congestion. As the Black students entered the building to a chorus of epithets, a gang of whites—in full view of the administrators—left the sit-in and chased three Blacks down the corridor.

In Charlestown, the boiling point was being neared. On October 20, twenty-five white students jumped and beat a lone Black student, pummelling a Black teacher who came to his assistance. The next day, eighty-five Black students refused to enter the school, citing the lack of safety as the reason. The buses took them to Freedom House, where student leader Clarence Jefferson, of the Charlestown Black student caucus, told the media the school was "like Vietnam." All eighty-five were suspended.

The lines were being sharply drawn. The Black students at Charlestown and South Boston high schools now had Black student caucuses, and were meeting at friends' houses. They then would turn to the media and community agencies for support. White student caucuses also existed. They had a base of organized support from ROAR, the Home and School Associations, the South Boston and Powderkeg information centers. Moreover, they had the support of politicians, the city council, and the school committee, as well as the encouraging atmosphere of "their turf." So in the schools it was hands off the white students, while the Black students, in their fledgling state of organization, were, it seemed, to be driven out. The scales in Boston were beginning to tip back in favor of the racists.

Thirteen hundred supporters of NSCAR attended the second National Student Conference Against Racism at Northeastern University October 10-12. It was a serious gathering. These activists had been tempered and educated by the Boston struggle or by arduous work elsewhere in the country to rally support for the Boston struggle. They appreciated that the struggle to defend school desegregation—one of the chief gains of the civil rights movement and the Black liberation movement—was a *defensive* struggle. The battle had been mounted by the bigots, and their continuing offensive was echoing in Congress and the White House. While the NSCAR delegates saw mass action as the key to a successful defense of Black rights, mass action was not the strategy of the nation's Black leadership. The NAACP pressed for school desegregation, but it fought almost solely through the courts. It did so alone, rarely seeking to organize the power of the Black community in action. Its support of the May 17 march and rally was an exception, not the rule.

Thomas Atkins liked the idea of street actions in general, but he placed confidence in legal activity to seek court enforcement of the laws on the books. For the most part, the established Black leadership in Boston and throughout the country saw the Democratic Party as *the* vehicle for securing Black rights. Results would come through participation in it, supporting "friendly" candidates.

In an election year, the consequences of such a strategy were especially frustrating. Looking to the Democrats meant increasing involvement in party campaigns and seeking platform promises of future aid. Any concessions to Blacks by the party, however, were designed to detour them from independent protest and action. Reforms were the fruit of struggle, not of reliance on the Democrats. Yet, such struggle threatened the authority of the Democratic Party itself over the Black community. In city after city, Democrats were administering the bipartisan social policy of cutbacks. In New York, this policy was directed against city workers and social welfare programs. In Boston, it was a campaign against school desegregation. Cutbacks were the theme of the national effort of both Democrats and Republicans. Black leaders who identified with either party would be swept along by this current of "austerity."

In Boston, two Democrats were vying for mayor. (Norman Oliver, the Black, probusing Socialist Workers Party candidate, had been eliminated in the fall primary election.) Kevin White and Joseph Timilty, experienced politicians, knew how to play the Black leaders off against one another. White's image had been badly tarnished by his performance in office. It was public knowledge that he had made not-so-behind-the-scenes deals with Louise Day Hicks. For some Black leaders, like Thomas Atkins, who was bitterly opposed to White, Timilty seemed like a preferable alternative. But this Democratic office seeker was a long-time foe of desegregation. He had taken special pains to seek ROAR's support, flying to Washington for the D.C. march to demand a constitutional amendment against busing.

Lesser-evil politics produced a bitter schism in the city's Black leadership over support to one or the other of the antibusing candidates. Demonstrations *for* busing did not fit into the mood against desegregation generated by the election campaign. Mobilizations *against* busing, however, were organized by the most racist wing of the Democratic Party to push both White and Timilty further in their direction. Neither mayoralty candidate was formally endorsed by ROAR.

On the national level, the approaching presidential primary campaigns were beginning to exert a similar pressure. All this weighed heavily on the city's Black leadership. Moreover, it appeared on the surface that the violence was abating somewhat. The crisis-laden months of the past school year seemed distant. Yet, the movement directly challenging Black rights drew inspiration from Boston and was gathering momentum nationally in the form of an increasing number of court suits.

So the need for protest and action in defense of desegregation was greater than ever before. But for a demonstration capable of mobilizing Boston's Black community and the increasing sector of whites repelled by racist violence, there would have to be an authoritative call from recognized and established leadership. NSCAR in Boston was beginning to win recognition as a militant, responsible wing of the movement for desegregation. However, it could not and did not want to go beyond its organizational and political capacities. It could not launch another December 14 or May 17 demonstration on its own. And there would be no call for action from the central leaders and organizations of the Black community. This was not for lack of efforts to persuade on the part of the NSCAR leaders in Boston.

Given these problems, the NSCAR conference realistically limited itself to adopting a proposal for a national educational campaign on the issues in Boston, utilizing teach-ins, picket lines, forums, and educational conferences.

Other work was coming to the fore, as well. In New York City, SCAR activists had been at the center of student protests against cutbacks in higher education. In city after city, SCAR chapters had played a key role in the successful defense effort for Joanne Little. In Denver, the SCAR chapter was involved in a campaign to win bilingual-bicultural education for Chicano students. Increased activity in behalf of Black victims of racist injustice was also projected. This involved twenty defendants, including Rubin "Hurricane" Carter in New Jersey, Stanton Story in Pittsburgh, J.B. Johnson in Saint Louis, and Gary Tyler in New Orleans. Common to all of them was that they were Black and had been convicted of crimes they did not commit.

Marion Fahey, the new superintendent of the Boston school system, fielded dozens of sharp questions from Black parents and students at a Freedom House meeting on October 18. Fahey was an archetypal product of the school department bureaucracy. Though a professional administrator, she had the manner of a second-grade teacher addressing her pupils—always seeing the bright side of things. She was a protege of John Kerrigan, and the school committee had split three-to-two in approving her contract. Many thought she would be Kerrigan's surrogate while he ran for city council. But she was not the type capable of Kerrigan's ugly, gutter-level tirades against desegregation. In private conversation many reporters likened her to television's Edith Bunker. She was good-hearted but a cog in the bureaucracy, unenlightened and uninspired. She could barely tread water in the choppy seas of the busing controversy. She inspired no confidence in the Black community.

Freedom House held conferences featuring as speakers figures in the school situation, administrators, school committee members—the "moderates"—as well as Black educators and community leaders. It was at one of these that Fahey was peppered with questions about the in-school organizing of white resistance. "There is nothing I can do to stop it," she apologized.

That night, more than a hundred parents and school-aged youth, some as young as eight, conducted a prayer vigil in the rain in South Boston. A cross was burned. The next night, a mob of two hundred battled police for three hours in a driving downpour. Three arrests and three injured cops.

The caldron of hate called South Boston High School was bubbling. On October 23, it boiled over at a South Boston-Dorchester football game, the latter team fielded by a high school where desegregation had been implemented with comparative peace. Fights erupted in the stands as racist catcalls and haranguing mixed with football cheers.

As Bubba Johnson, a popular young Black sportscaster, interviewed players after the game, the brawls spilled onto the field. A white gang jumped Johnson, and suddenly the skirmish was joined by scores, many of them Black and enraged at the treatment of the broadcaster whom they respected and considered a friend. The melee lasted an hour, with eighty police moving in to stem the outburst. No arrests.

State Legislator Raymond Flynn of South Boston called for the removal of school football from Franklin Park—in the heart of Roxbury—as if the site itself had been the cause of the turmoil. As a "neutral site" for games he proposed White Stadium in East Boston, where, a year before, the ROAR benefit game had featured a bus-burning at halftime. "Can you imagine," Ellen Jackson asked a meeting at Freedom House, "the nerve of that man calling East Boston 'neutral'?"

The following day was a Friday, the end of the school week. Hundreds of white students blocked the steps to South Boston High School. As the Black students pushed their way through the crowd, the taunts began. Then a brawl, fists and feet flying. Eleven Blacks and four whites were arrested.

> Burn, burn, burn the bus
> For all the world to see;
> Merrily, merrily, merrily, merrily,
> Walk to school with me.

These new words to "Row, Row, Row Your Boat" were being sung by a cheerful, rambunctious group of teenagers to listeners at South Boston's Marine Park.

It was a brilliant fall day, October 27, and a special boycott had emptied South Boston and Charlestown schools of white students. Their ranks had been bolstered by the closing of most of

South Boston's businesses and stores. It was "National Boycott Day," called by ROAR. Though the adjective "national" was inaccurate, the crowd was big and enthusiastic—six thousand, the largest antibusing march and rally since September 9, 1974. The movement had been heartened by the rising opposition to busing in the U.S. Senate and the swing to the right on the "forced busing issue" by all the major Democratic and Republican presidential candidates.

Among the speakers, a handful of local labor leaders railed against George Meany, who had rebuked Louisville union officials involved in the antibusing campaign. South Boston's State Senator William Bulger won the most applause. "There is not a shred of intellectual support left for forced busing in America," he boasted. "The signs of collapse are all around, including the Senate. We are here to tell you that if you are not with us you are against us, and if you are against us, we will fight you."

It was an angry crowd, chafing against the police, who kept their distance. Two hundred tam-o'-shantered Southie marshals served as a buffer between the bigots and the cops. They were now the South Boston Marshals Association, having outgrown their former simple, clublike organizational form of bar-based social groups.

The march chanted and shouted its way by G Street down Broadway. School was in session, the building empty but for Black students. The police packed the street, a dozen rows deep. In front of them were the marshals. The temper of the six thousand marchers rose to fever pitch with chants and glares as they trooped by this site of earlier battle. On the return route, as about five thousand began dispersing at the Broadway subway station, the tension gave way to outbursts of attack.

Black students were evacuated early from the Gavin Middle School, as a crowd within rock-hurling distance menaced the front entrance. Moments later a motorcycle cop was knocked off his vehicle as he drove near the throng. Reporters were greeted with a shower of spit. A city bus, stopped at a light, was rushed by twenty youths, who clambered aboard through the rear windows. Luckily, there were no Blacks aboard.

And, as the march mounted the last rolling hill, a section took up the chant the Black students heard every day in the high school corridors: "We don't want no boneheads," repeated over and over and over.

# 17

# Black Students
# Tell Their Story

Attorney Eric Van Loon was shocked by the testimony he and
the team of desegregation lawyers had gathered from the Black
students at South Boston High School. It was more damning
than anything he had imagined.

On November 18 the lawyers requested a hearing from Judge
Garrity to consider whether the school should be shut down. The
antibusing leadership reacted swiftly and angrily. It was an
attempt to "punish our community," Hicks proclaimed.

On November 21 the Black students appeared in the courtroom.
Some stumbled, confusing the names and faces of their victimizers, but the testimony streamed out as school committee lawyers
bombarded them with questions. The students' words constitute a
stark testament of their daily life in a school where desegregation
was opposed by a clawing, defiant white racism:

White students at South Boston High School are all the time saying
racial slurs to Black students there. My locker is on the second floor of the
building. When I am there between classes getting new books, the whites
who pass by are all the time saying things to me like "nigger" and "Kiss
my ass." These things are said all the time, and nothing is done about it,
even when the teachers or policemen hear the kids say these things.

Especially in the cafeteria, they call us "nigger" and say things like
"Kiss my ass" and "Go to hell." They also say things like "We don't want
you in our school."

One of the white student demands was that music be played over the
school PA system during the change of classes. They said they wanted
this "because music soothes the savage beasts." This is a racial slur, and
Dr. Reid printed it up on the school machine.

White kids were standing outside, chanting, "Two, four, six, eight,
assassinate the nigger apes." Later in that period, some of the white kids

came back into the school. When they came into my homeroom, some of the white kids continued to chant, "Two, four, six, eight, assassinate the nigger apes." Mr. Hamann told the students to be quiet, but most of them continued anyway. He did not tell them they were suspended or anything then, and I do not think that any disciplinary action was ever taken against them.

White students are all the time saying things to us like "Send the niggers home," or, "We don't want niggers in our school." When they walk through the halls as classes change, they sing the song with the words, "Jump down, turn around, pick a bale of cotton," and "Bye, Bye, Blackbird."

There is something about being in South Boston that does something to the white students. There is one white boy who was with us in the Burke last year, who was really friendly and nice to Black kids. This year at Southie, he runs with that Sean gang and is always getting into fights.

The "Sean gang" was one of the principal outfits which rampaged through the school, leading the attack on Black students. "Sean" is a white student leader of the antibusing toughs, who remained in school despite numerous suspensions, a conviction in South Boston District Court for desegregation-related attacks, and a pending federal indictment for assaults at Carson Beach.

I was sitting in my homeroom class early in the morning before first period. My teacher, Mr. Moore, was there and a Spanish student whose name I don't know and two other Black students. We were just sitting in our homeroom minding our own business, waiting for classes to start. All of a sudden, a lot of white boys, perhaps ten or twenty, came into the room and started to jump all of us. There was fighting all over the room, and we looked to our teacher, Mr. Moore, for help, but there was nothing that he could do about it. One of the white boys whose name I know is Sean.

Some days I see gangs of white boys, headed by a student they call Sean, just roaming around the halls of the school. Some days they all wear green army jackets, and it seems like there is trouble on days when that happens.

One day in early October, I saw a white student named Sean come into the school on crutches with his foot wrapped in a bandage. During homeroom, before first period started, I saw Sean unwrapping the bandage from his foot. I heard him say, "This is my new nigger beater. I am going to use this crutch on the first nigger that says anything to me."

There is a white student in my room named Sean. On many Thursday mornings he talks to other white students about meetings they have been at the night before. He has talked about this so many times that I believe there are regular Wednesday night meetings.

On Thursday morning, November 13, my homeroom teacher started to explain about voting in student council elections. Sean said, "White students aren't voting. We decided at the meeting last night that we're not voting, so don't anybody vote." Ms. Allen did not say anything to him, but she handed out the ballots. None of the white students voted except one white boy. [Sean accused him of voting for himself and] told him he better resign and then [the white student] told Ms. Allen he wanted to resign.

Neither the Boston police nor state troopers were spared in the testimony. They may have repulsed the crowds outside, but inside the building it was a different story:

During that meeting, a Black aide came in. She had been handcuffed by a state trooper. I asked her what happended and she told me that she had been walking with six Black students to the office. They had been jumped by white students, and one of them had grabbed for the guard's gun. The police jumped the Black students and also slammed the Black aide into a locker before he handcuffed her. . . . The police took all six Black students, but no white students, to the school office. When a white teacher told the police that the Black aide had not tried to get his gun, he apologized to her and asked her not to press charges against him. She also told me that he had hit her in the head with his stick. I know she was hit because I could see the knot on her head.

I was out in the hall near a state trooper. A white student passed me and said: "If there's one thing I hate, it's the smell of niggers," and spit on the floor. I said to the trooper: "You heard that." The trooper turned away from me and didn't do anything about it.

I am seventeen years old and a sophomore at South Boston High School. I went there last year, too. I have five brothers and sisters in school in South Boston, three in the Gavin, one at L Street, and a sister with me at G Street. I am Black.

All year long I have not been in any fights, and I have not been suspended.

One morning, Friday, October 31, 1975, I was walking to my first period health class, going right in front of the office. Three white boys were walking behind me, and one of them named John started to push me. A teacher named Mr. Marc Scarsella was standing right there by the office and saw this happen. Mr. Scarsella grabbed that white boy John real quick. But John grabbed me anyway and ripped my coat, and the other two white boys grabbed me, too, and I was knocked to the ground. I did not try to fight back. I did not raise my hands. I kept holding on to my books until I dropped them when I was knocked to the ground. A lot of state troopers came running over and grabbed me, and the white boys continued to hit me and kick me as the troopers held me.

Three or four of those troopers picked me up and carried me downstairs to the holding room. I didn't try to fight back or anything, and I would have walked down, but they carried me anyway. When we got downstairs, one of the troopers, Badge No. 665, who I have seen lots of times in front of the office, said, "Drop the nigger." They just dropped me on the floor like I was a dog or something. Then the troopers wanted to take my picture, but they didn't tell me what for, and I didn't want them to. I turned my head away and put my new leather coat over my head. One of the troopers who wears shades, whom I have seen lots of times, said something like "Break his arms" and "You grab one arm, I'll hold his other, and we'll break his arms if he won't stand for this picture." They tore my new leather coat even more.

Later a little short man who works in the school office came in and asked me to write a report about this incident. I told him what had happened and he wrote it down. I told him that Mr. Scarsella had seen the whole thing, and that I did not start anything, and that I did not fight back.

Mr. Gorovitch, the assistant headmaster, came in and told me I was suspended for fighting. He told me that I would have to go home, and they took me home in a van.

I have been trying to get along out there at South Boston this year and have not been involved in any trouble until this. Now this white boy John, who also pushed me and wanted to fight me last year, is starting that stuff this year.

The South Boston–Dorchester football game had made head-lines. Behind them was an epic struggle Black athletes had waged to get on the team. Many of them finally lost heart and gave up because of the unswerving discrimination they met. But six stuck it out and, under court pressure, were added to the team in mid-October. Coach Pearson is a Black assistant coach.

After Coach Pearson was added to the football coaching staff, I went out for the football team along with five other Black students. We rode to practice the first day on a separate bus, and we didn't have any pads to practice with. People spit on us during practice and threw rocks at us.

During practice, someone ripped one of the Black student's street pants, and stole my watch.

On Saturday, October 18, it was raining so we had practice inside watching a game film. When we came into the room, there wasn't anything written on the board, but I later saw that someone had written on the board, "Niggers can't take it." The words "Niggers suck" were also written on the board, once in red, once in yellow, once in blue. Coach Pearson pointed this out to the head coach, but the head coach said that that had been there before, and none of his boys would write that, and he left it on the board.

The day of the game at White Stadium was the first day we Black students were given practice equipment. They also had us ride to the game on a separate bus. . . . Black sportscaster Bubba Johnson was crossing the field after the game, but most of the players, Black and white, were over by the buses. Two white men came out of the stands and came after Bubba Johnson, but he flipped one of the white men on the ground. Some of the white players started to jump over the fence and run out onto the field to help the white man. I was standing near the buses and heard Coach Perdigao saying to the players, "Get back on the bus. Just get them in school tomorrow. Get back on the bus. Get 'em in school tomorrow."

I threw my bag of pads at the coach. After that day, three of the six Black players wanted to quit the team.

The testimony shook the judge. Bostonians became acquainted with this contemporary horror show through the newspapers, radio, and television. The Black students held their ground through a week of testimony.

Perhaps the most damaging testimony was that concerning James Scalese, the "monkey teacher" notorious for his imitations of apes. A young Black witness faltered in identifying Scalese (though other students, not called by the attorneys, corroborated his testimony). The legal moves to discredit the initial claims by the student featured rapid-fire questions and an attempt to browbeat the witness.

Ruth Batson fumed. She had been in the school the day of the incident and knew it to be true. She dashed off a letter to Garrity complaining of the mistreatment of the young witness and offered to testify. Garrity declined her offer. However, other Black students persisted in the matter. In their written statements and their oral testimony, they could not be budged.

I was walking with a group of Black students to a meeting we had arranged with the head of the state troopers stationed inside South Boston High. We walked by Tyson's homeroom, and his room teacher, Mr. Scalese, was not going to let him go to the meeting. Clyde told Mr. Scalese about the meeting, and we were starting to walk on down the hall to go to the meeting when I saw Scalese making monkey sounds in front of me. Mr. Scalese was standing in the doorway, making gestures and sounds like a monkey at us. I heard students inside the class behind him laughing and clapping and pounding their desks.

Before the bell had rung for first period classes, I was going to sign in at our classes and then go on to the meeting with the head of the state troopers along with several other Black students. With me were Tyson, Maurice, John, and my brother, Mel. At Tyson's homeroom (room 219, I believe), we encountered his homeroom teacher, Mr. Scalese. Mr. Scalese did not want Tyson to leave his homeroom, and tried to grab him by the arm. Mr. Scalese was standing in the door to his homeroom. I went over to him and was trying to tell him that Black students had a meeting with the state troopers, and that Tyson was needed at that meeting. Mr. Scalese then raised his hand up towards his ribs and armpits and made motions like a monkey. I heard laughter coming from the white students behind him in his homeroom. The four students named above were with me and also witnessed what this teacher did.

The day after the Black student caucus met with Dr. Reid at Lena Park Community Development Center, we had a meeting with the head of the state troopers stationed inside South Boston High School. At homeroom time, before the first period, I went by my homeroom to tell my homeroom teacher, Mr. Scalese, that I was going to this Black caucus meeting. Several of my friends were walking with me, including Maurice, Clyde, and Mel. Mr. Scalese tried to keep me from going to the meeting, and told me I should stay in my homeroom. He even tried to keep me in the room. He came to the door of the homeroom, and Clyde also told him about the meeting we had with the state troopers. I started to walk away with my friend, and heard strange monkey noises behind me, and then I heard the white students back in the class laughing and clapping their hands. I went on to the Black student caucus meeting in the cafeteria with the head of the state troopers.

The cumulative effect of the testimony was overwhelming. William Reid, headmaster of South Boston High School, told Judge Garrity, to the chagrin of the racists, that the Black students' testimony was "basically honest." Said Garrity, "I agree." But even while the Black students were testifying, the racists were on the move.

On November 22 a Boston ROAR contingent swelled the ranks of busing foes who marched five-thousand strong on the Democratic Party National Issues Convention in Louisville. A highlight of the gathering there had been Senator George McGovern's appeal to the "conscience of the Democratic Party" to back desegregation and busing. "I do not," he said, "want a great political party which nearly lost its soul in Vietnam to sell its soul on the issue of busing."

America's "soul" had been saved not by the Democrats, but by the rise of the massive and militant antiwar movement, which had radicalized a generation of young and not-so-young Americans. Drawing the lesson from that, McGovern saw that a soul-selling or capitulation to the racists on Black rights by the Democratic Party and the government could evoke a similar mass movement, based on the nation's Black community.

But the five thousand whites banging on the convention doors were demanding a soul that was already being bartered for antibusing votes by the silence of Kennedy and the campaign statements of George Wallace, Henry Jackson, and Jimmy Carter. And eleven days earlier, the U.S. Supreme Court had agreed to hear the appeal of antibusing forces against the community busing plan in effect in Pasadena.

This was the first time a school board appeal of such a kind had been accepted. Detroit had been the instrument for overturning city-suburb busing. Now, in Pasadena, "unworkability" and "white flight" were the code words accepted by the high court to judge in-city busing. The little city in California was beginning to make big news.

In Boston the Black leadership was closing ranks, demanding that South Boston High School be shut. This was not an admission of "the failure of desegregation," as William Bulger put it, but for most a necessary move because, as Percy Wilson put it, "there is no learning going on there." Adding, "Nor will there be in the near future." The desegregation order simply was not being enforced. South Boston was the racists' stronghold and symbol, "their turf."

Ed Redd, the NAACP's young executive secretary, concurred. "As long as the school stays open, it will be a symbol of resistance. . . . We are not going to allow Black kids to be subject to the jeers, the stares, the violence, and the harassment." Regardless of the outcome, Redd said, the hearings were "a victory in themselves . . . they got the truth out . . . there will be more attention paid to it [the school] and this will make things improve."

Ruth Batson saw the hearings as a way to make an example of South Boston. It had to live under the law of the land. There was no exemption for it. "Black kids would be kidding themselves if they saw it as a victory, 'Whew! We finally got out of South Boston.' But they would just get slammed if they ever crossed the threshold of that neighborhood again." And that threshold had to be kept open. She was for receivership, clearing out the school administration, and, more, stripping the school committee of all authority.

Ellen Jackson was tugged back and forth by the testimony. One day she was for receivership, the next for closing the school. It all depended on *how* the decision would be interpreted. She told a Coordinated Social Services Council meeting that the last thing she wanted was a view that closing the school meant the plan was not working. Otherwise, she said, the school should be closed.

NSCAR favored the closing of the school, but uncomfortably and with reservations. "We do not want to be in this situation," Maceo Dixon said. "But because of the criminal default of the city, state, and federal officials, the racists, both inside and outside the school, have been able to wage a relentless campaign with one goal: to keep 'Southie' open and *all white* by driving the Black students out." As NSCAR saw it, the crucial question was solidarity with Black students. "Until those students can go in safety to *their school* and be guaranteed a decent education there, that school should be closed down tight."

For Dixon, the key was not the neighborhood mentality but the absence of action in defense of school desegregation throughout the fall. Such pressure had not been kept up. The initiative belonged to the antibusing resistance, which had revived and, in so doing, had been boosted by national events, presidential candidates, and congressional action against desegregation. The situation in South Boston now was the bitter fruit of the racists' offensive, which, he felt, had not been adequately answered.

Judge Garrity spent two weeks drawing up his order. Twice he made unannounced visits to South Boston High School. He did not like what he saw. South Boston awaited his order with fear and a mounting readiness to act. Besides Louise Day Hicks's predictions of community opposition, carefully phrased for public consumption, and William Bulger's bolder formulations, there were such fulminations as those of Dan Yotts.

Yotts is one of the hotheads, a South Boston racist leader from "the grass roots." He and his wife, Nancy, managed the information center and are insiders in the machine to which the mothers' marches, the marshals, and the fanatical calls to action can be traced. Yotts writes a column for the *South Boston Tribune*, a neighborhood weekly. Days before Judge Garrity issued his order, Yotts was beating the drum in his "South Boston Information Center News" column. "Well, old gorilla-face Atkins is at it again in trying to stir up the chowder. Close Southie High, that's what mummy is spouting off. Well, if Garrity closes Southie and Atkins is not wiped out and NAACP headquarters with him, I'm going to be the most surprised and disappointed guy in Southie."

On December 9 Garrity announced his decision, a sweeping order that went far beyond the school building on G Street. That high school was placed under direct federal control. Headmaster Reid was relieved of his post, not for any wrongdoing, Garrity said, praising the beleaguered headmaster, but because a new administration had to be started. School Superintendent Marion Fahey was appointed Judge Garrity's receiver. The racist football coach, Arthur Perdigao, was transferred. Furthermore, Garrity stripped the Boston School Committee of authority in two key areas—desegregation implementation and school security—extending Fahey's authority as receiver to control of both.

Shock waves ran through the city. "We have been federalized!" Hicks burst out. That night, printed posters were plastered across the city: "Remember Black Tuesday" (the day of receivership—the day, Hicks would say, we lost Boston). That night, four white men in a car without license plates tossed a firebomb into the NAACP headquarters, shattering glass and destroying files. That night, the home of Black minister James Coleman was firebombed, bomb threats compelled evacuation of the National Center for Afro-American Artists, and bomb threats were telephoned to the home of Elma Lewis, director of the center. A wave of terrorism was reaching into Roxbury.

In anticipation of the Garrity decision, the South Boston Marshals had called upon a veteran for advice. Ku Klux Klan Grand Dragon David Duke came back to Boston, this time by invitation. He would stay for a month.

On December 12 a "spontaneous" stall-in on expressways and

bridges tied up early-morning rush hour traffic for an hour and a half. ROAR, disclaiming responsibility, called the action "heart-warming." The Klan claimed responsibility for several of the traffic snarls. No arrests.

That was the beginning of the "Day of Mourning" called by ROAR. White students stayed home from school in massive numbers in South Boston and in Charlestown, where, local antibusing leaders felt, Garrity's eyes would next be fixed. In South Boston two hundred bigots attempted to rush a school bus but were repulsed by police. That evening near midnight they returned, smashed through police lines, and occupied the school. They vandalized it, an act especially ironic because an incidental item in Garrity's receivership order was for a $120,000 repair project to improve school facilities. A police car was burned. The occupation lasted two hours; then the racists went home. An anonymously circulated leaflet fluttered in the nighttime breeze. "Our protest must take many forms," it read. "Some forms of protest will not be agreeable to everyone, but *protest we must!*"

The receivership decision was based on precedent. In the Jim Crow South a federal district judge had taken control of the entire Taliaferro, Georgia, school system when the local school board refused to desegregate. In addition Garrity applied constitutional guarantees for protection of the Black students *inside the school*, where, he ruled, their Fourteenth Amendment rights had been denied.

Thomas Atkins cautiously hailed the decision as giving South Boston "a chance to return to the educational fold." Further noncompliance by the school committee should merit their being "quarantined." As for the bombing of the Boston NAACP's headquarters, which had suddenly shifted attention away from the receivership decision itself, Atkins declared vigilante assaults would "not stop the NAACP from continuing to provide the service which has been our principal aim." Expressing his personal contempt for the racists and their violence, Atkins almost casually dismissed the bombing; his real outrage was over their courtroom attempts to overturn a law he considered almost sacred.

The CSSC meeting that morning rapidly turned to the bombing. It was felt that a response was needed. An emergency news conference was set for three hours later, and the press jammed the room. Ellen Jackson was angry. "We serve notice," she said, "that attacks on the Black community will not be tolerated." She read Dan Yotts's column aloud and demanded a Justice Department and FBI investigation.

"The question is now out in the open," Percy Wilson said. "To what extent are Boston's leaders and decision-makers going to allow themselves to be intimidated by a relatively small band of violators of the law and arch foes of the democratic process?"

Elma Lewis, an eminent older Black leader, spoke in a hushed voice. "We remember the South," she said, "and now, they come into our community. You know, we are a law-abiding community. We revere education, and we send our children into the jaws of death to get it. But this we will not allow."

Maceo Dixon termed the court order "a blow to the forces of racism and reaction who have played havoc with the lives of Black youth." Yet implementation remained the critical issue, and many were now worried about Marion Fahey as the receiver. "It was the public rage and anger of the Black community over the crude, racist treatment of its youth that compelled Judge Garrity to enforce the law of the land . . . even in South Boston," Dixon said.

Indeed, the pluck and pride of the Black students as they testified had exerted a great moral power. Backing that up was the feeling of the Black community, summed up in the words of the students who said and proved that "no one is going to drive us out."

The *Boston Globe* editorially backed the order, along with the *New York Times,* the authoritative voice for important sectors of the nation's most powerful circles. Though it was a hard blow to the racists, the order had contradictory effects. The toll being exacted by the racist resistance was staggering the city: to guard even the rudiments of the court's authority, Garrity had been compelled to impose federal control over a high school and some administrative functions of the school committee. To be sure, Phase II—except for seven schools in the system (those in South Boston, Charlestown, and Hyde Park High School)—was operating fairly well. Previous trouble spots, like Roslindale High School, had appreciably quieted. Education was going on in the decisive majority of the schools, a fact confirmed by Black and white parents alike. But in key areas, resistance was real and unyielding. It was encouraged by elected officials ranging from glorified ward heelers such as Palladino straight to Hicks, Mayor White, and President Ford.

Every federal judge in the country was watching Boston. What

Garrity had been forced to do in the attempt to enforce his sweeping desegregation order would not encourage a judicial readiness to move swiftly and sharply against racial discrimination through massive busing plans. This was especially true given the national mood—confusion about and opposition to busing. That mood had spread largely because there was no effective counterpressure, no organized mobilization demanding the enforcement of desegregation.

How important this last aspect was would be demonstrated with alarming clarity by the year about to begin.

# 18

# The Bigots
# Escalate the Violence

The January school opening was marked by about fifty walkouts by white students in Charlestown and South Boston. Again there were no suspensions.

On the evening of January 5, two hundred in South Boston braved subfreezing weather to march against desegregation. The offices of the school committee that day had been jammed with well-wishers, who chanted, "Here we go, Pixie, here we go," as Palladino, sporting a fake diamond tiara spelling "Stop Forced Busing," was sworn in. She replaced Kerrigan, the newest member of the Boston City Council, which had elected Louise Day Hicks as its president. Hicks's opening address sounded the latest theme of obstruction. Busing was "bankrupting" the city, and city employees might face "payless" paydays. This was a ploy that reelected Mayor White later adopted.

Events moved fast. On January 8, sixty-two Black students at South Boston High School were suspended for refusing to enter the building. They were protesting the immunity accorded to the white student walkouts. On January 13, South Boston High School's Puerto Rican students started a boycott to demand transfers to Roxbury High School, where there was a more ample bilingual program. In South Boston some twenty Spanish-speaking students had been jammed into one multigrade class, which was taught by a white, "bilingual" teacher in all major subjects. They had been forbidden to speak Spanish in the school.

On January 14 the First Circuit Court of Appeals issued an unusually sharp rejection of the antibusing appeals filed by the mayor, the school committee, and the Home and School Association, all seeking to overturn Phase II. The school committee was termed "intransigent and obstructionist." "These elected officials engaged in a pattern of resistance, defiance and delay," the three-judge panel declared, explicitly rejecting the contention that "white flight" was a bona fide argument for restricting desegregation. All the rebuffed attempts were promptly reappealed to the U.S. Supreme Court.

Alabama Governor George Wallace had come to Boston in his campaign for the presidential nomination. He spoke to packed suburban rallies and later in South Boston. On the night of January 9, he attracted devotees to the Statler Hilton Hotel. Wallace carefully avoided use of the word "busing." The Alabama demagogue didn't want to create a ruckus with over-inflammatory speeches. "I left the city cool," he would tell reporters.

But the revelers who packed the Statler Hilton ballroom—many of them making the trek from South Boston on school buses rented for the evening—roared agreement when he lambasted "tyrannical federal judges." It was an antibusing rally, with Palladino and Dapper O'Neill on the stage. Wallace didn't have to spell it out for the crowd; they knew where he stood.

As the third week of classes started, the racists launched a three-front attack within the schools. On January 20, 21, and 22, East Boston High School erupted in walkouts led by the white student caucus, protesting the coming desegregation plans that would make the all-white school a citywide "magnet" technical school in the fall of 1976. Boisterous, combative students, sometimes accompanied by parents, surged into the streets, blocking cars and fighting police in hundreds of skirmishes. They massed at tunnel exits and overturned automobiles.

On January 19, rumors began to fly through Hyde Park High School that a Black student had burned an American flag in the auditorium. Word went out that the incident called for retaliation. The message circulated through the school all afternoon. "'The niggers are going to get it,' that was what we heard," Black student leader Bernice Williams recalled.

The next day brawls broke out as white students prowled the corridors in the school. They were organized. The year before, the white toughs had used whistles, a tactic learned from allies in South Boston. This year a white leader, whom the Black students called "the king," simply shouted "niggers!" and his followers would come running. "We knew something was coming after the flag-burning," Williams said. "Those white students were just looking for something to start it off."

Black student leaders had arranged a meeting with Hyde Park headmaster John Best, who resembled former South Boston

High headmaster William M. Reid in his frustration, cynicism, and do-nothing attitude. As the meeting began, fights erupted in the hall. The Black students rushed from the meeting to reinforce their already embattled fellows. The school was in an uproar as hundreds brawled.

White parents made their way into the building. "I saw these parents come into the school and fight and beat up Blacks. South Boston students came in the front door. Even some Black parents got beat up by them. That stuff never made it on television," Bernice Williams said, recounting the conflict. Williams herself had been assaulted by ten whites and had fled into a phone for protection.

"The Black girls got it bad," according to Yvonne Fauntroy. The melee featured attacks on young Black women, many of whom were leaders of the students. "But we fought back too," she said.

Some of the assailants ran outside and came back with pipes and bats. Others emerged from the school shop—an area maintained as their private turf by white students—with hammers and razors. Some students had ice-pack bags full of rocks. The fighting was spectacular, spilling onto the school grounds, as Black and white students escaped the building by smashing out windows. The tiny police force was unable—and unwilling—to stop the rioting. One hundred racists rocked a school bus packed with Black students.

The police made eight arrests—all of white students—an index of the character of the violence. Later, Black students were collared in the school as white students pointed them out.

"We've got to get organized like those white students," Fauntroy concluded afterwards. "We fought to get into Hyde Park, and no one's going to drive us out." She was arrested upon her return to school, as the reprisals began.

Within hours of the riot, the bigots were on television. Hyde Park ROAR pulled together a news conference which featured the white students, some theatrically bandaged, others tearfully recounting their version of the events. Hicks declared the "Black attack" had been "premeditated." "One hundred armed Blacks [had] taken over the school," she proclaimed. The school committee hastily called an "open hearing" on the violence, highlighted by white student testimony before television cameras.

Palladino had been at Hyde Park High School that morning.

Two days later, on January 22, she arrived at Charlestown High School. It was set to go off. The fracas was carefully planned. After walking out of their classes, white student caucus members had, as one police observer put it, "run amok." One bunch went after a Black teacher, who fought them off—"he assaulted us" would be the claim. Then came a clash with police in the school. The Black students sat tight. The day ended with a two-hour sit-in near the front doors and the singing of "God Bless America."

Hyde Park High was closed. Charlestown was as tense as it had been since the opening of school in the fall. East Boston's racists had served notice with a stunning blitz of the city accompanied by a stupendous volume of propaganda.

On January 26, reduced attendance and increased police surveillance marked the cold, drizzling reopening of Hyde Park High School. In Charlestown, the white student caucus members began their day by throwing books at school administrators. They then proceeded to the "wrong" classes, disrupting them. When asked by school officials to leave, they scuffled with police, then walked out.

The young bigots marched to Boston City Hall. Near its rear entrance they spotted a Black man. Snowballs and epithets filled the air. Nearby police interceded. A white city worker reprimanded the teen-agers. They jumped and beat him before he could escape, all within police view. No arrests.

Then they trooped up to the city council chambers where Hicks, banning reporters, served them hot chocolate, doughnuts, and coffee. "They acted like perfect ladies and gentlemen in council chambers," Hicks told reporters, dodging their questions about the scuffles and attacks outside. The students left the chambers interspersing chants—"Here we go Townies, here we go!"—with their favorite hymn—"God bless America, land that I love. . . ." Then they jaunted to the school committee offices and finally home after a hard day's work.

Meanwhile in other areas of the country, the issue of desegregation was also coming to the fore. A two-year-old suit of the Cleveland NAACP had finally reached federal district court, where a hearing had been under way for two months. On January 15, two thousand Black and white marchers mobilized in Louisville at the call of the NAACP and the SCLC to commemorate the birthday of Martin Luther King. A major theme of the rally was support for busing.

In Detroit the watered-down "desegregation" plan, already under appeal by the Detroit NAACP, had begun peacefully on January 26. Strong representations had been made by Black leaders and organizations, led by the NAACP and Detroit SCAR, for safe passage for the Blacks. An antibusing motorcade of two hundred fifty cars, called by Mothers Alert Detroit (MAD), and a one-day boycott were all the bigots could muster.

In Milwaukee on January 19, after more than ten years of litigation, Federal District Judge John Reynolds ruled that an NAACP suit filed on behalf of Black and white parents was correct in its assertion that the city's schools were unconstitutionally segregated. The struggle for equal rights that had surged to a high point in the early 1960s with pickets, protests, marches, and a school boycott of more than twelve thousand had subsided in the intervening years. Now, after a slow, grinding court process, the battle was on the agenda again.

Yet, as these new battlegrounds emerged in city after city and court after court, Boston remained the national center of the storm. While the receivership order was keeping a lid on South Boston High School, the fires had fanned outward. And the fact that almost all thirty students suspended for a corridor battle on January 26 in that school were Black showed that, even in receivership, disciplinary action was still far from even-handed.

Ruby Bradley had seven children, and several of them went to Hyde Park High School. Though the reports they brought back were terrifying, she was determined that they should continue there. She was a welfare mother, unable to read or write, and her kids were going to get an education—regardless. The family had moved in early January to a newly refurbished apartment in Dorchester. Then, the racists decorated it. This was in white Dorchester, several blocks from the border of the Black community. It was one of those segregated neighborhoods that John Kerrigan and Louise Day Hicks had cited in passing as the cause of the peculiarly rigid racial composition of Boston's schools. The Bradley family would become an object lesson on the cost of attempting to desegregate such neighborhoods.

The welcome began with gangs of youth, ranging in age from eight to twenty, storming the house, smashing windows, and shrieking racist epithets. Landlord George Lincoln, a gruff-voiced white man who had come to detest the bigots, replaced the broken panes, more than sixty in all, as fast as they were shattered. Fires were set. The doors would be pounded on late at night.

News of the Bradleys' plight reached the Boston SCAR chapter, which called an emergency news conference. ROAR had been involved, at least through a neighbor of the Bradleys who had threatened to choke sixteen-year-old Anna Bradley.

None of the Bradley children had ventured out of the house to go to school. The police would cruise the area briefly, after frantic phone calls to them, and then leave without making arrests. On January 27 the house was firebombed. At the news conference, two days later, Ruby Bradley broke into tears and nearly fainted. "They threw bricks at the house, they climbed on the porch threatening us, saying, 'We're going to kill you niggers if you don't get out of here,'" she sobbed.

The room was hushed, the reporters asking their questions softly of the children. They also questioned State Representative Melvin King, George Lincoln, and SCAR leader Hattie McCutcheon, who participated in the conference. The Bradleys' plight was featured that night on television and on subsequent days in front-page articles in the *Boston Globe*.

The Bradleys' landlord, George Lincoln, looked so much like Southie that his presence at the news conference startled some reporters. He supported busing, but thought housing was the bigger issue. He was not political in the strict sense of the word, just gritty, moral, and angry. "You know," he would say later, "I want to see the protest grow in intensity and focus in on the bigotry in this city, on the tyranny against Blacks. I want to see us follow up and get the criminals and scream out our lungs about the constitutional rights of Blacks that are being violated. . . . The U.S. government has federal troops all over the world—in Korea and Germany and Japan. Well, I think we ought to have federal troops in Boston. . . . People have to get off their butts, you know. When Ruby Bradley isn't allowed to live where she wants to, when she is driven out, then all of our civil rights are on the chopping block."

The terror crushed the family. They had even been stoned in the taxicab that picked them up for the news conference. They finally moved, driven out of white Dorchester. There were hundreds of Ruby Bradleys in Boston.

On January 30, five hundred East Boston High School students suddenly stormed out of school, with one hundred marching on to the city council chambers in downtown Boston. Exuberant, spirited, they rushed into the building, smashing out a door. The

NSCAR news conference with Bradleys. Center, Mrs. Bradley and two of her daughters; left, George Lincoln; right, Hattie McCutcheon and Melvin King.

Boston NAACP headquarters, December 11, 1975.

day before, the Charlestown students, who had been "ladies and gentlemen" in the chambers on January 26, had finished their three-day suspension and returned to classes. They pledged not to speak, open a book, or raise their hands. The next day fights broke out. The "lulls" were now lasting only twenty-four hours.

On February 1, Marion Fahey, the federal receiver, committed the sin of sins in the *Boston Herald American*. She named Louise Day Hicks as a principal cause of tension in the schools, blaming "radical antibusing groups"—an unsubtle reference to ROAR—for fomenting recent disturbances. Further, she praised Garrity, a man "much maligned." Coming from Marion Fahey, a home-grown Irish grade-school teacher, a school department functionary and protege of Kerrigan, her precisely worded statement was blasphemy.

ROAR was incensed. One hundred fifty members jammed into the school committee offices, bombarding her with demands for resignation. How could she attack Louise? How could she blame ROAR? And praise Garrity!

As the Fahey affair raged, ROAR was preparing to live up to its reputation. February 3 had been set by the court-appointed Citywide Coordinating Council for community district hearings. These parents' gatherings were supposed to assess the first semester of Phase II and suggest modifications and changes for the fall.

At City Hall, ROAR members challenged the South Boston–Roxbury district hearing which was taking place there. Chanting and singing "God Bless America," the bigots broke up the meeting, beginning with a boisterous recitation of the "Pledge of Allegiance." Panel members were shouted down with death threats. A white woman from South Boston who attended the meeting to participate in it found the windows of her car smashed that night at home.

In East Boston the large hearing at the high school was swelled by several hundred ROAR disrupters waving signs and placards. They booed and whistled down parents attempting to comply with the order. "You're all a bunch of communists," Palladino shouted at the panelists, and her claque ate it up. Though this wrecking of parent involvement in the plan was a direct affront to Garrity, he preserved his silence.

On February 4 the school committee certified South Boston Heights Academy, which had been set up to circumvent the busing plan. The week before, a similar private school had been accredited in West Roxbury. Others in Hyde Park and East Boston would shortly follow.

Against this backdrop of renewed resistance, the White administration escalated its fiscal scare campaign. The city, said the mayor, was going broke, with no money to bail out the school department, whose deficit was caused "by desegregation." Schools might have to close early. Class size, slightly shrunk by the white boycott, required teacher layoffs to save money.

On January 27 Garrity had rebuked White for his "sabre rattling." "The constitutional rights of pupils, Black and white, are not going to take second place to routine expenditures," he had said. Then on February 3, in the wake of the mayor's "austerity" campaign, Garrity relented, approving seven to eight million dollars in cutbacks, including layoffs.

The reason for the expanding costs for the schools—twenty million dollars above those predicted—was, however, attributable to the White administration. By mollycoddling the racists, wheeling and dealing with them, encouraging resistance through court appeals, the mayor had fanned the flames of defiance. Huge police expenses had been the price of such a tactic. Now the antibusing Democrat was casting the blame on the Black community, specifying desegregation as the source of the money crunch.

Teacher layoffs jeopardized the status of newly hired Black teachers as well as other personnel directly involved in implementation of the order—bus monitors, teacher's aides, etc. Judge Garrity himself appeared to be waffling. While approving the initial cutbacks, he noted that he saw the school committee performing in a "round-the-clock effort for compliance" with the order, a statement which stunned desegregation supporters. His untimely compliment boded ill for the busing process.

By this time the Coordinated Social Services Council meetings had come to occupy an increasingly important place in the monitoring of desegregation. At them Maceo Dixon and Mac Warren had pressed discussions on the need for action—for, as they put it, "another May 17"—to check the growing offensive of the antibusing forces.

The violence had come close to home for Dixon. On the evening of February 6, his wife, Reba Williams, a staff member of NSCAR, had been attacked by three whites near their apartment on the edge of Roxbury. The next evening both of them had been insulted and threatened by a carload of bigots.

Ellen Jackson, Ruth Batson, and Dixon had decided after hours of discussion that a letter should be sent to Black leaders across the country seeking support for a national demonstration in Boston. CSSC meetings themselves, averaging forty to fifty in attendance, represented a cross section of Boston's Black community. Jackson and Batson were regularly present and were joined at times by such figures as Percy Wilson and Ed Redd. Ministers, community activists, parents, and teacher's aides also attended. As events buffeted the Black community, the CSSC's readiness to act rose. News conferences, letters, and appeals were all good and necessary, but now, it was felt, something more demonstrative—a massive action—was called for.

"The future of school desegregation in this city is in jeopardy," Jackson, Batson, and Dixon wrote. "We have come to the conclusion that what is critically needed today is a broad and massive movement to respond to the violent attacks of ROAR and other opponents of Black rights. . . .

"We view Boston as the center of the national desegregation struggle. And there is no question about the fact that this is how the national antibusing movement views this city as well. A failure to win school desegregation here will encourage further attacks on Black rights in cities across the country." The letter urged that messages of support for a national demonstration be sent to NSCAR and the Freedom House.

Nationally, NSCAR was involved in a broad range of activities, and it had been planned that its next national steering committee meeting would be held in New York City, the center of the nationwide student struggle against cutbacks in education. But the ominous developments in the desegregation struggle in Boston prompted an emergency rescheduling of that meeting to the latter city.

This NSCAR steering committee meeting, bringing in activists from coast to coast, would be the best place to launch a national drive to win support for the proposal, its sponsors felt. Meanwhile the Boston SCAR chapter would continue discussions on the idea with community leaders.

The joint decision, which created a key nucleus of support soon to include Percy Wilson, had not come too soon. The racists were preparing to up the ante. The South Boston Information Center had called a news conference, at which James Kelly told how the antibusing movement was prepared to "lash out" at the desegregation order.

Short, prematurely balding, and somewhat portly, he looked almost pleasant in a calm moment. Kelly was one of the new breed of racist leaders. He lacked Hicks's skill at syrupy goodwill which barely hid her contempt for Blacks. Nor could he match Kerrigan's strutting arrogance. Kelly had not functioned in the spotlight of the antibusing officialdom. He had moved to the fore as resistance came to mean something more than filing briefs, legal stalling tactics, and administrative evasions. Jimmy Kelly led the neighborhood from the streets. He was one of the tough, rugged bigots, who was familiar, more than one authoritative source had it, with the underside of South Boston life. The bars, the clubs, the all-white unions were his domain.

This combat veteran was ever present with the white student caucus ruffians, organizing this or that demonstration, calling the shots, taking orders from Hicks but making his own blunt statements. "Jimmy Kelly runs Louise," a longtime desegregation partisan once said privately. "She doesn't do anything without him." The reporters grimly endured Hicks, as they sat through her lofty, pained expressions of grief over the loss of Boston to the "judicial tyrants" and "social engineers." But Kelly pulled no punches. If you weren't against forced busing, you were for it and were the enemy.

Although draped in the semirespectability of the Home and School Association presidency, Kelly was more suspect as the leader of the shadowy information center. Now, with the court appeals having failed, with Phase II sinking in, and with the hated receivership order in effect, Jimmy Kelly was taking the gloves off. "We're being backed into a corner," he told the media on February 10. "We're not going to cower from Garrity. The only way Blacks in this country got reverse discrimination is that they went to the streets." And he added, "It could be a long, hot summer." Two days later the "lashing out" began.

The English High School auditorium was the setting for another CCC-called hearing, this one for parents whose children attended "magnet schools." Their children went to those schools through choice, and the parents would come to the meeting on the same basis. The district involved was the whole city, not such limited areas as those that paired an all-white community and an all-Black one. Nevertheless, because of the disruption of the two previous CCC hearings, police, FBI agents, and Justice Department officials were on hand.

The ROAR cadre had come early, many of them on school

buses—with police escorts—from South Boston and East Boston. Nearly two hundred of them circulated among the parents, taking seats throughout the auditorium. As the meeting began, a din rose from the disrupters. First they sang "God Bless America," eerily stopping the proceedings. The faces of the parents, many of them Black, froze. After more booing, hissing, shouting, the chairman of the panel pleaded for quiet, offering the ROAR members speaking time. But they were not there to talk. Parents attempted to rebuke them. More boos and shouts, as ROAR organizers patrolled the aisles, threatening outspoken parents. Then a strange buzzing sound rose through the uproar. Heads turned. ROAR members were fanning sheets of paper across the teeth of Afro combs. The tumult increased. ROAR members seized the floor microphones, berating the crowd, blasting Judge Garrity, busing, desegregation.

The meeting was suspended. The panelists moved off the stage as Palladino, grinning wildly and shouting, mounted it, waving her arms as she led her cohorts in chants and songs. The hoopla continued as police escorted the parents out, leaving the racists to themselves. An hour later they too had gone, but not before tearing up the auditorium, smashing windows, smearing racist epithets and obscenities on the walls, and vandalizing a bathroom in the majority-Black school.

That evening, in Charlestown, individuals earlier seen at the English High School disruption were identified as they jeered Senator Henry Jackson off the stage. Jackson, one of the Democratic Party's leading antibusers, was viewed as "insincere" by ROAR, many of whose rank-and-file activists supported Wallace in the presidential primary race. Jackson was regarded as a johnny-come-lately on the antibusing bandwagon; he had to be taught a lesson.

As the catcalls began, Jackson was stunned. "Are you trying to be funny?" he asked the crowd. They were not. Jackson was hustled off the stage by Secret Service agents.

These disruptions were big news in the city. But, as before, Garrity was silent about the bold attempt to sabotage his order.

As ROAR broke up the meetings across town, the family of Otis and Alva Debnam, joined by half a dozen friends in their Dorchester home, was keeping watch for vigilantes. For two weeks their windows had been smashed out. Gangs threatened the children. An elderly white who lived on the first floor had been stricken with a heart attack when a bottle shattered his bedroom window. The Debnams are Black. They had chased the hooligans off their porch, receiving little cooperation from the police. Boston knew about the Debnams because Gary Armstrong, a Black reporter from WNAC television, had pursued the story.

Sunday, February 15, was to be an early Father's Day in South Boston. This time the men would march. The antibusing demonstration, called by the highly secretive South Boston Marshals Association, was designed to show that "the men" were stepping forward, assuming leadership of the antibusing movement from the women whose "mothers' marches" had been so publicized in the fall.

The march looked like a military maneuver as scores of South Boston Marshals roamed the crowd with walkie-talkies. It was a bristling, beer-drinking throng, some of the men already drunk. The TPF kept its distance until the marchers attempted to move up G Street to the high school. The anticipated trouble broke out when the racists surged against the police lines. The marchers were armed with bats, sawed-off hockey sticks, golf clubs, tire irons, rocks, and bottles.

Refusing to be pushed back on G Street, the marchers menaced the police. A tear gas cannister flew from the ranks of the racists. Shoving and pushing escalated into hand-to-hand combat. For some of the marchers this was a long-awaited moment of vengeance. The battle royal lasted for two hours. The police had been less prepared for the fray than the rioters and waited in some instances up to half an hour for tear gas ammunition. The locals knew the winding streets, the alleyways, and by walkie-talkies they tipped off the various sections about police movements. The police pummeled marchers and bystanders. The whole G Street area became a zone of guerrilla warfare.

When the gas cleared, seventy-four police had sustained injuries. "We showed the TPF today," one local boasted, and indeed the marshals' march had given the cops a beating. Thirteen arrests were made. Their addresses were in South Boston, East Boston, Dorchester, and Charlestown.

The fighting was not confined to South Boston. It was Sunday and the school had been empty of Black students. So the real target was missing. Victims were found elsewhere.

Gary Gordon, a Black student leader from Tufts University in Medford, was waiting for a subway train at North Station that afternoon with a woman companion. They were going to see "The River Niger" at a Boston theatre. They were alone on the platform. About twenty young whites rushed off the escalator, hot for a fight. Gordon pushed his companion away, telling her to run. She escaped. Gordon was chased into a corner, beaten to the ground with golf clubs, table legs, and kicks. They left him in a heap, dazed. Moments later, his friend returned with city and transit police, who argued over jurisdiction. They had heard of the gang, which had moments earlier attacked a middle-aged Black man on a train.

No one knows how many other Blacks—waiting at subway and bus stops, riding the trains, watching television in living rooms in border areas, or walking the streets—had been assaulted. That week radio station WILD was flooded with calls. Attacks in Codman Square, near Roxbury, in Uphams Corner, a "division" area in Dorchester, in Hyde Park, at supermarkets. "People try to run me down with shopping carts," a Black parent anxiously complained at a CSSC meeting. Blacks were afraid to go downtown. Terror was on the loose in the city.

The next night in Charlestown, there was a small riot, with two hundred hooligans charging and fighting police, lighting bonfires, and smashing windows in the high school. A white reporter for the *Boston Globe* was seized and beaten.

Police Commissioner Robert diGrazia was incensed. On February 16, he announced a new, "get tough" stance. The low profile "policy of tolerance" was over. "A violent few," he said, had organized "a conspiracy against public order." He went on: "It may take five hundred or one thousand police officers in South Boston, but this violence will stop." The racists, undeterred, announced that another men's march would be held February 29, "whether we get a permit or not."

The three hundred NSCAR leaders, many from other cities, who gathered at Boston University on February 21 for the emergency steering committee meeting had trouble at first in comprehending that organized groups of white racists, often armed with clubs and similar weapons, could challenge the Boston police. But before the business matters on the agenda were taken up, victims of the terror gave first-hand accounts— Hyde Park High School student Melissa Wilson, Reba Williams of

NSCAR, and Lloyd Daniels, the assistant director of the Citywide Education Coalition, who had been at the English High School disruption—and the foreboding landscape of a city on the edge of confrontation became clear.

"NSCAR," Ruth Batson told the gathering, "has filled a void in this city. I speak for many people with whom I work." She noted how "absolutely essential this organization has been to those of us who have been working in the desegregation crisis." That role would become greater in the succeeding weeks, as the activists returned home to gather support for the national action.

While awaiting confirmation of the specific date of the action, NSCAR projected a series of national events for April 3 and 4; the latter day, a Sunday, would be the ninth anniversary of the assassination of Dr. King. The theme: "March for what Dr. King died for."

In the CSSC, Dixon had become the advisor on matters concerning the proposed action. He and Ellen Jackson canvassed a variety of community leaders and agency heads for their backing of the march. "This has to be a community effort," Percy Wilson advised, "and very disciplined." He was alluding to the December 14 confusion and the provocations by ultralefts at Carson Beach. "No one should get their ass caught on a limb. Folk are wary of demonstrations since Carson Beach."

On February 23 Mayor White issued a permit to the South Boston Marshals for their threatened march and acceded to their demand that the only police present be locally assigned beat cops—no TPF. White had refrained from comment on the February 15 riot—a deafening silence that many interpreted as a rebuke to Police Commissioner diGrazia, undercutting his warning to the organizers of the melee.

White's deepening public sympathy with the bigots paralleled his stepped-up efforts to make the city's financial difficulties into a battering ram against the Garrity order. His statements that desegregation-related spending was the cause of a cutback of 615 city jobs brought thousands of city workers into the streets on February 19.

The demonstration was called by the local affiliate of the American Federation of State, County and Municipal Employees (AFSCME) which represented the bulk of such workers. The demonstration reeked of antibusing politics. The composition of the work force was 96 percent white in a city more than 25 percent Black and Puerto Rican. In Boston segregation and patronage in city employment went hand in hand; civil service was a white job trust, politically subservient to antibusing officials on a neighborhood and citywide level. Dapper O'Neill got the biggest cheers at the rally. Later, city council member John Kerrigan promised his full backing to the city employees if they organized "a general strike against forced busing."

White's was a deadly ploy. City debts over and above technical and security costs for a decade-delayed desegregation order flowed from the same sources as the financial crises developing in other American cities. Interest payments alone to the ruling rich of Boston—the banks and corporations which held its tax-free bonds—amounted to nearly $50 million a year. The burden imposed by the hundreds of millions of dollars Boston citizens paid out in taxes for the multi-billion-dollar federal war budget was never considered by the mayor in assessing the roots of the financial crisis.

The cost of school segregation so long forced upon Black youth, the cost of segregation in housing and employment, the price of the most minimal remedying of blatant institutional racism—were all made secondary in the anti-Black demagogy of a mayor looking for a way to gut the Garrity order. The blame was all put on busing.

Notwithstanding the ferment of antibusing activity, ROAR was beginning to be torn by long submerged disputes. On February 25 the split was publicly consummated: Hicks Loyalists vs. Palladino "rebels." In addition to the city council president's long-standing resentment of rivals who attained prominence, she and the East Boston ROAR leader differed over presidential nominees. Hicks supported Henry Jackson, Palladino backed Wallace. Hicks had disregarded the vote at a ROAR meeting against support for a Senate bill sponsored by Jackson to provide federal funds to compensate Boston for busing expenses. Palladino opposed the measure, terming it tantamount to accepting desegregation. Hicks, however, controlled the secret ROAR executive board; Palladino was purged. The fractious contest resulted in the discontinuance of ROAR meetings in the city council chambers.

Palladino, nominally backed by Kerrigan and O'Neill, formed ROAR United, while Hicks, retaining her base in South Boston, Charlestown, and Hyde Park, led the formation of ROAR, Inc. Though the organizational split reflected a combination of political disagreements and personal clashes, there was no fundamental difference between the two groupings. Palladino was no stranger to inflammatory rhetoric; Hicks maintained the loyalty of hardened partisans of violence like James Kelly and the South Boston Marshals. Overshadowing their disputes was their common opposition to Black rights.

On February 29 two thousand racists took to the streets in South Boston, continuing their monopoly of action, in the second "men's march." This one was peaceful, a model of decorum. The leaders of the antibusing movement were not without tactical sense. On February 15 they had vented the wrath of their ranks, bloodying the cops. Now they would behave in an attempt to prove that they had been victimized two weeks earlier.

Fifteen hundred men trooped up G Street to the cheers and applause of five hundred women. They marched behind a color guard of the South Boston Marshals bearing ROAR, American, and Confederate flags. The speeches were militant, the crowd orderly. The word was out, as one marshal told a group of eleven-year-olds who had drawn a bead on a local cameraman. "No bullshit today," he warned, taking a small bat from one of them. The speakers were all men—the pols, the locals—all banging away at busing and urging a big vote in the presidential primary, now three days away. Senator William Bulger was in form. "Resist," he had shouted, "fight, no matter what form the fight takes."

ROAR's James Kelly stole the show. The Black community, he explained, "is a culture with a serious drug problem. It's a culture full of handbag snatchers. It's a culture full of flag burners and a culture that spouts a Black national anthem." A few shouts went up, clear and audible, "niggers, niggers." "We cannot accept that culture," he shouted as the crowd burst into cheers, "we will never accept that culture." These words were not reported by Boston's major media.

ROAR had announced a march on Washington for April 24, with the Louisville United Labor Against Busing taking primary responsibility for it. With the men's march considered a success, the racists would now go to the primary polls and send a message to America. Then they would march again.

Ellen Jackson termed the March 2 presidential primary "deadly—there is no one for us." Indeed, while Henry Jackson and George Wallace openly courted the antibusing vote, all of the Democratic liberals—Birch Bayh, Fred Harris, Morris Udall, and Sargent Shriver—had steered clear of the issue. If they mentioned it at all, busing was a "last resort," "unfortunate," and "to be avoided."

Jimmy Carter had opened a headquarters in Roxbury, prominently displaying endorsements from Martin Luther King, Sr. Above the bank of telephones was a sign for the volunteers: "Don't talk about issues." The silence was resounding.

George Wallace won Boston in the primary, but finished behind Henry Jackson statewide. It was Wallace's last hurrah, and Jackson would peter out after the New York primary. But the impact of their racist campaigns was unmistakable. There would be no articulate defense of desegregation coming from the array of Democrats. Jimmy Carter's "ethnic purity" statement was no slip of the tongue: he opposed "forced busing."

The absence of debate among Democrats and Republicans did not mean that desegregation was not at issue in the campaign. To the contrary, the suppression signaled a unanimity of opposition, a desire to deter and discourage Black leaders from demanding it and from engaging in the fight necessary to achieve it.

The predictable outcome was noted by the American socialist leader Eugene V. Debs a half century ago: "When you vote for the lesser evil, all you get is the evil."

# 19

## "People Have to Take Sides"

On March 9, after nearly a month of preparation in Boston and around the country, the April 24 national march on Boston in support of school desegregation was announced. Backed by such key leaders in the city as Ellen Jackson, Ruth Batson, Percy Wilson, state legislative Black caucus chairperson Mary Goode, and caucus members Doris Bunte and Robert Forbes, the call had also been endorsed by more than a hundred prominent partisans of desegregation from coast to coast.

The announcement of the demonstration was indeed timely. On the night of March 9, vigilantes firebombed school buses parked in a company lot, causing $50,000 damage. An official of the firm, noting that such harassment "had been going on for some time," termed the midnight arson an attempt to "obstruct implementation of the court order."

That same day the Massachusetts House of Representatives overwhelmingly passed a measure supporting the antibusing constitutional amendment. The vote, Black State Representative Melvin King stated, was an effort to "turn back the clock not to pre–civil rights days, but to pre–Civil War days." Its intent, he said, is to "put the niggers back in their place. It encourages a movement back to Jim Crowism, segregated schools, and segregated facilities."

Still more potshots against Black rights were in the offing. A heated meeting of the suburban Newton school board culminated in the cutting of a modest educational exchange program with Roxbury sponsored by the METCO system. This action symbolized the erosion of support for "voluntary integration" under the hammering of ROAR's campaign in the city.

METCO bused two thousand Black students out of Boston to suburban schools. Spurred by the racist resistance in Boston, antibusing bigots had begun to organize in the suburbs. METCO programs were being cut back, solely at the expense of the Black students. The success of the campaign against METCO was significant because Newton was the keystone of suburban liberalism.

Two thousand miles away in Dallas, the effect of Boston was being felt. On March 10 a long-awaited desegregation order was handed down by Federal District Judge William Taylor. The approved plan, submitted by the big-business-dominated Dallas Alliance, required busing for less than a seventh of the system's 145,000 students. This segment of Black and Chicano students was to be bused from predominantly or entirely Black and Chicano schools to majority nonwhite schools, in grades four to eight only. Early grade desegregation was scrapped entirely. All-white areas—the centers of the best in-city education—were "incorporated" in the plan through partial and token "voluntary" steps which included magnet schools.

Racist resistance had been loud and visible in Dallas. The bigots looked north for inspiration. "Judge Taylor," antibusing city council member Rose Renfroe said, "is no Judge Garrity."

The Dallas decision registered the impact of the Boston situation. The scope of resistance to desegregation was becoming the excuse for watered-down plans announced by recalcitrant judges and an inspiration for local antibusing organizations and segregationist school committees. Antibusing pressure was on the rise from Pasadena to Dallas, from Milwaukee to Louisville.

This crisis had motivated NSCAR's initiative in seeking to unify Boston's Black leaders behind April 24 as the first step toward organizing a national show of support for endangered desegregation rights. Backing for April 24 was growing fast, in spite of the distraction of the primary campaigns. By March 23 more than three hundred prominent individuals and organizations had endorsed the demonstration, a number greater than that secured for either the December 14, 1974, or the May 17, 1975, march. Scores of Black student leaders and organizations in New England and nationally endorsed the action.

April 24 already had a presence in the city through posters and leaflets, news conferences, and press statements. The fuel for the machinery of organizing the demonstration was provided by NSCAR. This was a situation the student organizers had hoped they might avoid. But however much local Black leaders backed the idea of the action, central responsibility fell on the youngest elements of that leadership.

The idea of a counteroffensive was popular in the Black

community. "I want people to come to Boston from all across the country on April 24," Ruth Batson said, "to show that we won't surrender to the kind of racist attacks that have been going on here. We have to do everything possible to turn the tide, to leave no method untried to stop the racist offensive. . . . There is a terrible void in this city. It seems the only people you hear from are those who support racism.

"We have to end this idea of 'not taking sides,' which has been very detrimental to the struggle," she noted. Ruth Batson had been taking sides on the desegregation issue for twenty-six years. She agonized over the divisions in the Black leadership over busing, desegregation, personalities, in-groups, image. "People have to take sides. Everyone needs to know there are people in Boston who support justice. We need that spirit revived, that old abolitionist spirit that Boston used to have."

Though possessing great moral influence, Ruth Batson lacked, as she put it, "clout, authority." Moreover, she had to take some courses relating to her work at the Boston University Mental Health Center, which increasingly limited her role in the CSSC and her activity for the April 24 march.

Outside of Boston, April 24 was being organized principally by NSCAR chapters, several of which had strong ties with the NAACP. This was the case in Detroit, for example. There, NAACP executive director Joe Madison was an outspoken supporter of school desegregation. At twenty-five he was one of the youngest NAACP leaders in the country and something of a maverick and militant. He had developed a warm working relationship with SCAR, had spoken at its second national conference in Boston, and was a proponent of direct mass action.

Through its collaboration with the Detroit NAACP, SCAR had also begun to work with Tom Turner, Black president of the Detroit Metropolitan AFL-CIO Council, which represented three hundred thousand unionists. Turner had become convinced of the need for April 24 both as a member of the national board of directors of the NAACP and as a trade unionist who saw the increasingly corrosive effects of antibusing racism in the labor movement. Turner came to Boston for an early news conference to publicize the march.

Efforts to involve the Boston NAACP, of which Dixon and Mac Warren were both members, proved less fruitful.

The NAACP's national leadership had taken a stand against becoming part of or endorsing the coalition building the action.

In answer to the Jackson-Batson-Dixon letter, Margaret Bush Wilson, chairperson of the board of directors, set forth the following reasons for the decision of its Boston branches:

"For tactical reasons I express reservations about your suggestion for another march in the near future in support of public school desegregation in Boston," she wrote. "First, the NAACP-NASCAR demonstration [on May 17] was a success and showed Boston, as well as the rest of the nation that there is a considerable reservoir of sentiment within our citizenry that favored our prescribed course toward achieving racial justice and equality in American schools.

"Second, the enemies of equal justice are seeking all opportunities in this election year to inflame passions and foster hatred in an attempt to bolster the standing of the most reactionary candidates. We must avoid handing them an opportunity to capitalize on latent fears.

"Instead, I see an urgent need for us to organize massive voter registration and education campaigns on the college campuses across the nation, and in minority communities around the country. NASCAR, with its national-wide network, can play a key role in this regard. In a critical year, like 1976, we cannot allow a repeat of the experience of 1972, when voters stayed away from the polls in large numbers. The political process offers immeasurable opportunities to bring about positive social change, but such opportunities can only be realized if the people most affected appreciate the value of their vote."

The abstention of the NAACP, nationally and in Boston, served to undercut the authority of the call for the upcoming demonstration that the unified leadership sought by NSCAR would have given it. To counterpose voter registration to mass action was to miss the point and lose an opportunity. A Black community on the retreat in the face of an antibusing offensive which included the tacit or eager participation of all the Democratic and Republican party presidential candidates, let alone their underlings, would not be roused to register for the "lesser of the many evils."

In fact, a mass mobilization of the Black community and its allies against the racists, in a year of heightened political interest, could only result in greater political awareness and help restrain the traditional politicians from their headlong lunge for the antibusing vote.

The mood of Wilson's letter, however, foreshadowed the

modesty of active support that would be forthcoming from the established Black leadership in Boston, despite widespread and genuine sympathy for April 24. The Boston NAACP was the most important of all the eighteen hundred local units of the organization precisely because of its centrality in the busing struggle. Because it was more in the spotlight, its simple endorsement of the action would have brought forth further effort by the NAACP and others.

As Margaret Bush Wilson's letter showed, pressures of the elections bore down heavily on the branch, which was still recuperating from financial losses incurred through May 17. Also, some leaders of the branch believed that an antiracist action could provide a focus for the unification of the bigots. Others felt the lingering sting of Carson Beach, and still others, who liked the idea of the event, hesitated to immerse themselves fully in another demonstration. Thomas Atkins did not endorse April 24, although he did not discourage rank-and-file participation in it. Dixon sought his advice periodically.

The end of March and beginning of April were marked by an episodic calm that belied the existence of a divided city. The schools were free of major incidents. The hoopla of the presidential primaries was over. The memory of the riotous clash of police and South Boston Marshals in South Boston was fading.

It had been a bitter, cold, and frustrating winter. Spring still felt months away. The racist movement was like a caged beast: stalking, menacing. The absence of eruptions did not mean peace. It meant planning behind the scenes. A slow fuse was smoldering towards a hidden case of dynamite.


Theodore Landsmark put on a three-piece suit on the morning of April 5. He was a young Black lawyer working with the Third World Clearing House. This Black, Puerto Rican, and Chinese organization was seeking representation as the "hiring hall" for minority workers on city-funded job sites in Boston to ensure proper application of affirmative action quotas. The clearing house had grown out of a three-year struggle of minority workers, now organized into the Third World Workers Association. The direct actions of the groups preceding the formation of the TWWA had won commitments for 30 percent minority worker placement on jobs in the Black, Puerto Rican, and Chinese communities and 10 percent placement citywide. The promises were not being enforced.

Now, the TWWA, to redress that specific grievance and counter the overall impact of racism in the building trades, had increased their demands to 50 percent and 30 percent. Landsmark was going to City Hall to meet with Mayor White about the matter. The young attorney was softspoken and persuasive. As a college student, he had been in the South for the struggles against Jim Crow.

Monday morning was a sunny, warm day, a relief from the grey, rainy weather of the past weeks. Theodore Landsmark was prepared with facts, figures, and arguments to back up the demands of the clearing house.

Over the weekend both adult and young ROAR leaders in Charlestown and South Boston had been meeting. They, too, sensed that renewed protest was called for. This would be a school boycott exceeding the long-term stay-out that the diehards had previously conducted—and that already in fact existed for those white students attending the segregated academies. It was conceived as something stunning, a clean sweep of the schools.

The word was passed rapidly, and by Sunday night the instigators knew that the next day South Boston High School, Gavin Middle School, and Charlestown High School would be virtually empty of white students. They scheduled a student march to City Hall, where Louise Day Hicks would again be ready with hot chocolate and doughnuts. There the Southie kids could raise their newest demand. They wanted assurances that Jerome Winegar, a liberal educator from Saint Paul and reputedly a member of the NAACP and the American Civil Liberties Union, would not be hired as the new headmaster of South Boston High School.

They, too, were ready for work on Monday morning.

# 20

# A Countermobilization
# Begins to Take Shape

They chanted the fight song boisterously marching to City Hall. "Here we go Southie, here we go!" They bore signs against Winegar: "Go home Jerome" and "Winegar is a communist." Neatly typed demands were ready for Hicks.

Two hundred of them trooped into city council chambers. Again cameras and reporters were barred. There was the hot chocolate, coffee, and doughnuts for the "young ladies and gentlemen" who recited the "Pledge of Allegiance" in the chambers where their parents had met for a year and a half, plotting against Judge Garrity's order. Joseph Rakes, a South Boston High School student who had led the marchers with an American flag, held it aloft as the young bigots intoned the pledge.

They were husky young men, raised in neighborhoods where manhood meant fighting gang battles for the turf, rising in amateur boxing, being a starter on the football or hockey teams. And the young women were not shy but feisty companions. Their mothers were housewives, sometimes holding down a part-time job, raising big families.

"The white girls are dressed to kill," a South Boston High School Black student had said, smiling at the double meaning of her description. The smiles, the Irish good looks—turned-up noses, red and blonde hair, and blue eyes—would contort into snarling hate as the Black students walked by.

Beneath the camaraderie, jokes, and high school gossip, there was a steaming rage against Blacks. No conversation could last for more than a couple of minutes without racist expletives. The common motive that welded them was: *Get the niggers!* The social stability of their schools, athletic teams, beaches, neighborhoods, and hangouts had been disrupted. The cops were everywhere, and, though not bad guys when you thought about it, because they had a job to do, they still could be pigs.

The information centers were boiling with activity. The secret meetings, the planning sessions for boycotts and walkouts, the attacks in the corridors, the bull sessions which recounted the disruptions (how that nigger got his face smashed), the publicity, the television—this was the *life*.

These were a minority of activists among the white students, the hard core, the most pugnacious, who rode herd on the rest. The "young ladies and gentlemen" indignantly complained to Louise Day Hicks about the unfair treatment they received in school, how the Blacks were slow and kept their studies back, how Jerome Winegar was an NAACP member and could never be headmaster. She reassured them, summoning up her maternal image of concern and frustration over the fate of these innocents hurled into battle with the ghetto kids who just couldn't keep up.

Enthused by this field trip, the white students bounded out of the chambers, giving surly looks to the handful of reporters in the outer corridors, and made their way downstairs. They were going to see Judge Garrity. As they left the building, a group of Blacks who walked by were met with insults and epithets. Several white students, trying to pick a fight, threw apples at them.

Theodore Landsmark did not know that the young bigots had been in City Hall meeting with Hicks. Walking towards the front entrance of the building as the white students were leaving, he inadvertently found himself in the middle of an antibusing demonstration. So he suddenly became the spark that lit the short fuse on the violence that had been building up for weeks. "Get the nigger, kill him!" someone shrieked.

The chase began, as Landsmark was swarmed over by the students. To shouts of "Get him," "Kick him," he was grabbed from behind. Passersby backed away, horrified.

Joseph Rakes lined up his steel flagpole as Landsmark struggled to escape. "Lynch him!"

Mayor White watched from his sixth floor window as the attack unfolded. He attempted to leave his office to intercede. This could be bad, very bad. Two aides blocked the door. It could be worse, they counseled, if you went. White continued to watch.

Rakes aimed to kill. The flagpole was a *spear* now, a lance, and he was going to drive it right into the center of that "nigger's" brain. Rakes, built like a halfback, slammed the pole into Landsmark's face. Blood spurted from the victim's nose. He was down and rolling. Kicks in the face, in the head, in the ribs. He was punched and pelted. He thought he was going to die.

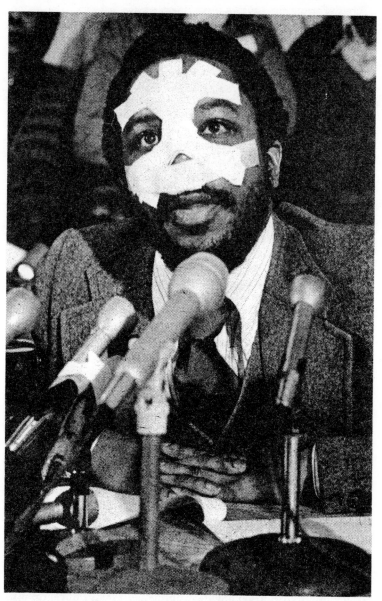

Theodore Landsmark after beating at City Hall.

WCVB, the ABC affiliate, filmed the entire attack, running it in slow motion for viewers and for the police. Stanley Foreman, the *Boston Herald American* photographer who had a reputation for being in the right place at the right time as well as for standing his ground, froze the image of Rakes beginning his spear thrust. There they were, the "young ladies and gentlemen," grinning, exulting in the assault. Landsmark was under them as the cops came, peeling the hooligans off his body, pushing them away, and arresting—one.

Flushed with the scent of the kill, the racists regrouped and marched towards the McCormack Federal Building. On the way, two Black women were briefly assaulted at a subway stop. Security officers blocked the doorway to the McCormack building. Disappointed, they picketed for a short time, then went home to tell their friends about the conquest at City Hall Plaza.

Theodore Landsmark was stunned and bleeding. His body was bruised, and his nose had been broken by Joseph Rake's bicentennial spear. He was rushed to a doctor. The morning news had been about the success of the boycott in the South Boston and Charlestown schools. Now it was the Landsmark beating which flashed across front pages from coast to coast.

The *Boston Herald American* devoted front page and page three articles to the assault, terming the assailants, "vicious, racist hoodlums." For the past several months the paper had been covering the antibusing movement from a less favorable angle than before. At the same time it was routinely scooping the *Globe* on certain news about the desegregation controversy, and the writing of its reporters more pungently conveyed the essence of the antibusing drive.

Now the racist underbelly of that movement was exposed to the city in its most naked way since the assault of André Yvon Jean-Louis eighteen months before. The city recoiled in horror: an American flag was used as a weapon in a broad daylight attack at City Hall Plaza.

The next morning, after perfunctory apologies from Mayor White, the response would begin in earnest. But that night sniper's bullets smashed into the parked car of a Black family in Charlestown. As one Black man ran for aid for his wounded brother, a white gang clubbed, beat, and robbed him.

Two hundred Blacks, a wide-ranging assemblage of community leaders, turned out with the staffs of Black community agencies to swell an angry news conference called by the state legislative

Black caucus. William Owens blasted city officials and antibusing leaders. They, he said, "were the cause of the racist attacks by white youth on Black adults, youth, and young children. . . . [The students who attacked Landsmark] were truant from school to attend a gathering in the city council chambers, where they were given inspiration for this vicious behavior."

Owens read a Black caucus demand that Massachusetts Attorney General Francis X. Bellotti and U.S. Attorney General Edward Levi "conduct immediate investigations into the roles of those Boston city councillors, school committee persons, and state legislators who are inciting young people to mob violence. We must come to the realization that if city and state officials will not protect us, we will ask for federal protection, and short of that, we must protect ourselves," he said.

Rev. Rafe Taylor, a widely respected Black minister with a flair for fire and brimstone, thundered about the crisis. "They have blown up buses, stoned houses, attacked our children, and harassed Black mothers. The streets of Boston are not safe for people of color. War has been declared on us."

Taylor suggested the time might be near for "our community to consider whether the laws that prohibit us from bearing arms are legitimate." This and similar formulations, spoken in outrage and born of frustration at gross police inaction, were seized upon by racist leaders who demogogically claimed the Black community was "arming itself."

The crowd cheered and applauded the militant statements, but there was no call to action in them. Owens, amidst rumored differences within the Black caucus, had assumed center stage. But the main line of his protest was that he was' considering withdrawal of "political support for Mayor White," a decision which could mean he would "call for his resignation." The suggestion was barely applauded, but that, in fact, seemed to be a theme of the gathering: Pressure White to act by threatening to call for his resignation. White easily shrugged off the empty threat. Next in line of succession to the mayor was the city council president—Louise Day Hicks.

A reporter asked Owens if he supported the April 24 demonstration. "That, I understand, is a probusing march. I am against busing," he said tersely. Instead of pressing for an action-oriented response that could tap the rising anger of the community, Owens even urged out-of-town Blacks to *stay out* of Boston.

As the questions for Owens ended, Maceo Dixon took the microphone. "These criminals tried to kill the first Black citizen they saw, because they knew from experience that the police and the elected officials would turn their heads the other way. Who's going to be next?" Dixon asked. A "massive public outcry" was necessary "to put the racists in their place." This would be done April 24, which had rapidly become a focus for the protest that was starting to mushroom despite Owens's statement.

That afternoon fifty white students refused to enter the Gavin Middle School in South Boston, marching to the L Street Annex, where they stoned an empty school bus, a police car, and radio and television news vans. Miles away, on the Boston Common, Edward Soars, a Black, and his cousin were playing chess. Though it was rush hour, that did not faze a group of four white men who had been hassling the two Blacks all afternoon. Now, armed with a crowbar and a knife, they pounced. They kneeled over Soars, as hundreds of motorists watched, beating and kicking him.

Municipal Court Judge A. Frank Foster saw the attack. He leaned on his horn, blaring at the hooligans. They started to run. Foster sped through a red light, chasing them down, and alerted a patrolman who refused to arrest the thugs because he had not seen the crime. Warrants were later issued.

"When I saw this, and then this Black man's face splattered with blood, I did all I could think of to draw attention," Foster said. "I can't wait to get this case in court."

The state legislature, the governor, the chamber of commerce, all condemned the Landsmark beating. The walls of opinion were closing in on the racists.

ROAR's James Kelly could not be budged. "The outrage over the incident [is] more deplorable than the act itself," he told a news conference at the South Boston Information Center on April 7. The real issue was "Black crime" and "forced busing." "If I was an eighteen-year-old student, I'd do the same thing," he said, referring to the Landsmark assault. The reporters grimaced. One from the *Boston Globe* asked if that meant sticking a flagpole in someone's face. A South Boston Marshal snarled back, "I'd like to stick it in your face!" Then Kelly warned the media representatives to beware. "It could be a long hot summer. You might come down here. Watch what you write. It might not be safe."

On April 8, 125 racists cheered Dennis McLaughlin, a longshoreman, as he announced formation of the Charlestown Marshals Association "to fight by any means necessary to protect our community" against Blacks and subversives who, he charged, "are arming themselves."

On the heels of that, South Boston Chief Marshal Warren Zaniboni announced the organization of a hundred-member dusk-to-dawn neighborhood car patrol with citizen's band radios. There were, Zaniboni stated, "threats on our community" from Blacks and "communists." Zaniboni, a Hicks patronage flunky, was employed as a transitional aide in South Boston High School. The stated purpose of the aides was to help implement desegregation! The Charlestown Marshals followed suit on the car patrol seventy-two hours later.

The war was on. The city, it seemed, was going up for grabs.

The events of those April days reverberated through the April 24 coalition offices. The phones were never quiet as media calls came in and requests for funds went out. Support that previously had been shaky became solidified, and a broad list of speakers for the rally was readily nailed down. Rev. Ralph Abernathy would come, to be joined by Detroit's Tom Turner and Joe Madison. Percy Wilson would chair the rally, and the Boston speakers included Ruth Batson and Black caucus members Mary Goode, Doris Bunte, and Robert Fortes. Local religious, student, and labor leaders rounded out a program that reflected the history and breadth of the struggle.

Ruby Bradley and Otis Debnam would give eyewitness accounts of the terror in the city. High school students, parents, and teachers would also speak. It was going to be a big demonstration.

In a conversation the night after the Landsmark attack, Ruth Batson commented, almost taken aback by the thought, "I think this may be a turning point." It was. Editorial opinion in the Boston papers was lambasting the bigots, calling for swift police action against them. For all the fearfulness, the mood in the city presaged a shift against the racists. The April 24 coalition went on the offensive.

Maceo Dixon wrote a letter to Louise Day Hicks on April 8 asking permission to use city council chambers for a public meeting of the coalition on April 19. Hicks was under extraordinary pressure. In the wake of public outcry, she had stepped back as Kelly and the leaders of the marshals came increasingly into the spotlight. To deny the April 24 coalition the council chambers in this situation would be to paint ROAR into a smaller corner.

She relented. Frederick Langone, the city council member from the Italian North End, agreed to sponsor the meeting. He appeared at a State House news conference, flanked by Dixon and April 24 Chief Marshal Mac Warren, declaring his belief in free speech—and his opposition to forced busing. The news conference and the setting of the meeting were major news in the Boston media. It would be the first probusing, pro-Black rights gathering ever held in the lair of the racists. It was full steam ahead for April 24.

Meetings of Warren and Mark Severs (a coalition activist helping to coordinate defense and security for the march) with city and police officials had been amiable at first. There was virtually no problem about the march route, which would begin with an assembly at Franklin Park, in Roxbury, and proceed on major thoroughfares in the Black community through Boston to City Hall Plaza. The city would even provide a sound system—a unique offer from the White administration.

On April 3 the coalition received a death threat from the South Boston Defense League, signed by "Michael O'Connor." "We look forward to fight scum such as you," it read. "In fact it is what we live for most right now. Despicable slime like you must be eliminated and it will be." With publicity mounting for the action, more letters and phone threats came in. At one security meeting, top police officials claimed they had never heard of the South Boston Defense League, an admission of ignorance that had ominous implications.

Warren and Severs had gone to great pains to explain the difference between NSCAR and the Committee Against Racism, which, though essentially defunct in Boston, had a name which was greeted with animosity in virtually all quarters of the city. CAR's provocative and adventurist tactics had isolated them in the antiracist movement, a situation which made them easy targets for victimization by racist gangs and police.

NSCAR, in the past, had been confused with CAR because of the similarity in names. Now rumors sifted back to the coalition that police believed CAR was not only involved in the action but leading it.

In the wake of the April 5 attack on Landsmark, Owens had called what would be a small, all-Black meeting in City Hall to discuss the situation. A "security" subcommittee was set up. Shortly, it convoked an all-male meeting in Mattapan to organize street patrols to "calm" the situation in Roxbury.

Warren attended one meeting at which a ban on "socialists, communists, and capitalists" was passed. Warren was a recently announced Socialist Workers Party candidate for Congress in Roxbury. As he spoke, a member of the All African People's Revolutionary Party shouted out Warren's political affiliation. He was escorted from the room. The red-baiting attack was an unhealthy sign in a tense period for the Black community, when unity was needed against the racists. The exclusion of radicals boded ill for achieving that.

The AAPRP, a small Pan-Africanist group headed nationally by Stokely Carmichael, counterposed desegregation to Black community control of the schools. It opposed busing and political collaboration between Blacks and whites in principle. It had tangled with NSCAR before, provoking a minor disruption at the organization's national convention seven months earlier. Groups of its members had physically threatened Black and white staff members working in NSCAR's Roxbury office.

In the midst of crisis and frustration in the Black community, the influence of the AAPRP could be especially deleterious. The barring of Warren at the security meeting was part of an ongoing red-baiting campaign against the April 24 demonstration; the narrow nationalist organization opposed the march.

Floyd Williams, the owner of a Roxbury funeral home and a key figure in the security meeting, chimed in with the scare campaign. Warren, he announced, was prepared to lead a team of armed Blacks to City Hall to assassinate Mayor White. Williams, on the insistence of Ellen Jackson, later retracted the ludicrous slander, but not before the damage had been done. Between the problems with the police and the political assaults on the integrity of the demonstration, a perilous pattern was emerging.

The hue and cry over the Landsmark beating did not stop the rash of attacks on Blacks. Though the major media ignored the stories, racist strikes against the Black community itself had begun. Carloads of white vigilantes, encouraged by the inflammatory rhetoric of ROAR and the "marshals" organizations, entered Roxbury.

Windows on Columbia Road and Blue Hill Avenue were

smashed out. Housing projects were the scene of nightriding forays. The Black community came under siege. In the predawn darkness of April 18 two Black bus drivers waiting outside their South Boston station were assaulted by a gang of five whites. They were whipped with a car antenna and kicked to the ground. Their shouts brought two white drivers running to their aid, one of them from South Boston. The police arrived and arrested one thug. The two Blacks and a white defender were hospitalized. The news ran through the city.

At this moment the popular outcry against the bigots was reaching a peak. Such antiracist sentiment could have been channeled into a stunning demonstration demanding an end to the two years of City Hall betrayal of Black rights. The physical battering being administered to the Black community, however, served to intensify the political pressure on the Black leadership to stay out of the streets. This was the toll of a strategy that pinned its hopes on the election of "friendly" Democrats, around the theme of Margaret Bush Wilson's letter weeks earlier. The hesitancy flowed from the logic of trying to compel enforcement of the law through verbal protests made individually to City Hall. April 24, a day of action in the streets that could rock the already strained relationship between the city's Black leadership and the city government, meant a massive, direct confrontation with Mayor White and the "downtown" Democratic Party apparatus. The hands of the official Black leadership were tied by participation in and reliance on the Democratic Party.

Thus the alternative of independent struggle came solely from the organizers of the April 24 march, from its NSCAR core: a young, new wing of the city's Black leadership, which on its own, however, lacked the political authority of the broader, established Black leadership.

The frenzy of the bigots was a sign of desperation and weakness. Yet it caused deep anxiety in the Black leadership. They correctly sensed a deepening racial polarization in Boston and feared an explosion, something worse than ever before.

The heightening tension was evident April 19 in the city council chambers meeting sponsored by the April 24 coalition. The hall was packed. The vast majority of those present, however, were white, a sign of the fear of Blacks to travel downtown in the evening. Even several of the Black leaders scheduled to speak failed to show up. A big publicity campaign for police protection and the fact that there would be seventy-five marshals present from the April 24 coalition and NSCAR had been widely noted by the media.

April 24 organizer Mark Severs, in casual conversation with the police, learned of their belief that the meeting was sponsored by CAR and that they were there for show. Severs was alarmed. Was this to be some kind of setup? He told Mac Warren, and they discovered through leaks from the police department that a memo was being circulated stating that April 24 was a CAR-led project.

The meeting itself was a big story on Boston's three major television network affiliates, drawing all three anchor men to the council chambers. As the antiracist activists filtered into the austere chamber, they appeared awed by the eerie quality of the room with its grey concrete walls. It was like discovering a mummy's tomb or entering a secret bunker. This was where ROAR had met a hundred times.

But as Dixon settled into Louise Day Hicks's oversized, throne-like chair, the tension began to ease. "It's good to be here," he said, smiling broadly. "This is not the first meeting, nor will it be the last." Cheers and bursts of applause greeted the remarks. Afterward a dozen speakers sat in the chair, blasting the racists, ROAR, Hicks, Kelly, all by name, and whoops of delight resounded off the walls.

A few bigots who came to the meeting left demoralized. ROAR leader Rita Graul stood outside with a knot of racists. This time no incidents, only a few insults. Their sanctuary had been violated.

Thousands of leaflets and posters had been distributed by the antiracist activists for the final push. The media coverage of the meeting would give an enormous boost for the action. The buoyant, exuberant crowd felt this was like a victory rally.

Nonetheless the scent of trouble was real. The action still had to be held together in face of the ominous attitude of the police, the political sniping, the threats, the fear and pressure bearing down on those Black leaders who did support the action. As the march supporters drifted away from City Hall that night, April 24 was 130 hours away.

The Orchard Street housing projects in Roxbury had been shot up by racist gangs roaring through the area sometime that day, according to residents. Ground down by poverty and the worst slum conditions in the city, the project residents were steaming with anger. After two years of violence, capped by the reported and the less-publicized attacks of the past two weeks, this vigilante attack was the final blow. The teen-aged bands that hung around the projects were seething.

That night they blocked the Amtrak rail lines with debris, stoning the train as it stopped and pelting the crew as they removed tree limbs and other material from the tracks.

That night a thirty-four-year-old white mechanic named Richard Poleet, driving home to Jamaica Plain, stopped at a red light near the projects. The youths stoned his car, dragged him from the driver's seat, and beat him. As he lay bleeding on the ground, they crushed his face and skull with cinder blocks.

That night Richard Poleet's brain stopped normal functioning. He was kept alive by machine as he entered a deep coma. He would never know that he had been in the wrong place at the wrong time, an innocent in the war zone, who suffered a beating that would trigger a stupendous campaign of anti-Black hysteria when the news spread the next morning.

# 21

# NSCAR Is
# Forced to Retreat

It was as if war had been declared. South Boston ROAR leader James Kelly set the tone. He hinted at reprisals. No one, Kelly declared, could stop residents from lashing out. He warned that his neighborhood was now "a defensive perimeter" and that "a Black is not safe in South Boston." Kelly's Charlestown counterpart, Thomas Johnson, echoed the warning, telling Blacks to stay out of the part of Boston dominated by the Bunker Hill Monument. The Charlestown Marshals, he said, would "protect the community by any means necessary."

The racist leaders' implications of the danger of "Black invasions" were inflammatory fabrications. These were pretexts to justify in advance—as "defensive" measures—violence against *any* Black citizen in those parts of the city. A state of siege had been proclaimed.

The lynch mob clarion sounded by the bigots was accompanied by stupendous media coverage of the Poleet attack. It flooded city newspapers and radio and television reports. The *Boston Globe* featured blow-by-blow eyewitness accounts of the beating and interviews with Poleet's family, employer, and friends.

The attack on the white auto mechanic was construed as proof that "Black violence" was just as vicious as two years of racist terror—if not more so. At the same time there would be no word of editorial rebuke of the public boasts of white vigilantism and the paramilitary parading of the antibusing movement.

The stunning impact of the publicity generated by the Poleet beating staggered the city's Black leadership. From the state legislative Black caucus to the NAACP, statements by community leaders denounced and deplored the assault. The horror expressed at the brutal crippling of an innocent man momentarily eclipsed the broader and more fundamental facts of the whole situation.

The Black community had been the victim of terror and

violence for nearly two years. For months the wave of racist lawlessness had been escalating. No Black felt safe anywhere in Boston except in Roxbury, and white nightriders had penetrated even to the heart of the Black community there. That had been the message of the midnight bombing of the NAACP office months earlier. Following the unchecked outbursts of racist violence since desegregation had begun, Black retaliation in kind had been short-lived and sporadic.

The sorely tested restraint of the Black community had finally been broken by a handful of teen-agers in the Orchard Street projects after Mayor White's failure to lift a finger against the bigots.

In the aftermath of the Landsmark assault, Percy Wilson recalled, "we had to beg [Mayor White] for an arrest." The official outcry that met the attack was nothing but bombast—coming from the elected officeholders who had contributed decisively to the mounting tension by months of silence and inaction.

While an unruly gang of youths, incensed by the unpunished nightriding that had terrorized sections of Roxbury and perhaps their own project dwellings, had gone after Richard Poleet, the cinder blocks that pounded him had, in effect, been delivered into their hands by Louise Day Hicks and her ilk. Richard Poleet's ebbing life was a most tangible result of the White administration's accommodation to two years of antibusing lawbreaking.

Fear and panic gripped the city as airwaves and newspapers blared reports on the state of the hospitalized victim and the pledges of frontier retribution from the ROAR posse leaders. The "evenhandedness" of the media equated "Black violence" with "white violence."

As the racist movement clamored for war against the Black community, the Black leadership sought reconciliation of the contending forces. State Representative Melvin King's remarks were typical. "What's most important," he told the *Globe*, "is that people with differences over busing have to come together and say that they have no differences on the issues of violence and safety in the streets. Otherwise, we don't have a city."

There could, however, be no effective appeal to the good will of the bigots. Far from rising above "differences over busing," Hicks, speaking for the central racist leadership, stridently blamed the Garrity order for any and all violence against Blacks. Racial amity had been destroyed by desegregation, she maintained. And in fact, violence was not an excess of the antibusing movement but at the very heart of it from the first day of desegregation, when hundreds of whites had gleefully stoned buses transporting the Black students.

In one way, Hicks was right. Bound up with the staccato of attacks—and now, retaliation—was the busing question: Would Black rights be enforced by the city government, from the right to desegregated education to the right to walk and live in safety? Or would busing be pushed aside in the name of "safety" and an unoriented opposition to "violence"—deference to an abstract unity—and be ultimately junked?

Hicks wasted no time. Evasive in her refusal to rebuke the monstrous movement she had nurtured, she had tenacity; and no amount of turmoil confounded her ability to go for the jugular. She was the racist politician par excellence. This was the moment she had been waiting for since the hot chocolate and doughnut breakfast for the boycotting student hooligans two weeks before had made crystal clear to Boston that ROAR's lion was indeed a beast.

She called for a Justice Department investigation of the Poleet beating. "A young man," she stated, "lies close to death from the stones thrown by the disciples of Mel King." Hicks slanderously claimed that the Black legislator had made a call for "retaliation" after the Landsmark beating. (No trace of such a remark could be found, and King denied ever making it.) She blasted Thomas Atkins, who, in a debate with her at the University of Rhode Island, had said that the Black community could control "its crazies." Atkins, she said, and "nobody else in the Black community can control [them]."

She released copies of letters to Senators Brooke and Kennedy. "It is imperative," Hicks wrote the lawmakers, "that you now seize the initiative on behalf of every citizen in the city of Boston to persuade Judge Garrity that his forced busing orders are the root cause of racial violence and they must be rescinded immediately if the city is to be stopped from its headlong rush into insanity."

Boston "justice" echoed the hysteria erupting on all sides against the Black community. Police, aided by television footage of the Landsmark beating, ended up making four arrests. All were released without bail, and the first two convicted would be given suspended sentences of probationary counseling, as they made public apologies for the grisly assault. The arrest toll for the Poleet beating reached six, with bail for two young principals—both pleading innocent—at $25,000.

The blindfold had been pulled tight on Lady Justice. Joseph Rakes, the flagpole-wielding assailant of Theodore Landsmark, was out on his personal recognizance while, in the Orchard Street projects, Black youth feared that big price tags on their necks could be in the offing should the dragnet of suddenly zealous police sweep them up.

At news of the Poleet beating, police were mobilized in Roxbury, and squads of motorcycle cops roared through Mission Hill and a dozen projects. White gangs in Uphams Corner, Mattapan Square, and parts of Mission Hill—all border areas—hooted and tossed bottles at Black passersby. Dozens of incidents of stonings of Black motorists failed to make the papers. Gangs of motorcycle hoods, screaming obscenities, sped through parts of Mission Hill and Mattapan. As the agonizing week wore on, the media reported a seeming tit-for-tat battle as white and Black motorists ran afoul of rock-throwing gangs both in Black Columbia Point and in white Hyde Park.

The city was completely polarized, the streets in the neighborhoods teeming with people. Boston was out of control.

With hysteria rising, the thin threads holding together the April 24 coalition forces began to snap. Maceo Dixon and Mac Warren were interviewed on WILD on the morning of April 20. They had hoped that the "Relate" program broadcast would help publicize the upcoming demonstration. After an initial discussion, the phone calls began coming in. The first three were disastrously similar in content and tone—hostile, vicious attacks on the action:

It was led by whites.

It would cause violence.

It was dominated by communists.

It was not supported by the Black community.

The two young Blacks patiently responded to each charge. But, Dixon recalled, "It was a campaign, orchestrated. Like they wanted to smear the action." Later callers berated the earlier opponents, but the damage remained. In the midst of peaking emotions, a tiny handful could smear the image of the demonstration.

"They could have been disruptive agents," Warren recalled. "It is a time-honored tactic, this rhetoric of splitting, of white-baiting a demonstration, tainting it with the potential for violence, calling it communist-led, and so on. The aim is to discredit the leadership, blast away at its legitimacy, divide the ranks of an organization, a movement, and confuse its potential friends and allies."

Dixon and Warren were shaken by the broadcast. They had been conscious of what would happen if such a polarization took place. They knew the dynamite of the desegregation issue could be touched off by the police, by ultraleft elements who favored confrontations, and, most importantly, by racists who would seek to provoke incidents so that the police would attack the demonstrators. The April 24 demonstration posed special difficulties. The death threats and hate mail to the coalition had not abated. The city was rent by fear and hostility. At the same time the police feigned ignorance of the most extreme racist organization, the South Boston Defense League, which was now routinely mailing warnings to the coalition.

Allies of the march organizers, through their contacts with the police department, confirmed rumors that cops assigned to monitor the demonstration had been told it was being led by the confrontationist Committee Against Racism, an alarming forewarning of what could be in store if trouble broke out. The fact that the police officialdom persisted in such an attribution of leadership to the march was another ominous matter.

Strict discipline would be necessary within the march as it assembled and moved out of Roxbury, and even stricter at City Hall, where, no doubt, more than a few bigots would gather. Given the near-frantic atmosphere in the city, a rock or a bottle thrown within the demonstration or at the marchers could break the demonstration wide open. In Roxbury that could mean white police in the Black community providing the detonator for clashes inspired by hotheads or provocateurs or a combination of both. At City Hall it could be like Carson Beach, with the cops seeing what was not there—a "CAR" demonstration. Again the cops could ignore the rock-throwing bigots and go after the demonstrators, who probably would have a nucleus of confrontationists in their midst.

With national attention focused on Boston, the April 24 march, with its broad range of backing and a program of speakers reflecting the wide scope of support, would challenge the city administration to enforce the law in a way that the bigots would be hard put to counter. But the city government and police could not be relied upon to maintain order.

Nearly one thousand marshals had been trained in Boston and

in the areas from which supporters were journeying to the march, but even a crack monitoring operation might not avert a determined effort to disrupt the demonstration.

At the same time, the wide support for the action among Black leaders in the city did not extend to the most authoritative organizational level. Although support for April 24 was extensive, the united effort of community leaders and organizations needed to ensure the complete success of the demonstration had not been achieved.

As Dixon and Warren returned to the Tremont Street office of the April 24 coalition, a bigger shock was in store. Reporters had been calling. Was the march still on? Dixon learned that two important backers of the demonstration—Black State Representatives Doris Bunte and Robert Fortes—were prepared to withdraw their support. Both had been scheduled to speak at the rally. There was no malice on their part. The city, they believed, was boiling hot, the situation was too volatile. But they also felt the squeeze coming from the mayor's office: it was time to "cool things down."

The political pressure directed by Mayor White and the media was not new. It had been applied since desegregation had begun and was directed at the Black community. It said, simply, "restrain yourself." For a long time the Black leadership had been confronted with demands to go slow on desegregation. When busing began, marches and demonstrations—at least those *for* Black rights—faced official condemnation. White had personally attempted to stop the Carson Beach picnic. What had kept that important protest alive was the decision by local NAACP President Thomas Atkins to push forward. Now the situation was far more explosive than the August days leading up to the Carson Beach picnic. And the central authority and responsibility for the April 24 march rested with the young leaders of NSCAR. The NAACP was not participating.

April 24, on a collision course with the White administration and the "downtown" Democrats, represented the emergence of a new, militant wing of the city's Black leadership. This threatened to upset the established relationship the rulers of Boston had imposed on the Black community.

With the uproar over the Poleet beating, the united voice of Boston's power brokers was telling the official Black leadership that any departure from the theme of "equal blame" for the violence would be met with condemnation. Stepping outside these narrow boundaries set by the Democratic administration would mean ostracism and charges of irresponsibility, of adding fuel to the fire. This squeeze play was tightening the pressure on the Black leadership to appear "responsible."

The erosion of support exposed the action to greater and greater difficulties on the level of security and safety. Any major withdrawal of endorsement or speakers would be taken as a sure sign that something was amiss and would discourage broad participation. The coming action would appear more and more isolated, becoming a smaller, and therefore more vulnerable, target for disruption and victimization. A march that turned into a rout would be a demoralizing setback for the Black community. It would make it harder than ever to call for subsequent mobilizations. Polarization, provocation, and police rumors all pointed to confrontation, and for that to mark the action would be extremely harmful for the development of the movement. Dixon and Warren began asking themselves: Can *we* guarantee a legal, peaceful march and rally?

The tumult around the Poleet beating ushered in a retreat of the city's Black leadership under the impact of the hysteria about "antiwhite violence." Black leaders were told in no uncertain terms to become "civic leaders." This meant dropping any partisanship for the Black community and blaming a handful of Black youth for acts of retaliation that were the fruit of two years of racist violence. If the city blows up, was the campaign message, it's *your* fault.

In Charlestown and South Boston the marshals continued dusk-to-dawn patrols, as the antibusing leadership's voice rose in volume against Garrity and "forced busing." Against their shrillness Kevin White appeared as the moderate, standing above the warring camps—while opposing Black rights in the courts and by mayoral inaction.

Conversations of Dixon, Warren, and the key community and coalition leaders working on April 24 painted a gloomy picture. Political pressure, intertwined with the awesome security problem, made it inadvisable, they agreed, to carry through the demonstration. The police had virtually stopped talking to the coalition leaders. And the unremitting red-baiting of the action, coupled with the death threats, stirred further apprehension.

A morning meeting on April 21 at Freedom House was attended by Maceo Dixon, Mac Warren, and other April 24 activists, along with Ellen Jackson, Percy Wilson, Otto Snowden, Ruth Batson, Pat Jones, and other key Blacks backing the action.

The candid discussion confirmed ebbing support for April 24 and a widespread buckling to the mayor's "antiviolence" campaign. The established Black leaders felt that calling off the action would help "cool things down." The real nucleus of the coalition, its key support, was present at the meeting. They agreed unanimously that the march should be called off.

The authority of these leaders had been the basis for launching the demonstration in the first place. But from the start they, along with NSCAR, had been somewhat isolated. The NAACP had refused to join in the coalition and was unwilling to commit its desperately needed national muscle. This had also been the posture of other major Black organizations—the Nation of Islam, the Urban League, the Southern Christian Leadership Conference (SCLC had endorsed the action itself but had not participated in building it). Lack of such vital support had weakened the march from the start.

Now the result of that abstention was making itself evident. On April 21, at the Freedom House, Dixon, flanked by a dozen Black leaders, announced that the April 24 march would not take place. The room was filled with anguished supporters as well as media people. In spelling out the retreat, Dixon did not kneel before the hysteria. "The reason why this city is hot, tense, and racially polarized rests with Mayor Kevin H. White, City Council President Louise Day Hicks, Governor Michael Dukakis, and President Gerald Ford," he said. "They are responsible for the over two-year campaign against school desegregation and for the physical and violent attacks against Blacks and Puerto Ricans.

"Let me make clear that Louise Day Hicks and Mayor White, the chief antibusing bigots in this city, don't give a damn about Mr. Poleet or any other white that gets hurt. What they are concerned about is gutting the school desegregation order in this city," Dixon charged.

In recalling the cancellation, Atkins noted it was "the only thing to do." The Black leader had felt since February that NSCAR would be "set up." "Elements in the Boston police would have loved nothing so much as half of an excuse to rain thunder . . . on who they perceived as the CAR people." The pressure to crush the march, Atkins said, flowed from the absence of key leadership support, which "heightened the vulnerability" of the effort. But, he noted, he had no serious second thoughts, even months later, about the NAACP's posture toward April 24.

The news about the cancellation was widely covered—the biggest play the April 24 demonstration had yet received. Now April 24 would be just another day.

The tension that broke the back of the planned demonstration was only seventy-two hours old.

"It hit like a locomotive," Dixon recalled. "Looking back, seeing it all take place so fast, so rapidly, says one thing: The government, the mayor, the racists, the media created a furious, frenzied mood. They lashed out against anything that told the truth. We were the target, and there was no way out for us. . . ."

News conference cancelling April 24. From left: Pat Jones, Ruth Batson, Percy Wilson, Maceo Dixon, Ellen Jackson, Mac Warren.

Mayor White's peace parade. Far left, Edward Kennedy; far right, Edward Brooke; Kevin White is third from right.

# 22

# Mayor White's
# Peace Charade

Two hours after the Freedom House news conference ended, Mayor White announced a "Prayer Procession for Peace" on April 23. That was *his* demonstration. There would be no speeches, and placards and signs were banned. It was a religiously tinged event, set to begin near the State House and proceed to City Hall.

It was to be a silent demonstration, designed to show a civic concern for the crisis, a desire on all sides for "ending the violence." Busing, desegregation, the attacks of the past years were not at issue. Just violence. It was the mayor's trump card, an attempt to show, according to an anonymous aide, "that he is in control." The idea had emanated from the offices of *Boston Globe* Editor Thomas Winship, and for the next two days the media drummed up support for the action.

On Thursday morning an enormous bomb blast ripped through Suffolk County Court House, hospitalizing twenty-one people. First reports, in Boston and nationally, indicated a "racial link" to the blast. Later, a group identifying itself as the "Sam Melville–Jonathan Jackson Collective" took credit for the explosion, claiming it was set off in the cause of prison reform. The bombing added a new and weird dimension to the violence stalking Boston, creating a stark backdrop to the mayor's march set for the next day.

That evening, as millions of other Americans watched the NBC television dramatization of the 1931 frame-up of the nine "Scottsboro Boys" of Alabama for the alleged rape of two white women, Boston's WBZ-TV yanked the program from the air. The station logos were replaced by admonitions to "Pray for Peace" imposed on images of the seal of the City of Boston.

Kevin White spared nothing to make the march a big show. Phone calls from his office fanned out to Senators Kennedy and Brooke, to congresspeople, mayors, and state legislators, urgently requesting them to turn out for the event. Humberto Cardinal Medeiros would offer a benediction, along with Protestant and Jewish leaders. City and state workers were offered extended lunch hours or a day off to attend the march. Downtown businesses, especially banking and insurance concerns, would empty for the procession.

The racists boycotted the march. Asked if she would attend, Hicks responded sharply: "No, no, never, never." Bulger falsely described the march as "probusing." The only presence of the antibusing movement was a knot of maroon-jacketed South Boston Marshals, perched on a City Hall balcony, hooting as the marchers passed below.

The Black leadership was divided over whether to attend. Ruth Batson was repelled by the whole idea; she viewed it as a deceitful maneuver by the mayor.

Despite disagreement with placing an equal sign between Black and white violence, Thomas Atkins led the NAACP in backing the event. The mayor, he said, had done "the right thing for the wrong reasons." Freedom House leaders Otto and Muriel Snowden and Ellen Jackson also turned out.

For Percy Wilson, the procession "was basically a joke in the Black community." He emphasized the timing connection between cancellation of the April 24 march and the announcement of the "peace procession." Some people, he was not sure who, "wanted April 24 called off and knew about the mayor's march. . . . I felt awful about [the cancellation]. . . . We were had, that much I'm sure of."

Some inkling of the behind-the-scenes work came out later. Ruth Batson had received a phone call from an aide to the mayor, who unsuccessfully tried to persuade her to come to the event. As an inducement the aide told her that Maceo Dixon was attending. "I was shocked," she recalled. Dixon had told the mayor's staff he had no intention of supporting the event. It was one of White's lesser lies, the kind that point to bigger ones beneath the surface.

Dixon, in fact, had given a brief news conference the morning of the procession to denounce the mayor. For him, the demagogic denunciations of violence and pleas for peace were the height of cynicism. "The same people who called for people to pray for peace shielded the racists for two years," he said. "I know some people went out of good will. That was fine. But the essence of the thing was a cover-up."

The mayor's march was large. Downtown banks and businesses, as well as several area colleges, declared a virtual holiday, along with state government offices. Most important was the message to city employees. "The word sent out in city departments," Atkins recalled, "that this was going to be a holiday." If, however, released employees were found to have stayed home or "gone shopping," there was an implied threat, Atkins said, that "we can't be responsible for any failure to produce a paycheck on time."

More then twenty thousand marched, many participating out of honest concern. The event, however, was essentially a manufactured hype to promote the viability of the White administration and safeguard the prospect of long-awaited millions of bicentennial tourist dollars which seemed to be going up in smoke. The mayor's office claimed a crowd of a hundred thousand.

For the religious leaders who led the prayers, the violence emanated from corrupted mortals forged in the world of flesh and greed. Yet it was saddening to listen to such predictable remarks coming from Rabbi Roland Gittlesohn.

The Jewish leader had been a clear-headed stalwart in the campaign for school desegregation, whose impeccable arguments in favor of busing offered reason in the midst of emotionalism. He had been to marches in the past, but then the goals were lucid, the demands explicit, and the impact positive. Today, the sun shone on a charade, a face-saving stunt for Mayor White to gloss over the betrayal of Black rights with which the name of Boston had become synonymous. The "good people" had come out. But the "issue" was centered around innate human frailty, and there was no definition, no explanation of the prime source of the violence. The man who had called the event was as much against busing as Louise Day Hicks and, in his own way, because of his official position, had done more damage than she.

Roland Gittlesohn was standing where Coretta King had stood more than a year and a half before in the wake of the Phase I violence, when she had declared in ringing tones that the "issue in Boston is racism." Gittlesohn had also spoken then.

Now he called for "segregationist and desegregationist alike to join hands" against the "violence" which threatened Boston. The words themselves, born of the best intentions, inadvertently played into the mayor's cynical attempt to portray Boston's Black victims as equally guilty with their victimizers. Between the lines of the prayers and speeches lurked the real message: If only busing would stop!

April 24 was a quiet, beautiful day in Boston, the kind of day that brought out sightseers and picnickers, that invited strolls through the Boston Common, a good day for a ball game, for the beach, for a drive in the country—and for a march. The evening after the mayor's procession there had been more incidents, but they seemed to be abating.

Indeed the impact of the event had a certain double edge. The mayor had said the violence would stop. Now, he would have to make good the pledge, and, backed by a united concern of the city's opinion makers—business and political leaders who had marched at the head of twenty thousand people—he would have to deliver, especially with the nation watching. Certainly, he would not openly challenge the racists; and, in all likelihood, police teams, already present in big numbers in Roxbury, would mete out swift punishment to Blacks. But, still, the bigots seemed at least temporarily reserved, though the Charlestown Marshals had called a demonstration for May 2.

In Washington the vaunted march for the antibusing constitutional amendment, led by United Labor Against Busing in Louisville and backed by Boston ROAR, flopped. ULAB leader Jack Shore had promised a turnout of upwards of forty thousand. But fewer than two thousand marched on the Capitol on April 24.

The endless week was over. School was set to reopen. Bomb threats—which had become epidemic after the courthouse bombing—shifted from downtown establishments to the schools. Several buildings were emptied on April 26 and 27. Attendance was down among Black and white students alike, as a special alert poised police for action.

On April 29 a bomb threat precipitated the evacuation of Hyde Park High School. As the Black students streamed out, they passed between two large cordons of whites. Amidst pushing and shoving, a rock sailed into the Black students, and a huge melee erupted, involving upwards of two hundred fifty students. Even as punches were being exchanged, groups of white students rushed to nearby hedges. Piles of stones were stored underneath the bushes. The Black students were bombarded. Later that day twenty Black students met with Superintendent Marion Fahey. They had heard the day before of the false alarm. They had been set up and ambushed. This would be the last in-school incident of the year.

On May 2, fifteen hundred bigots took to the streets of Charlestown in a "men's march" against busing. It was smaller than previous mobilizations for several reasons. First, the primary elections were occupying bigots who were working for local, state, and national candidates with antibusing platforms. Second, the racists, despite much smoke and noise in Boston, were exhausting themselves politically. Many had put their hopes in the courts, but all the appeals had upheld Garrity. Though desegregation might be resented and opposed, a legal overturn appeared doubtful. Despite sympathy expressed in Washington, the antibusing constitutional amendment had not gathered any significant momentum.

At the same time, perhaps as many as two thousand white students, the children of a hardened antibusing element, were now attending segregationist academies throughout the city, removing them from the arena of conflict. Another two thousand white students had circumvented desegregated schools through illegal transfers, which were relatively easy to obtain in the bureaucratic maze of a school department whose personnel were against desegregation.

In addition an untold number of white students had registered in parochial schools, while some others had gotten into suburban schools or had simply registered at schools other than those to which they had been assigned. All but 7 of the city's 162 schools fell outside Judge Garrity's guidelines for racial composition, and the vast majority had been without turmoil. A large number of white parents had acquiesced in the order. With them the fear-inducing demagogy of Hicks and Bulger had not caught on.

In fact, a late spring survey of reading scores in elementary and middle schools had shown a *one-year rise* in scores. The racists had not been able to deliver.

The size of racist demonstrations had, in general, tended to dwindle over the past two years. With rising frustration, large marches had given way to a system of anti-Black violence and terror, to strong-arm tactics in the antibusing neighborhoods, and, consequently, to increasing secrecy and underground operation of the antibusing movement. These developments repelled many supporters and narrowed the base of the drive. The harrowing, fearful month of April caused the racist violence of

Racist men's march.

Mothers' prayer march.

the antibusing movement to be viewed with enmity by the majority of white Boston.

The frustration flowing from this reality was manifest at the Charlestown march. Contingents of jacketed marshals stood out in the throng—maroon for South Boston, blue for Charlestown. New buttons appeared: "KKK" and "White Civil Rights— NAAWP [National Association for the Advancement of White People]." Several youngsters wore "niggers suck" on their T-shirts. This was the hard-core crowd who knew the trenches and were ready for combat. It listened anxiously to speakers who set a tone of antibusing hostility but counseled peaceful approaches and a show at the polls in November. War was in the air, and the troops were ready; but they were far fewer (the Charlestown Marshals had predicted a crowd of eight thousand) than expected, and the Democratic Party generals were not about to sound the charge. Not after the week just past.

Nonetheless, the antibusing movement still had a bite. Twenty-four hours after the Charlestown march, Judge Garrity bore its marks.

For months he had been hearing testimony for Phase II, the "final plan" for the city, the finishing touches to dismantling the dual school system. A key part of that had, at one time, involved the fate of East Boston High School. But both the bigots and Black leaders knew that plans to convert East Boston High from an all-white district institution to a citywide magnet technical school, with 75 percent of the students bused in, was contingent on the completion of the multimillion-dollar Madison Park complex, near the heart of Roxbury.

The two schools were to be paired, offering white East Boston students who would be bused out the option of attending the sparkling modern complex. Madison Park, however, was unlikely to be completed for the fall of 1977 and had fallen a full year behind schedule. This sluggishness was not uncommon in Boston school construction.

Garrity's announcement of the exception of East Boston High School from Phase II was not unexpected. He designated the newly completed Barnes Middle School in East Boston, however, as a citywide magnet vocational high school. This switch implied permanent exemption of the old high school. East Boston Technical High School, with a curriculum drawn up in collaboration with the Massachusetts Institute of Technology, was assigned a composition of 50 percent white and 50 percent Black and other minorities. Garrity noted that he would reconsider the status of the old high school in a year.

While the explanation of the pairing with Madison Park was understood, it meant another full year, perhaps more, of segregation of East Boston High School, another year of the opposition digging in. Although Garrity could have altered plans for the inclusion of the school, he chose not to. The reason was to be found in words that kept cropping up in court: "stability and continuity." The judge did not want to rouse opposition.

For this reason he let stand the two thousand illegal transfers that had been challenged by NAACP lawyers. One dozen schools would have a segregated character, remaining virtually all Black. Spanking new West Roxbury High School, slated to be a desegregated magnet school, was instead designated a district high school, remaining a virtually all-white institution in one of the city's most affluent neighborhoods.

Garrity also ordered modifications allowing stricter admission standards for the city's three "accelerated" high schools, which selected students on the basis of competitive examinations. The changes came at the expense of earlier revisions he had made to open the schools to more Black students and would begin to reestablish strict "academic segregation" in the city's best schools. Such modifications, the *Boston Globe* noted, "seem designed to keep white, middle-class families in the city . . . and will open more seats for whites next September."

Thomas Atkins hinted at an appeal of the transfer decision, while criticizing the status of West Roxbury High School; but no action would be taken.

The remainder of the Phase II plan firmly established the patterns of desegregation initiated during Phase I and strengthened by Phase II. But the tone of the order, and the exemptions and modifications, signaled that Garrity had departed from the sweeping 1974 decision to eliminate segregation "root and branch" in Boston's schools. South Boston State Senator Raymond Flynn was quick to discern the elements of retreat in the plan. Phase II was "a confession of failure," he said, "a declaration of defeat that busing is not working in Boston." Antibusing school committee member Kathleen Sullivan was "encouraged because [Judge Garrity] has finally heard the school committee's message, which is that the school system must be stabilized as much as possible."

Stability, however, meant more than the absence of disruption, which was the racist answer to desegregation. It meant the first signs of white continuity in all-white schools, the germ of *resegregation.*

While Garrity was issuing Phase II for the fall of 1976, the alarm was being rung by Mayor White for an early school closing that spring. The money, he declared, had run out. Conflict between White and Garrity had been developing since the new year, with the mayor resorting to financial sabre rattling to attack the desegregation order. Now, the school department's budget was exhausted, and White claimed city financial reserves could not spare a bailout. So the schools would have to close early.

The timidity attending Phase II plans evaporated a week later in federal district court as Garrity confronted White in person and angrily rebuked him. In this dramatic showdown Garrity, not known for raising his voice, was insistent that the city come up with the $13 million necessary to keep the school's open. The early closing would be "catastrophic." Indeed, Garrity's acquiescence in the blackmail would have been a signal blow to the court's authority and an encouragement to antibusing elected officials across the country.

Garrity did not believe White and would have none of the talk of an early closing. He would not allow desegregation to be "grievously jeopardized." He ordered "all actions necessary" to make up the difference.

White, in a flurry of activity, proposed to the city council—in a maneuver designed to provoke a confrontation between that body and Garrity—a whopping, one-time $16.40 (per thousand dollars of assessed value) property tax increase. The council balked and rejected the request, setting the stage for a long-sought showdown between federal authority and city political power. The racist council members proclaimed a willingness to go to jail for contempt rather than to "bleed the city dry," accelerating "white flight."

Garrity, however, sidestepped the bold challenge. He utilized a nearly forgotten clause in the statutes of the Commonwealth of Massachusetts requiring state subsidy to meet federal court orders in the case of local financial insufficiency. The theatrical charade of last-ditch circumvention by the mayor and council had brought stern warnings from the city's ruling circles. Speaking in a united voice, they had warned, in the words of a

*Herald American* editorial, of an early "long, hot summer" if the schools were prematurely closed.

But even as Garrity found the loophole guaranteeing a normal school closing date, the same institutions made clear, through radio, television, and newspaper editorials, that the judge had refused to consider the onerous fiscal impact of desegregation. This process would have to stop if the city was to avoid financial disaster over the long run.

While Garrity was preparing his courtroom tongue-lashing of Kevin White, another storm was brewing. For months the Black, Chinese, and Puerto Rican construction workers organized in the Third World Workers Association had been pressuring firms which had city contracts to enforce affirmative action quotas on job sites—and increase them. Sometimes tense protests would temporarily close construction areas. On the morning of May 7 negotiators from the TWWA were meeting with officials from the Barletta Construction Company. The site had been closed the previous day in anticipation of negotiations.

The meeting, held in a trailer near the site, was interrupted by white officials from the Building Trades Council. As the negotiations neared termination, a dozen racist unionists charged into the trailer, shouting and brawling. Outside a gang of twenty white workers, not employees of the company, had swelled to nearly two hundred, half of them sporting the maroon jackets of the South Boston Marshals. They were led by South Boston ROAR chieftain James Kelly. Boston police quickly intervened to squelch an incipient riot.

The near confrontation had taken place in the South End, a majority Black and Puerto Rican neighborhood. The marshals had been armed with bats and clubs. Moments later key white union officials were alerted by the racist heads of the building trades. By noon two thousand white construction workers were swarming towards City Hall in an angry mood. They stormed the building, chanting and shouting, refusing to leave the lobby and smashing glass doors as they burst in. Led by Kelly and Building Trades Council President William Cleary, they speciously demanded "protection" from the TWWA, and charged, again falsely, that city money was behind the protests of the minority workers' group.

Only the preachments of Louise Day Hicks—"I love you all and I know you love me"—gained sufficient quiet for Mayor White to attempt to address the white workers. Loudly and repeatedly

Two thousand construction workers jam City Hall lobby; Hicks tells them "these Third World people want nothing but chaos."

hooted down, the nervous mayor was led into a smaller room amidst bodyguards, to confer with some business agents. Outside the building, speakers from the police and fire-fighters' unions, both heavily influenced by ROAR, offered solidarity to the construction workers in their opposition to affirmative action. "Remember, we are on your side," the spokesperson for the cops told the workers who had attempted to smash through police lines into the mayor's office.

Indeed, busing was not the only issue in Boston. ROAR was also in the unions, parading its marshals in minority communities to battle job-seeking Blacks, Puerto Ricans, and Chinese. They were able to seize City Hall in a stunning mobilization. The racists were active on all fronts in their challenge to Black rights. Rebuffed so far on school desegregation, they would be present wherever struggle broke out.

Hatred of school desegregation was the most pronounced driving force of the anti-Black movement. It would soon have a new, albeit short-lived, hope of victory. The optimism would be generated by two highly placed men in Washington—the president of the United States and his attorney general.

# 23

# The Racists Lose
# a Round in Court

The rumors had begun in early May, 1976, as leaks from the White House spread. President Ford was pushing Attorney General Edward Levi to come up with an appeal of a federal busing order, to find one that the government could side with and, by so doing, get a hearing by the United States Supreme Court.

Ford and Levi, along with Solicitor General Robert Bork, had begun secret deliberations on the matter in November of the previous year. Their strategy sessions coincided with the hearings in Judge Garrity's court, which had exposed the terrifying treatment of the Black students of South Boston High School by racist administrators, teachers, police, and white students. The nation's chief law-enforcement officials were plotting a further, more ominous move to sabotage Black rights.

The U.S. Supreme Court had to decide whether to hear any one of three separate antibusing appeals from Boston—filed by Mayor White, the Home and School Association, and the Boston School Committee. The Boston Teachers Union had also appealed sections of Garrity's desegregation order which mandated parity hiring of Black teachers until the figure of 20 percent Black employees was reached.

On May 15, in the wake of a personal investigation by Senator Edward Brooke to verify the rumors, the *New York Times* broke the story in an exclusive article. By then, partisans and foes of the desegregation order had been alerted and were beginning to mount campaigns to influence the decision that would eventually be made by Levi.

For the attorney general to enter the litigation as a "friend of the court" in behalf of one of the Boston appeals would mark a drastic departure from the position of the Justice Department on the desegregation issue. It would identify the federal government openly with white resistance to Black rights. It was no small step.

Since desegregation had begun in Boston, Ford had issued

statements opposing "forced busing." He clearly felt the heat of his conservative challenger Ronald Reagan on his right flank. Moreover, like virtually all the candidates for the presidency in both the Republican and Democratic parties, he was a champion of social and economic austerity for the average American. The latest cutback trend, directed mainly against the Black community, fitted into such a context, while at the same time appeasing and animating racist sentiment.

As a piece of legal work Judge Garrity's order was itself a rather moderate document. It ploughed no new terrain in the realm of law. It was based fundamentally on the *Brown* decision of 1954 and practically on the 1971 *Swann* and 1973 *Keyes* decisions, which had authorized and upheld busing to achieve desegregation. Both of these latter decisions had come from the Burger Supreme Court which was now faced with the Boston appeals.

Phase I had been upheld by the circuit court of appeals, and the Supreme Court had shut the door on a review hearing. Phase II had likewise been unanimously vindicated by the second highest court in the land. This judicial fortification made the Garrity order appear untouchable.

The impregnability of the Boston desegregation decision may, in fact, have punctured the ballooning expectations held by antibusing forces earlier in the spring. School Committee Chairman John McDonough had boasted to the *Herald American* that a score of city governments would file "friend of the court" briefs backing the Boston School Committee appeal. By the time of the Levi controversy, only two city governments had come forward: those of Cleveland, Ohio, and Wilmington, Delaware.

What made Boston a special object of Ford's attention was the amount of resistance that had met the Garrity order—a resistance to which he had deliberately contributed and for which he had been publicly reprimanded by the U.S. Commission on Civil Rights the year before.

In this presidential election year political capital was to be made by taking a stand against further desegregation. The Boston appeals directly challenged desegregation. That showdown aspect was both the strength of the racist appeals and at the same time their greatest weakness. Boston's bigots, overjoyed at the prospect of a positive decision by Levi, sent delegations to Washington to meet with him. Louise Day Hicks and School Committee Chairman John McDonough basked in the national capital spotlight. Boston Democratic Congressman Joseph

Moakley, whose gerrymandered district included South Boston, the North End, and Roxbury, contributed his support.

On the other side a louder outcry from Black leaders challenged Levi head on. First, the national NAACP blasted the move. On May 19, NAACP Executive Director Roy Wilkins declared that intervention would ally the government with "lawless mobs who have been responsible for the violence and ugliness directed at Black children." It would mean, NAACP Chief Legal Counsel Nathaniel Jones said, that opponents of desegregation could "stone their way into the attorney general's office, into the Supreme Court, that, no matter what the law of the land, if they hang tough, be mean and violent, the Justice Department will come to their rescue."

That same day, more than five hundred representatives of community agencies and coalitions meeting at the offices of the National Education Association in Washington, D.C., at a "Desegregation Without Turmoil" conference, called on Levi to "cease and desist" siding with the bigots. At the conference the delegates watched a videotaped message from AFL-CIO President George Meany, who lauded "The big yellow buses [that] have improved the quality of education for millions. . . . Some politicians and candidates have ignored the issue of equal justice and quality education. Demagogues have vented their spleen on busing, as if busing were the real issue. The facts prove that busing is not the issue. . . ." Though Meany did not mention Levi by name, the timely objective of his remarks was clear. "In every city where the courts have ordered action to desegregate the schools, the churches, civil rights groups, and, certainly, the unions must be mobilized. They must accept responsibility."

On May 20 leaders of the congressional Black caucus personally protested to Levi. Brooke again spoke out. Edward Kennedy quietly noted his opposition to the "friend of the court" strategy. Within the Justice Department, civil rights division chief Stanley Pottinger publicly objected.

The outrage even compelled Secretary of Transportation William Coleman, Ford's only Black cabinet member—who had come to prominence by helping to formulate and argue the *Brown* case as an NAACP attorney years before—to urge Levi to stay on the sidelines. Backing the appeal against Garrity's order, he delicately advised, "would be ill-timed and unsound in law."

Levi was deluged with opposition from his academic peers across the country. "The academic community really rose up," an anonymous insider told the *Boston Globe*.

A sharply worded protest was sent from Boston by a wide array of Black leaders on the initiative of the Freedom House. On May 21 the National Student Coalition Against Racism held a news conference at which NSCAR Coordinator Maceo Dixon and Massachusetts Civil Liberties Union Director Ellen Feingold termed Levi's very consideration of intervention a "capitulation to violence."

NAACP leaders, including Roy Wilkins and Clarence Mitchell, met with Levi in a gathering marked by heated exchanges. As Wilkins rose to leave the attorney general's office, he looked at Levi, asking, "Why now, why now?" Levi turned from the elder statesman of the NAACP, refusing to answer.

On May 20, while campaigning in Kentucky, Ford hinted Levi might use an antibusing appeal from Louisville to test desegregation. The Justice Department officially denied the Ford trial balloon. Shortly afterward, a Ford spokesperson retracted the president's remark, terming it "hypothetical."

Levi weakened under the pressure of the massive protests, postponing the date on which he would announce his decision. The projected intervention in collusion with Boston's racists had created an uproar that started in the Black community and reached into the highest circles of the government. There, differences existed not over how to support Black rights but how to *oppose* them. In a game with very high stakes, Ford had tipped his hand too early.

The *New York Times* noted the inherent significance of a federal decision to back a Boston antibusing appeal: "The first message—even worse than that issued by President Ford in 1974 when he 'respectfully disagreed' with Judge Garrity's original order—would be to encourage resistance to the orders of the Federal courts. The signal would simply read that if one disagrees loudly enough, throws enough bricks, breaks enough windows and injures enough people, the Justice Department ultimately will back down and ask the courts to bend the law to accommodate violent resistance to it. . . . Black Americans will be put on notice that the Department of Justice . . . has concluded that there are no remedies for their rights and that the last twenty-two years have been nothing more than a cruel hoax."

The *Times* editorial—coinciding with the anniversary of the *Brown* decision—bespoke two great fears. First, the perpetration of a spectacular federal betrayal of Black rights—a "cruel hoax" undoing the gains of twenty-two post-*Brown* years—would spur

Black America into a militant response to such a monumental grievance that would bring forward a more aggressive leadership and a higher level of consciousness. The accommodation by Levi and the courts would at once signal to Blacks that the highest judiciary—the institution viewed as least susceptible to racism, and hence a hope of last resort—was a mortal foe. A concurrent surge by the racists would upset the status quo through more Bostons, more struggles, more polarization and political confrontation.

Moreover, a stunning "legal" setback for Black rights would imperil the image of U.S. foreign policy in Asia, Africa, and Latin America—particularly in Africa, where already Blacks in Angola, Rhodesia, and South Africa hardly viewed the American flag with friendship. Any efforts by the State Department to curry favor with Black regimes, to appear at least "neutral" regarding racism and apartheid in the unfolding struggles between the African masses and white settler regimes, would not be enhanced by domestic assaults on the rights of Afro-Americans.

*Appearing* to enforce the law in Boston was a better option than knuckling under to a white resistance that was declining in active size and had a national reputation for anti-Black violence. Accordingly, on May 25, Levi made his decision public. There would be no support for any of the Boston antibusing appeals.

Louise Day Hicks wasted no time in replying. "People," she warned, "might lose their heads." For ROAR's James Kelly the situation had come down to bare knuckles. "Perhaps it is time to start some intimidation of our own," he said in denouncing the protest that had been raised by supporters of desegregation. "The Black power base was built on violence and we have to resort to the same tactics if necessary, and it appears that it is necessary." Kelly was advising the diehards that there was "no other recourse except for violence."

That night, the windows of nine downtown department stores, shops, and banks were smashed out. The Boston Tea Party Ship Museum was set on fire, resulting in $75,000 damage. A "Michael O'Connor," in behalf of the South Boston Defense League, took credit for the action through telephone calls to the Boston media. Shortly afterward racists bombed the Paul Revere House and Plymouth Rock.

The terrorist organization, Kelly told reporters, called him periodically although, he claimed, he had no idea who they were. But they had "supplies to do anything . . . and intended to create havoc in Boston."

As Levi announced his decision, the White House made public Ford's intention to propose legislation placing a five-year limit on busing orders and narrowing the scope of orders that could be issued. On the executive level the campaign against desegregation was not dead.

The stage was set for the Supreme Court. Lawyers for the Boston School Committee, the Home and School Association, the mayor, and the Boston Teachers Union had presented arguments in favor of the high court hearing the appeals, and attorneys for the Black plaintiffs had responded. On Monday, June 14, the Boston cases appeared on the Supreme Court's regular list of its actions on pending hearings. Opposite each one were two words printed many times before: "*Certiorari* denied."

The news interrupted television and radio broadcasts in Boston, filling the front pages of the papers. Kevin White was "disappointed." Louise Day Hicks was angry. "The people of Boston have been had, and they will respond." Pixie Palladino was angrier. "Now people are up against the wall with no place to go." James Kelly was angriest. "As long as there is forced busing in this city, violence and racial confrontation are unavoidable. . . . There is no longer justice for the white people in this country."

For Thomas Atkins the outcome had been predictable. "The Supreme Court confirmed what we already knew—that none of the appeals of Judge Garrity's decision had any merit." He urged the antibusing forces to relent and "work together" with the Black community in implementing the law.

Some segregationists would hold out a last hope—appeals of Garrity's receivership order of December 9, 1975, and *pro forma* opposition to Phase II. That was always the bottom line. All the other expectations had been dashed: Racial balance would never come; Phase I would never come; the buses would never roll; Phase II would be overturned; Levi would help us out; the courts would answer.

Now it all seemed hollow. The *Boston Herald*, saddened by the Supreme Court decision, printed a chronology of the years of controversy with the final entry June 14, a date that suddenly loomed large.

Thayer Fremont-Smith, after years of legal toil representing the Home and School Association in opposing desegregation, appeared tired. One Black leader, a longtime adversary, put it exultantly: Fremont-Smith "waved the white flag." The antibusing lawyer had said there is "nothing we can do about it. I'm afraid people will have to live with the . . . order for the sake of the children that are attending school."

Following the court decision, groups of racists splashed balloons full of red paint on the walls of Boston City Hall and Faneuil Hall. Attached to the mouths of the shriveled, paint-smeared bits of rubber were hand-stamped calling cards: "Stop forced busing." In Boston, at least, the bubble had burst.

The city's racists had unsuccessfully tried to batter down the front door of the Supreme Court. Formalities aside, Gerald Ford had entered his own "friend of the court" comments. But they were not enough.

On June 14 the U.S. Supreme Court acted again, in a more substantive way than simply refusing to hear an appeal. The Pasadena antibusing case had been on its docket for more than a year and a half. Now came the ruling.

In the process of desegregation of Pasadena's dual school system, white population shifts in the city had occurred, negating assignments designed to reflect a "unitary" and "racially neutral" student composition in the district. Dubbed "white flight" by local antibusing school board members, the changes resegregated the schools. Federal District Judge John Real, who had ordered the initial desegregation plan, instituted yearly adjustments in the busing order to effect compliance with his decision that no school have more than 50 percent Black and other minority students. Swept into office by antibusing senti-ment, the school board appealed the decision to the Ninth Circuit Court of Appeals, which, however, upheld the ruling.

The Pasadena case was known as the "white flight" appeal. It implied that residential shifts—in many cases to avoid busing— were an effect of court-ordered desegregation. Consequently, it argued, there was no constitutional basis for continuing adjust-ment of the implementation orders.

By a six-to-two margin (newly confirmed Justice John Stevens disqualified himself, having recently left the law firm represent-ing the foes of the busing order) the high court issued a decision favorable to the school board, referring to the historic *Swann* case for precedent. That 1971 decision had noted that "it does not follow that communities served by unitary systems will remain demographically stable, for in a growing, mobile society few will do so. Neither school authorities nor district courts are constitu-tionally required to make year-by-year adjustments of the racial composition of student bodies once the affirmative duty to desegregate has been accomplished and racial discrimination through official action is eliminated from the system."

By sleight of hand the high court majority now noted arguments raised against the school board for noncompliance with aspects of the initial order concerning hiring and promotion procedures for Black teachers and administrators. Such noncompliance would contradict the achievement of a "unitary system" described in *Swann*. But, for the judges, that, in and of itself, "does not undercut the force of the principle" articulated in the decision.

The judges did not address themselves in particular to "white flight," but rather to judicial authority in the adjustment of desegregation plans. "No one," the majority held, "disputes that the initial implementation of this plan accomplishes . . . racial neutrality. . . . That being the case, the District Court was not entitled to require the school to rearrange its attendance zones . . . to assure that the racial mix desired by the court was maintained *in perpetuity*" (emphasis added).

In other words, *initial* "racial balance" of the schools—the first step towards desegregation and elimination of the dual school system—was to be the decisive measure of remedying discrimination. Should population shifts create segregation once more, there was no option for judicial intervention. The court's work was over, unless proof of school department activity obstructing balance could be found.

The court did not overturn the original busing order but sent the case back to the court of appeals for modifications and possible reversal. The verdict had no impact on the Boston case, yet it seemed to hold out a gleam of hope, as that city's school committee chairman, John McDonough, noted. Segregation, he said, "was caused in the first instance by population shifts and housing patterns. . . . Just as segregation occurred naturally, resegregation will occur." Because of the Pasadena decision, he boasted, "this time, the courts will not be able to do anything about it."

Summer began and school in Boston ended on June 22, a virtually cloudless, languid day, the kind of day made for cutting classes. The second year of desegregation was over.

For the majority of students, Black and white, it had been a productive year. Only a handful of schools had been centers of turmoil. "If only the parents would leave us alone"—this was the common refrain among white students not engaged in the organized disruption.

Despite the monumental obstructions put up by the antibusing movement—from street and school violence directed at Black and Puerto Rican students to consistent defiance from the school committee and the mayor's office—desegregation had taken hold in most of the city's schools. In two years Boston's dual school system had been virtually uprooted. Gone was the systematic exclusion of Black students from the city's better schools. The segregationist feeder patterns had been broken. The "open enrollment" scheme, which shackled Black students to the most deteriorated and poorly staffed schools in Boston, was abolished. The technical quality of the education and preparation of Black students had risen.

Regardless of the tirades of the bigots, "white flight" was a largely bogus claim. While white student enrollment had dropped overall, making the school system majority Black and Puerto Rican, the figures utilized by the racists to claim an exodus of twenty thousand white students were inflated.

Before desegregation had begun, the names of some white students had cropped up as many as three, four, and five times on computer printouts of citywide enrollment rosters. This had resulted in greater federal aid. After desegregation started, the school department eliminated the replications, and the bigots claimed these phantom students as part of "white flight." A rigorous, court-ordered analysis of attendance figures revealed the extent of this statistical swindle—untold thousands, according to one desegregation attorney.

The real drop of white students, hovering around seven thousand, represented the organized strength of the white student boycott and re-enrollment in the "segregation academies" and suburban and parochial schools, all amounting to about 10 percent of the school system's population. Late summer 1976 surveys indicated a decline of student enrollment in the suburbs, further disproving "white flight."

The population of South Boston, the neighborhood of strongest resistance to desegregation, actually *rose* slightly over one percent during the first year of desegregation. This was hardly an indication of "flight." With the beginning of the third year of desegregation in Boston, the student composition was 47 percent white, 41 percent Black, and 12 percent "other minority."

Among the Black students there existed a deep sense of determination. Many of them recognized that the act of simply going to school was important. A heightened sense of awareness pervaded Roxbury. "Now," Ellen Jackson remarked, "people realize that what happens in the schools touches every part of our lives. You go into a beauty parlor, a barber shop, and people say, 'What can *I* do?'"

There was, according to Thomas Atkins, "more ferment" in the schools—in the positive sense—than ever before. Court-mandated parent councils, notwithstanding the controversy of desegregation itself, had infused unprecedented parent involvement into the school system. The magnet schools had enthused students, teachers, parents—Black and white—in a year virtually without incident for them.

Only 7 of the system's 162 schools were deemed crisis-ridden by the attorneys for the Black plaintiffs in the desegregation case. Yet, for all the advances accomplished over the past two years, the toll was—and remains—high.

While the most visible aspects of institutional racism within the system had received a body blow, the city was hardly calm. Into the summer, Black families in Dorchester and Hyde Park faced physical attacks as an almost daily routine. Part of the agonizing ritual was the police inaction.

By mid-summer the Debnams, a Black family in Dorchester, had spent more than fifteen hundred dollars on windows and had fended off a demonstration of one hundred racists at their doorstep. This took place despite relatively consistent publicity and police awareness of their plight dating back six months.

They were not alone. By June all forty-three Black and Puerto Rican families living in the Maverick area projects of East Boston had been driven out of their homes. The racist gang responsible called itself "KKK Junior." Random beatings, unreported harassment, and violence against Black families in predominantly white neighborhoods pockmarked the city. Blacks did not venture near Carson Beach.

The city suffered a polarization imposed by the bigots, tolerated by the city government and the police, and covered up by the media in deference to a sham housecleaning operation designed to woo bicentennial tourists to a "safe Boston." Despite the hush-up, expectations of merchants and hotel operators for whopping profits failed to materialize. The polarization was so pronounced that Ferguson Jenkins, the star Black pitcher for the Boston Red Sox, commented on the scarcity of Black fans in Fenway Park.

# 24

# Boston Today—
# the Struggle Continues

Today—January 1977—Boston exists in a contradictory condition. On the one hand, key elements in one of the most rigidly segregated school systems in America have been dismantled. Though its teaching and administrative staffs do not comply with the racial composition ordered by Judge Garrity, though segregationist bias is rife within the school department bureaucracy, though the Boston School Committee maintains a posture of defiance, significant aspects of the dual system have been removed. As a product of years of struggle by the Black community, this is a victory.

Yet the city itself contains highly volatile ingredients. The ROAR apparatus remains, if somewhat deflated, along with the South Boston and Charlestown Marshals. A mood of violence is tangible in those racist communities. Blacks are not safe in a majority of the city's neighborhoods. Tension prevails.

Consequently the desegregation of the Boston schools cannot as yet be considered complete or permanent. And, since any definition of freedom includes the right to live and move safely anywhere in the city, Black rights remain under challenge.

Some in Boston exhibit a strong sense of optimism. For example, Thomas Atkins sees an unrelenting "forward march" nationally. The city's racists, he notes, have been "met and we have beaten them." Redress of grievances of segregation will be delivered affirmatively by the government "in the courts, the legislative chambers, and administrative rooms." For Atkins, "street action" is subordinate, to be used to "dramatize and facilitate activity" in those governmental arenas. The legal route remains the essence of the strategy he advocates.

For others, like Ruth Batson, the struggle in Boston is not over "until there are no more 'incidents,' until we feel safe in the streets." The big tests for desegregation are still in the offing: Philadelphia, Los Angeles, Chicago. "I can't imagine that what has happened here will happen there," she says, "I can't imagine a return to before 1954." Still, Batson is not comfortable with the promises of the "politicians," from Mayor White to Jimmy Carter. What will stop retreats, she affirms, is "public outcry and uproar, the kind of thing that happened when Levi said he was considering Boston for appeal."

Ellen Jackson spent an agonizing spring and summer plagued with serious illness. She worried about the third year of school desegregation in Boston. "We are more unprepared," she says. Funding cutbacks have crippled community agencies in general and those concerned with desegregation in particular. Money from the government is drying up. "It is a penalty, a punishment," she says, for supporting desegregation. Her staff has been cut from twenty to six by funding slashes. Ruth Batson's Crisis Intervention Teams have likewise been reduced. This is a microcosm of what is happening nationally. "All the gains are under attack," Jackson says. She continues working, despite poor health, unsure of what lies in store.

Percy Wilson sees "five very tough years [in Boston] for the climate to change." The fight around school desegregation, he says, points to a new locus of confrontations, "a test of the housing patterns" which segregated Blacks in the first place. "Boston is a Birmingham, a Selma, and it has to be broken," Wilson points out. "Every pressure has to be mounted to make that happen, because where Boston goes, the country will go."

This sampling of the city's recognized Black leaders share a common respect for a new force in the struggle, the National Student Coalition Against Racism. The multiracial group, Atkins says, has had an "overwhelmingly positive, overwhelmingly constructive impact," notwithstanding important differences in strategy and assessment with the NAACP. Should it continue to grow, "it will be a major national force." NSCAR, Ruth Batson says, "has filled an enormous vacuum. . . . I'm for it because I'm for *action.*"

The new antiracist student group has challenged long-held beliefs of many Black leaders, and its ideas provide a center of discussion and debate. Ellen Jackson notes differences on the need for demonstrations. "Some of us have been that route, and we aren't sure any more, or are just exhausted." But, she says in the same breath, NSCAR, in the context of the crisis facing the national Black community, "may be the new SNCC [Student Nonviolent Coordinating Committee]."

"They put pressure on us and we put pressure on them," Atkins emphasizes. A source of such pressure, NSCAR Coordinator Dixon says, is his organization's view of the state of the Black movement and the way forward. "Big blows have been dealt Boston's racists," he says. "They are demoralized. Still there is the mood of resistance, the hatred. There is the hard core— ROAR, the marshals, the organized racists *inside* the schools. There is a tentativeness of things in Boston. There may be moments, weeks, even months of calm. But the *national* desegregation picture is completely unresolved. The elections have slowed down further developments. However, busing is too volatile an issue. The uneasy calm reminds me of the time around Lyndon Johnson's 'peace candidacy.' Goldwater was the war-monger. Then LBJ was elected, the electioneering hot air was over, and bang—the war escalated and the resistance started.

"Black people have never won anything in this country without a fight. The Supreme Court annointed Jim Crow in 1896. In 1954 segregation was declared illegal on paper. But what *implemented* the new 'law of the land' was not the court decision by itself but an entire decade of militant struggle and protest that came after a virtual mobilization of the national Black community. That rising up had the sympathy of people all over the world, and it shook this country to its roots. That's the real basis of every gain we've won.

"The government is trying to rip all those gains back. It is saying Black rights are too 'costly.' Well, we think that no matter what happens today or tomorrow, the Black community and the levels of government that back up bigotry are on a collision course. And the only way we are going to survive, to put teeth in the Bill of Rights, is to fight, to organize, to march, to protest, without putting an eyedropperful of trust in the courts, the Congress, or whoever is president."

A former SCAR leader, Mac Warren, remains a supporter of the coalition. He ran for Congress in Roxbury on the Socialist Workers Party ticket in the fall of 1976. Ellen Jackson and Ruth Batson endorsed his campaign.

The election was peculiar. Democrat Joseph Moakley, the

incumbent, is a leader of antibusing forces in Congress. Through gerrymandering, his district includes South Boston, the North End, and other parts of white Boston, as well as Roxbury. Running as a bogus "independent" and "friend of the Black community" in 1972, he pushed aside the ballot-designated Democrat, Louise Day Hicks, who was endorsed by George McGovern.

"That, in a nutshell, is the crisis of our community," Warren says. "Choosing between lesser-evil Democrats. Being lined up between Hicks, who had McGovern's backing, and Moakley, our 'friend.' The tying of the Black community to a racist party by Black leaders who think change is going to come through one of its 'progressive' wings is deadly. Then we are placed between a hammer and an anvil. Our power is broken.

"Boston is where it is today precisely because of the Democratic Party, both in its lesser and greater evils. To win desegregation in Boston we had to fight that organization's representatives. Our biggest gains came in the early 1960s when we were in the streets. Things stagnated when those protests stopped. Everything was delayed except for the construction of a few community agencies, which are now being gutted by cutbacks. A few [Black] Democrats were elected from the community. They are powerless in real life, especially since, as a rule, they continue to look to the Democratic Party—not to the power that could be organized in the streets that is the community's real basis of strength.

"If you expand the view beyond Boston, the same thing is true nationally. Looking back, what stopped the racists from rolling over us here was not Judge Garrity. It was the manifestation of our power as a mass movement, at least the potential it had."

Warren reviews the milestones of antiracist demonstrations. November 30, 1974. December 14, 1974. May 17, 1975. Carson Beach, August 9, 1975. "Together, their force was greater than that of the bigots. Together, they said we are going to fight. That gave the court backbone and pushed the mayor. But these are not enough because today I can't go into Joe Moakley's office in Southie without getting beaten up. And the national picture, for Blacks, is not upbeat. At best we're in a holding action, a shaky position to be in. At worst, we're in retreat. Our leaders aren't leading. The biggest assist to school desegregation in Boston, let alone in America, may very well come from across the ocean, from the effect of the struggle heating up in Southern Africa. . . ."

The results of the next stage of the struggle will depend a great deal on the kind of leadership the movement gets. Thomas Atkins notes that the "war on poverty" of the 1960s "poured a lot of money in the community but bought off a lot of energy, diverted a lot of effort, isolated a lot of leaders."

Ruth Batson, after two decades of participation in the desegregation struggle, grapples with the problem of the "vacuum" of what she terms "our so-called leaders" and the dangerous notion that "we can wish away the situation in the city" because "peace" is declared by the mayor and the media.

Percy Wilson points to NSCAR's independence as its source of strength. It has "no ties to the mayor," it has no funds that can be taken back. It is not beholden to anyone for favors. "It has to go out there and do it, be a beacon for folks to follow."

Although the national effects of the school battle have yet to be definitively tallied, a tentative balance sheet has begun to emerge. "Forced busing" has become the pivotal issue defining the federal government's retreat on Black rights. It was the codeword for racism in the 1976 platforms of the two major parties. For the Republicans, a constitutional amendment against busing for the purpose of school desegregation was the election year cry. For the Democrats, busing—the *central* means to desegregate the schools—was a "judicial tool of last resort." President Carter has shown himself to be a foe of court-ordered busing.

The year 1976 brought piecemeal setbacks for school desegregation. While the tumult raised by the Boston bigots has encouraged resistance from Pasadena to Queens, from Dallas to Wilmington, the national trend has been an *erosion* of Black rights, not spectacular assaults. This began with the Supreme Court's Pasadena decision and has traveled across the country: a "voluntary" busing plan in Saint Louis; the all-Black busing order in Dallas; a similar "voluntary" scheme in Milwaukee; a year's delay of city-suburban busing in Wilmington, Delaware; a New York State Board of Regents decision withdrawing a desegregation order for two Queens high schools. Chicago, America's most segregated city, remains without a school desegregation order, although there is a plan to end segregation of faculties.

Major court decisions noting the need for desegregation have been made in Cleveland and Buffalo, but with no plans as yet.

Fully six hundred school districts are within the purview of existing or anticipated desegregation orders.

The bulk of post-Boston plans, however, have been marked by an avoidance of thoroughgoing measures against segregation. They have placed the burden of busing solely on Blacks; stressed "voluntary" and/or "magnet" approaches rather than systematic, mandatory plans; and utilized "open enrollment" gimmicks— which are unconstitutional under Supreme Court guidelines— instead of the forceful reorganization methods required to root out the effects of long-standing segregation.

This pattern is tied in with the government–big business campaign to make the Black community into a scapegoat for the economic crisis. The racist alliance that runs America whips up racism with the claim that the gains won by the civil rights and Black liberation struggle came out of the pockets of white workers; they use this lie to justify the cutbacks, which hit Blacks, Chicanos, Puerto Ricans, and women especially hard. These groups—the last hired, first fired—are slated to bear the worst of the economic downturn. School desegregation is only the first battle front.

In the past, Boston gave birth to rebels against British tyranny, to abolitionists, to Black Civil War regiments. It was a place were Blacks began to struggle for equality nearly two hundred years ago. Martin Luther King, Jr., and Malcolm X both lived there for a time.

Malcolm X once said, "We won't organize any Black man to be a Democrat or a Republic because both of them have sold us out." His conclusion that "both parties are racist" has been confirmed in the school desegregation battle.

In summing up the experience of the civil rights movement, King, who mistakenly supported the Democratic Party, stressed the need for mass action: "The 1960 sit-ins desegregated lunch counters in more than 150 cities within one year. The 1961 Freedom Rides put an end to segregation in interstate travel. The 1956 bus boycott in Montgomery, Alabama, ended the segregation on the buses not only of that city but practically every city of the South. The 1963 Birmingham movement and the climactic March on Washington won passage of the most powerful civil rights law in a century. The 1965 Selma movement brought enactment of the Voting Rights law. . . ."

Independence from the Democrats and Republicans and the need for mass actions—these are not just historical lessons, they are essential weapons. A new generation of Black leaders, armed with these ideas, has come forward and gained battle experience in the Boston struggle.

A partial victory has been won, but the racist offensive has not been defeated. The battle of Boston will go on. And there will be more Bostons—new attacks on Black rights, new tests for the Black movement and its allies.

As the "cradle of liberty" enters its third year of desegregation, the war is far from over.

# Appendix

*The following is the introduction to the Boston desegregation ruling by Judge Garrity. It summarizes the court's findings and the goals it established for racial balance in the schools. Legal citations have been deleted for ease of reading.*

### Tallulah MORGAN et al., Plaintiffs,
### v.
### James W. HENNIGAN et al., Defendants.
### Civ. A. No. 72-911-G.

United States District Court,
D. Massachusetts.
June 21, 1974

School desegregation suit brought by black parents and their children who attend Boston public schools against the Boston school committee, its individual members, the superintendent of the Boston public schools, the Board of Education of the Commonwealth of Massachusetts, its individual members, and the Commissioner of Education for declaratory and injunctive relief against the acts that allegedly violate the constitutional rights of the plaintiff class. The District Court, Garrity, J., held that the evidence established that the school authorities had knowingly carried out a systematic program of segregation affecting all of the city's students, teachers and school facilities and had intentionally brought about or maintained a dual school system; that the entire school system of Boston was unconstitutionally segregated; that the Massachusetts Commonwealth Board of Education and its Commissioner of Education were not responsible for the maintenance of a dual system but would be retained as parties for the purposes of remedial relief; that the school committee would be permanently enjoined from discriminating on the basis of race in the operation of the Boston schools;

and that they would be ordered to formulate and implement plans to secure for the plaintiffs their constitutional rights. The Court further set forth remedial guidelines.

Order in accordance with opinion.

Evidence established that the Board of Education of Commonwealth of Massachusetts, its individual members and the Commissioner of Education were not responsible for racial segregation in the schools of Boston because of conflicts concerning application of the Racial Imbalance Act of Massachusetts or because of state court litigation.

The Massachusetts Racial Imbalance Act and Constitution of the United States are not in conflict and the Massachusetts Act is facially valid.

Evidence established that racial segregation in the schools of Boston was not the result of the actions of the Boston school committee, its individual members or the superintendent of schools having complied with the Massachusetts Racial Imbalance Act.

In a school desegregation case, the court's primary task is to determine whether the defendants have intentionally and purposefully caused or maintained racial segregation in meaningful or significant segments of the public school system in violation of the Fourteenth Amendment.

Evidence established that in the matter of facilities utilization and construction of new structures within the Boston school system, the defendants were covertly resisting the elimination of racial imbalance and endeavoring to perpetuate racially segregated schools.

Evidence established the intent of the Boston school committee in its determination of which of two high schools new building would replace was to keep the student body of one of the high schools predominantly black.

Evidence established that Boston school committee made districting changes for the purpose of perpetuating racial segregation in the Boston public school system.

Evidence established that racial segregation of elementary students in the Boston public school system was facilitated by the existence of multischool districts.

Evidence established that implementation of feeder patterns for Boston high schools and the creation of transfer options were made for the purpose of promoting racial segregation.

Evidence established that the open enrollment and controlled transfer policies adopted by the Boston school committee operated as an aid to racial segregation rather than as aid to integration.

Independent of student assignment, where it is possible to identify a "white school" or a "Negro school" simply by reference to the racial composition of the teachers and staff, the quality of school buildings and equipment, or the organizations of sports activities, prima facie case of denial of equal protection is shown, and the first remedial responsibility of school authorities is to eliminate invidious racial distinctions and produce schools of like quality, facilities, and staff.

Evidence established that Boston school committee knowingly pursued policies which resulted in racial segregation of teachers and administrative personnel which reinforced the racial identifiability of schools and which increased the racial segregation of students.

Evidence established that in the Boston school system the black teachers are segregated in black schools.

The Fourteenth Amendment bans intentional racial segregation in public schools whatever may be the desires of black teachers or parents.

Evidence established that the personnel policies of the Boston school committee resulted in predominantly black schools being staffed with less qualified and experienced teachers and with ever-changing faculties, all to the detriment of black pupils who generally were receiving an education unequal to that being given white pupils.

Evidence established that the lack of blacks in administrative positions in the Boston public school system was due to racially discriminatory hiring and promotion practices knowingly followed by the Boston school committee.

Evidence established that the racial segregation in the college preparatory or "examination schools" and the vocational schools was intentional on part of the Boston school committee.

Where plaintiffs had made detailed showing of intentional segregation of students and staff at all grade levels and in all parts of the city and a showing of racial segregation in the "examination schools" and vocational schools and programs, a prima facie case of unlawful segregated design on the part of school authorities was made with respect to the "examination schools" and vocational schools programs.

School authorities had burden of proving unlawful intent in the creation of segregation in the "examination schools" and vocational schools programs within the system.

If school officials had followed for at least a decade a persistent course of conduct which intentionally incorporated residential segregation into the system's schools, that conduct was unconstitutional.

When school districting and a neighborhood school system are fraught with segregative exceptions, the defenses of de facto segregation due to segregated housing patterns and adherence to a neighborhood school policy need not be considered in a desegregation suit.

Evidence established that the segregation in Boston schools was not the inevitable consequence of segregated housing patterns and the increase in the city's black population for which the Boston school committee was not responsible.

Evidence established that neighborhood school policy of Boston school committee was so selective as hardly to have amounted to a policy at all and that several practices of the committee, including extensive busing, open enrollment, multi-school districts, magnet schools, citywide schools and feeder patterns, were antithetical to a neighborhood school system.

No section of the city of Boston was "separate, identifiable and unrelated" so as to remove from school authorities the affirmative duty to effectuate transition to racially nondiscriminatory school system.

Evidence established that the Massachusetts Board of Education and the Massachusetts Commissioner of Education did not intentionally contribute to or participate in any substantial way in creating or maintaining racial segregation in the Boston public schools.

In view of the ultimate responsibility of the Massachusetts State Board of Education and the State Commissioner for the education of pupils and the Boston public school system, their continued presence in the desegregation suit was necessary for the purposes of formulating and aiding in the execution of appropriate remedy for racial segregation although they had not contributed to the racial segregation that pervaded the Boston schools.

In resolving whether city school committee acted with a "purpose or intent to segregate" public school system, either with desire to bring about or continue segregation in the schools or with knowledge that such segregation was certain, or substantially certain, to result from their actions, the court need not ascertain the ultimate reasons why the schools officials made certain decisions.

Racial hostility is not the applicable standard in determining whether the maintenance of a dual school system is unconstitutional.

Segregation in public school system need not have been inspired by any particular racial attitude in order to be unconstitutional.

The intent to segregate school system need not be the sole purpose for the actions of school committee; it need only be one of them in order to make dual school system unconstitutional.

A course of intentionally discriminatory decisions by school officials, all arrived at independently, which over the years has produced a dual school system is unconstitutional although there is no proof of a common scheme linking each decision.

Discriminatory policy which results in a dual school system may be shown in a number of ways such as by direct evidence of discriminatory segregative steps or by indirect evidence, including the absence of valid educational, fiscal, administrative or other governmental justifications for decisions having clearly foreseeable segregative consequences.

If actions of school authorities were to any degree motivated by segregative intent and segregation which resulted from those actions continues to exist, fact of remoteness in time does not make those actions any less intentional.

Evidence established that the entire school system of Boston was unconstitutionally segregated as result of pervasive practices of school authorities which were intentionally segregative.

Boston school committee and superintendent of schools would be permanently enjoined from discriminating upon the basis of race in the operation of the Boston public schools and would be ordered to begin forthwith the formulation and implementation of class to secure the constitutional rights of black pupils.

Boston school committee and the superintendent of Boston schools had affirmative obligation to reverse the consequences of their unconstitutional conduct and to eliminate all vestiges of the dual system "root and branch"; neutral conduct was not constitutionally sufficient.

In ascertaining school officials' compliance of obligation to proceed now to secure the rights of plaintiffs in desegregation case, the remedial plan is to be judged by its effectiveness.

The primary responsibility for desegregation of a school system lies with the school committee or board of education.

If, in fulfilling the responsibility for desegregation, policy preferences hinder or obstruct the conversion to the unitary school system, they must give way since they would hinder vindication of federal constitutional guarantees.

A preference not to bus, or for neighborhood schools, or any other policy preference, can be validly maintained by school authorities only if it will not interfere with the authorities' constitutional duty to desegregate.

No amount of public or parental opposition will excuse avoidance by school officials of constitutional obligations to desegregate and the constitutional principles which mandate duty to desegregate cannot be allowed to yield simply because of disagreement with them.

School authorities are clearly charged with the affirmative duty to take whatever steps might be necessary to convert to a unitary system and this means that busing, the pairing of schools, redistricting with both contiguous and noncontiguous boundary lines, involuntary student and faculty assignments, and all other means, some of which may be distasteful to both school officials and teachers and parents, must be evaluated and, if necessary to achieve a unitary school system, they must be implemented.

Ideally every school in Boston school system should have the same racial proportions, although as practical matter there was no prospect of achieving the 2:1 ratio in every school.

Where school officials have been found to have committed discriminatory acts as to a specific school facility, no desegregation plan which ultimately leaves the racial identifiability of that facility untouched will be constitutionally sufficient.

The time allowed for compliance with order to desegregate school system must be only that reasonably necessary to design and evaluate plans to be presented to the court and thereafter only the time reasonably necessary, administratively, to implement the desegregation plan which is ultimately approved by the court.

# Index

Abernathy, Ralph D., 89, 95

Abortion, 122, 126, 134

Academies, segregationist, 206, 249

Affirmative action, 221-22

AFL-CIO, 100-101, 103

Alexander, Michael, 167

All African People's Revolutionary Party, 231

Amalfitano, Tracy, 106-7

*An American Dilemma,* 40

American Federation of Teachers, 102. *See also* Boston Teachers Union

Antibusing amendment, 97, 130, 174, 217

Antibusing demonstrations
—1974: 24, 78, 97-98
—1975: 130, 163, 165-66, 185-86, 193
—1976: 202, 204, 211, 212, 215, 223-26, 248, 249, 251, 254-56

Appeals: of Phase I, 101, 117; of Phase II, 199-200, 257-62

Armstrong, Gary, 211

Atkins, Thomas, 27, 56, 63, 119-20, 252; and court suits, 53, 131, 134, 196, 262; and demonstrations, 28, 120-23, 153-54, 158, 160, 182, 242, 246

Barrowright, James, 150

Batson, Ruth, 52, 64-66, 267-68, 271; and April 24 action, 202, 219; and crisis teams, 147-49, 176

Best, John, 200-201

Biden Amendment, 174

Bilingual-bicultural education: in Denver, 184; in Boston, 199

Biracial councils, 106, 149

Birmingham, 46

Bivins, Ollie, 67

Black Educators Association of Massachusetts (BEAM), 172

Black schools, 55-56, 59

Bolling, Royal, 68

Bond, Julian, 89

Bonner-Lyons, Patricia, 28, 124

Bork, Robert, 257

Boston: housing, 21-22; liberal image, 18-19; map, 14; neighborhoods, 14, 19-20; racial composition, 19, unemployment, 20-21

*Boston Globe,* 125, 168, 197, 235, 252; poll of Blacks on busing, 165; reporter beaten, 212; ROAR attacks, 33

*Boston Herald American,* 33, 34, 206, 226, 254, 262

Boston School Committee, 23, 29, 161; and Phase I, 117; and Phase II, 118-19, 146-47; sabotage of Racial Imbalance Law, 56; and teachers' strike, 172

Boston State College, 61

Boston Teachers Union, 101-2, 171-72

Boston Technical High School, 60

Boycotts, 54, 75, 165, 185-86

Bradley, Ruby, 203-4

Breeden, James, 53

Broderick, Chester, 142, 165

Brooke, Edward, 54, 130, 159, 257, 259

*Brown* v. *Topeka Board of Education,* 9, 41-43

Budd, Reginald, 151

Building trades council, 21, 254

Bulger, William, 82, 131, 186, 193, 215, 246

Bumpers, Robert, 150

Bunte, Doris, 217, 240

Busing, 60, 89, 164-65; in other cities, 103, 139, 162-64, 193, 203, 218

Byrd antibusing amendment, 174
Byrne, Garret, 122

CAR, 126, 135, 155-56, 230
Carroll, Julian, 163
Carson Beach: 26, 145, 149-50, 151-54; community picnic, 155-61
Carter, Alma, 85
Carter, Jimmy, 216, 271
Carter, Vernon, 55, 89
Cass, Melnea, 68, 112
Catholic Laboure Centre, 107
Chopper, Phillip, 164
Ciano, Michael, 126
Citizens for Participation in Political Action, 71
Citywide Coordinating Council (CCC), 111, 146-47, 209-10
Citywide Education Coalition, 64
Civil disobedience, 92, 95
Civil Rights Act of 1964, 47
Civil rights commission, 161, 174
Cleary, William, 254
Coalition of Black Trade Unionists, 103
Coleman, William, 259
Columbia Point, 26, 67
Commission of Inquiry on Racist Violence, 150-52
Committee Against Racism (CAR), 126, 135, 155-56, 230
Committee for Quality, Integrated Education, 71
Communist Party, 124, 125
Concerned Parents, 163
Congress on Racial Equality, 48, 49
Connor, Sue, 163
Constitutional amendment, antibusing, 97, 130, 217
Construction workers' protest, 254-56
Coordinated Social Services Council (CSSC), 147-48, 180, 196, 207
CORE, 48, 49
Crisis intervention teams, 148, 176
Cutbacks, 182-83, 213

*Daily World,* 143
*Death at an Early Age,* 56
Debnam, Alva and Otis, 210-11, 266
Declaration of Clarification, 29
*De jure* school segregation, abolition of, 52
DeMascio, Robert, 162

Democratic Party, 71, 124-25, 193, 251, 271; and Black community, 48-49, 65-67, 182-83, 215-16, 232, 240-41; machine, 19-20, 21
Demonstrations. *See* Antibusing or Probusing demonstrations
Detroit, 74, 161-62, 203
DiGrazia, Robert, 142, 159, 212, 213
Dixiecrats, 44
Dixon, Maceo, 74, 91, 194, 197, 246, 260, 269; and April 24, 1976, 207, 208, 228, 229, 233, 238, 239, 242; and Carson Beach, 153, 158, 160; and crisis teams, 148, 176, 180; and May 17, 1975, 121, 140-41
Doogan, John, 129-30
Dual grade structure, 59
Dukakis, Kitty, 132-33
Dukakis, Michael, 35, 67, 154, 165
Duke, David, 31, 195

*East Boston Community News,* 114
East Boston for Quality Education (EBQUE), 111, 115
Eastland, James, 10
Edelin, Kenneth, 121-22, 126, 134
Eisenhower, Dwight D., 45
Emergency Committee for a National Mobilization Against Racism, 70-71, 72-73, 92-96
Equal Rights Amendment, 132
"Examination schools," 60

Fahey, Marion, 184, 195, 206, 248
Fair Employment Practices Commission (FEPC), 40
Faith, Michael, 81-82
Faneuil Hall, 132
Faubus, Orval, 45
Federal troops: in South, 45, 46; in Boston, 28, 64, 67, 73, 91, 140-41
Feeder patterns, 59, 60
FEPC, 40
Fisher, Harvey, 167
Flannagan, Newman, 122
Flannery, Harold J., 58
Fleming, Arthur, 161
Flynn, Raymond, 97, 122, 154, 185
Forbes, Robert, 217
Ford, Gerald, 35-36, 161, 174, 257, 260, 262
Foreman, Stanley, 226

Fortes, Robert, 160, 240
Foster, Frank A., 228
Franklin, Brenda, 151
Freedom House, 28, 63, 64, 184
Freedom House Coalition, 64, 147
Freedom House Institute on Schools and
　Education, 63, 147
Freedom Rides, 45
Freedom schools, 54
Freedom Stay Out Day, 54

Garrity, Wendell Arthur, 58, 111, 207;
　Phase I, 24, 62, 147, 258, 275-80; Phase
　II, 118-19, 129, 137, 146-47, 253-54;
　South Boston High hearings, 187-92,
　194-95, 196
Gittlesohn, Roland, 76, 247
Goode, Mary, 217
Gordon, Gary, 212
Gordon, James, 163
"Grandfather clause," 39
Graul, Rita, 165, 233
"Great Society," 48
Groves, Walter, 164
*Guardian,* 52
Gurewitz, Donald, 67, 120-21

Hall, Prince, 51
Hicks, Louise Day, 23-24, 154, 162, 237,
　254-55; and Phase II, 137, 147; and
　ROAR, 30, 141-42, 214-15; and South
　Boston High siege, 82-84; use of public
　office, 54, 136, 199, 202
Hollis, Benjamin, 145, 151
Home and School Association, 23, 137,
　173, 209
Housing discrimination, 21-22

Intervention teams, 148
Irish immigration, 19

Jackson, Ellen, 57, 86, 176, 180, 194, 268-
　69; and demonstrations, 208, 246, 268
Jackson, Henry, 210
Jackson, James Lee, 55
Jean-Louis, André Yvon, 15-18
Jefferson, Clarence, 181
Jenkins, Ferguson, 266
Johnson, Bubba, 185, 191
Johnson, Lyndon B., 48
Johnson, Thomas, 173, 235
Johnson, Thomas, Jr., 114
Jones, Nathaniel, 259
Jones, Pat, 63

Kelly, James, 208-09, 228, 235, 254, 261
Kennedy, Edward, 24-25, 131-32, 259
Kennedy, John F., 46
Keppel, Francis, 129
Kerrigan, John, 29-30, 117, 118, 119, 165-
　66, 199, 214
*Keyes* v. *Denver School District No. 1,*
　58
King, Coretta Scott, 75-76
King, Martin Luther, Jr., 12, 41-44, 47,
　55, 272
King, Melvin, 53-56, 156-58, 160, 204,
　217, 236
Klein, Joe, 31
Kozol, Jonathan, 56, 88, 89
Ku Klux Klan, 31, 38, 130, 163-64, 195-96

Landsmark, Theodore, 221, 222, 224-26
Langone, Frederick, 230
Levi, Edward, 257, 262
Lewis, Elma, 67, 197
Lincoln, George, 203, 204
Little, Joanne, 143
Little Rock crisis, 45
Louisville, 103, 162-64, 193, 202
Luscomb, Florence, 133

McCormack, Edward, 129
McCutcheon, Hattie, 204
McDonough, John, 258, 264
McDonough, Patrick, 122
McGovern, George, 193, 270
McLaughlin, Dennis, 229
Madison, Joe, 162, 219
Malcolm X, 48, 272
Maoists, 123, 158
March on Washington, 39, 47
Marshall, Thurgood, 40, 43
Massachusetts Citizens Against Forced
　Busing, 130
Massachusetts Citizens for Life, 122
Massachusetts Commission Against
　Discrimination, 60
Massachusetts State Labor Council,
　100, 103
Masters' Plan, 129, 130-31
Mayor's march, 246-48
Meany, George, 103, 259
Meatcutters, Amalgamated, 99-100
Media: coverup, 33-35, 108-9, 125-26; and
　Phase II, 166; sensationalism, 235, 245

Men's march, 211, 212, 215
Meredith, James, 47
METCO (Metropolitan Council for Educational Opportunities), 56, 217-18
Miah, Malik, 120-21
*Militant,* the, 69
Mitchell, Clarence, 260
Moakley, Joseph, 258-59, 269-70
Montgomery bus boycott, 12
Morash, Evelyn, 111-16
Mothers' marches, 169-70, 173
Myrdal, Gunnar, 40

NAACP (National Association for the Advancement of Colored People), 37, 162, 195, 259; and Boston school suit, 52-55, 57; and demonstrations, 64, 133, 153, 219-21, 246; history of, 37-41, 49-50
National Boycott Day, 185
National Center for Afro-American Artists, 67
National Education Association, 101, 259
National Guard, 69, 163, 165
National Student Coalition Against Racism. *See* NSCAR
National Student Conference Against Racism: first, 97, 121-28; second, 171, 182
Nazis, 31-32, 130
Nelson, Avi, 78, 97, 98, 142
*New York Times,* 34, 197, 257, 260
Nixon, E.D., 44
Noble, Elaine, 132-33
NSCAR (National Student Coalition Against Racism), 124, 183-84, 230, 232, 268-69; and April 24, 219; steering committee meetings, 134, 142, 171, 208, 212

O'Bryant, John, 172
O'Connell, William, 54
October League, 158
Oliver, Norman, 138, 183
O'Neill, Albert "Dapper," 30, 122, 136, 141, 214
O'Neill, Thomas "Tip," 130
On-the-job training programs, 61
"Open enrollment," 57, 59, 61, 252, 265
Operation Exodus, 57
O'Sullivan, James, 106

Overcrowding, 61
Overton, Volma, 139
Owens, William, 68, 70-71, 92-96, 227, 231

Palladino, Elvira "Pixie," 112, 131, 137, 199, 201-2, 210, 214-15
Parent Teacher Association, 23, 137, 173, 209
Parks, Paul, 56
Parks, Rosa, 11, 44, 92
Pasadena, 139, 193, 263
Pearson, Coach, 190, 191
Perdigao, Arthur, 191, 195
Phase I, 24, 101, 117-18
Phase II, 118, 129, 130, 137, 146; appeals of, 199-200; limits of, 251-52; preparation for, 165
*Plessy* v. *Ferguson,* 37-38
Poe, Tania, 68
Poleet, Richard, 234
Police, 84-85, 159, 161, 171, 212, 239; and opening of Phase II, 166-69, 171; and ROAR, 30-31, 142; treatment of Blacks, 33, 155-58
Pottinger, Stanley, 170, 259
Powderkeg Information Center, 144, 173
Powers, Frank, 173, 176
"Prayer Procession for Peace," 245
Probusing demonstrations
—1974: 68-69, 70, 71-72, 75-77, 93-97
—1975: 120-23, 133, 138-41, 171
—1976: 202, 217, 218, 229, 232-33, 242-43
Progressive Labor Party, 126, 134-36, 155-56
Provisional teachers, 61

Racial Imbalance Law, Massachusetts, 23, 55, 56
Rakes, Joseph, 223, 238
Randolph, A. Philip, 39
Rarick, John, 141
Rauh, Joseph, 140
Real, John, 263
*Real Paper,* 31
Red-baiting, 231
Redd, Ed, 193
Reeb, James, 52, 55
Reid, William, 80, 175, 192, 195
Renfroe, Rose, 218
Renici, Michael, 114

Rest, Obalajii, 152
Restore Our Alienated Rights, *See* ROAR
Reynolds, John, 203
Right to life groups, 122
Ring, Lawrence, 59
ROAR (Restore Our Alienated Rights), 29-30, 66, 104-5, 116, 214-15, 256; demonstrations, 66, 97, 130, 141-42, 185-186, 206; and Phase II, 165-66; violence by, 107-8, 131-32, 152, 204
*Roberts* v. *City of Boston,* 51-52
Rock, Leon, 150
Rockefeller, Nelson, 174
Roosevelt, Franklin D., 39
Rowe, James, 149
Russell, Pat, 173

St. Clair, James, 59
Sargent, Francis, 35, 67, 69
Save Boston Committee, 29
Scalese, James, 191-92
Scarsella, Marc, 190
School boycotts, 54, 75, 165
School committee. *See* Boston School Committee
SCLC (Southern Christian Leadership Conference) 48, 49
Seaborn, Colly, 117
"Sean gang," 188-89
Severs, Mark, 230, 233
Shanker, Albert, 102
Sheats, Samuel, 139
Sherbill, Ray, 74
Shore, Jack, 248
Smith, Thayer-Fremont, 262-63
Smothers, Clay, 98
SNCC (Student Nonviolent Coordinating Committee), 47, 48, 49
Snowden, Muriel, 63, 246
Snowden, Otto, 63, 246
Soars, Edward, 228
Socialist Workers Party, 67, 69, 138, 183
South Boston Defense League, 135, 152, 230, 261
South Boston Information Center, 30, 208
South Boston Marshals Association, 186, 195, 211, 213
*South Boston Tribune,* 108, 195
Southern Christian Leadership Conference, 48, 49
Southern Manifesto, 10
Staples, Verna, 146
States' rights, 10

Steele, James, 124
Stevens, John, 263
STRESS, 74
Student Committee for the December 14 March, 74-75, 87-88, 92-97
Student Nonviolent Coordinating Committee, 47, 48, 49
Substitute teachers, 61
Sullivan, Kathleen, 252
Supreme Court: 39-40; Boston appeals, 137-38, 146, 262; 1954 *Brown* decision, 9, 42-43; other school suits, 58, 161-62, 263-64
*Swann* v. *Charlotte-Mecklenburg Board of Education,* 58

Taliaferro, Georgia, 196
Taylor, Rev. Rafe, 227
Taylor, William, 218
Teachers, 60-61, 171-72. *See also* Boston Teachers Union
Teach-ins, 69, 74, 88-92
Third World Clearing House, 221
Third World Workers Association, 221-22, 254
Thomas, Katherine, 149
Till, Emmett, 43-44
Timilty, Joseph, 170, 183
Tracking, 10. *See also* "Feeder patterns"
Transfers, discrimination in, 57, 59, 61, 252, 265
Trotter, William Monroe, 52
Truman, Harry, 42
Tucker, Lem, 29
Turner, Tom, 219

Ujima Society, 67
United Labor Against Busing (ULAB), 164, 215, 248
U.S. Commission on Civil Rights, 161, 174
U.S. Supreme Court. *See* Supreme Court

Van Loon, Eric, 180-81
Vocational schools, 60-61
Voting Rights Act of 1965, 47

Wallace, George, 30, 46, 200
Wallace, Richard, 91
Warren, Mac, 143, 148, 150, 176, 269-70; and April 24, 1976, 207, 230, 231, 238, 239

Wells, Ray, 143
Weng, Rexford, 99-100
White Citizens Councils, 10
"White flight," 263, 265
White, James, 81-82
White, Kevin, 65, 161, 183, 224, 245; and
    demonstrations, 68, 153, 154, 245, 256;
    and fiscal scare, 207, 213, 214, 253;
    and media, 33-35; and Phase I, 25-28,
    35; and Phase II, 137, 165, 170
Wilkins, Roy, 33, 140, 260
Williams, Floyd, 231
Williams, Reba, 207
Wilmington, Delaware, 139
Wilson, Margaret Bush, 220-21
Wilson, Percy; 63, 64, 246, 268, 271; and
    Carson Beach, 158, 160

Wilson, Woodrow, 39
Winegar, Jerome, 222
Woolworth sit-ins, 45
World War II, 40-41

Yotts, Dan, 195
Young Socialist Alliance (YSA), 67, 69,
    74, 120, 124
Young Workers Liberation League
    (YWLL), 124-25, 143
Youth Against War and Fascism
    (YAWF), 68, 70, 73, 93

Zaniboni, Warren, 229